MICHAEL ELLISTON

THE ORIGINAL

FRONTIER

A SERIOUS SEEKER'S
GUIDE TO ZEN

REDFeather™
MIND | BODY | SPIRIT

4880 Lower Valley Road, Atglen, PA 19310

Cover design by Ashley Millhouse
Type set in Futura/Minion

ISBN: 978-0-7643-6088-6
Printed in India

Published by Schiffer Publishing, Ltd.
4880 Lower Valley Road
Atglen, PA 19310
Phone: (610) 593-1777; Fax: (610) 593-2002
E-mail: Info@schifferbooks.com
Web: www.schifferbooks.com

For our complete selection of fine books on this and related subjects, please visit our website at www.schifferbooks.com. You may also write for a free catalog.

Schiffer Publishing's titles are available at special discounts for bulk purchases for sales promotions or premiums. Special editions, including personalized covers, corporate imprints, and excerpts, can be created in large quantities for special needs. For more information, contact the publisher.

We are always looking for people to write books on new and related subjects. If you have an idea for a book, please contact us at proposals@schifferbooks.com.

ACKNOWLEDGMENTS

I would like to thank those fellow Zen teachers who graciously provided commentary for the cover and foreword. They are luminaries of Zen in America, published authors in their own right. It is impossible to acknowledge all who participated. Apologies to anyone left out.

Borko Jovanovic, PhD, associate professor, medicine, Northwestern University, published author. "Emphasizing contemporary American life and frontier spirit may be a major contribution to the field."

George Wrisley, PhD, associate professor, philosophy, University of North Georgia, published author. Provided caveats from the scholarly side.

Keisei Andrew Dietz is a Zen disciple, longtime practitioner, and published author. I owe him for much of my clarity regarding the intersection of Zen, creativity, and design thinking.

James Smith, Zen priest and educator, Nova Scotia. "Like a well-written user's manual for software (or your lawnmower), just what you want in hand as you begin or continue Zen practice."

Lloyd Williams, motivational speaker, professional coach. "Comparison between Prajna Paramita and E = mc2 is very good. I like the content and find it easy to read, illustrations clear and understandable. This will be a valuable book."

Kevin McNeil, PhD, clinical neuropsychologist, Saint John, New Brunswick. "As though Elliston was inside my head, guiding me step by step through meditation, pointing the way, the 'middle way' through it all, answering questions I didn't even know I had."

Jimmyle Listenbee, Zen priest, Oxford, Mississippi. "Accessible, full of unpretentious insight but not chatty, a thorough yet uncomplicated guide, a unique resource for beginners and seasoned practitioners alike."

Liz Lawlor, Zen priest, lifelong teacher, Ness City, Kansas. "The Original Frontier gives encouragement to continue my zazen practice and never give up, practical instructions and teachings, down my path of 'sitting still enough, long enough.'"

Seigetu Roger Cochran, PhD, sociology. "A unique (and good!) approach to Zen for both new practitioners and maturing students in Zen. Original Frontier explains clearly how the senses interact with the mind in establishing a Zen practice."

Kuwasan Ann Glasmann, Zen priest and classical harpist, Montana; with her husband, former professors of music. "I, finally, am reading the words of a teacher that fulfill the needs of a student like myself. Goes on my shelf to pull out many times, as my practice changes and deepens."

Last I would like to express my deep gratitude, admiration, and respect for my wife, **Diane,** without whose tender loving care and patience this project could not have come to fruition.

CONTENTS

FOREWORD

By Norman Fischer

The book you have in your hands will carry you along. Its author, an American who's spent a long lifetime practicing and wondering about Zen, writes with ease and seems to have thought through just about any implication, conception, or objection to Zen practice anyone could possibly have. Also, he spent many years studying with an important (if not so well known) Japanese Zen teacher and represents that master's teaching eloquently and faithfully—which in itself would make this book well worth your reading. But there's more. To say something about this "more," I want to sketch some historical background.

Michael Elliston's teacher, Rev. Soyu Matsuoka, like the other Japanese Zen pioneers in America, was born in the early years of the twentieth century. He came to the United States in 1939. To leap across the ocean to America from Japan was, at that time, a far more enormous and daring undertaking than we can imagine from today's perspective, when people travel all over the globe, and far-flung cultures seem to know each other's business. Prewar America and prewar Japan could scarcely have been further apart. Which raises a question: What compelled Rev. Matsuoka and his contemporaries to do this outrageous thing?

To appreciate this, you have to understand the enormity of the year 1868 in Japanese history. This was the year of the Meiji Restoration, a massive political and cultural reorganization that lasted for generations, through which the Japanese undertook, with all their disciplined force, to end the project of trying to keep the Western barbarian influence at arm's length (an effort they were forced to give up when Admiral Perry's warships sailed into Edo Bay in

1853) and instead absorb Western ways in order to surpass them.

Zen priests such as Soyu Matsuoka who came of age in those days of cultural foment couldn't help but question their tradition in light of the West. Studying with searching and critical eyes both Western religion and philosophy as well as Zen, they felt compelled to revise, renew, reenvision. They intuitively seemed to understand that they could not do this freely within their own cultural context, that they needed to see more directly through Western eyes. And so the most lively and daring among them gave up their secure careers at home to live permanently in the West—without any idea of how they would survive or what they would do. They were determined to bring Zen to the West—a Zen they knew they'd have to discover in the process.

I point this out in order to indicate that though the Zen transported from Japan by Rev. Matsuoka and others was authentic and traditional, it was also a Zen intentionally torn free from its traditional Japanese context and was, therefore, at the same time, completely different. This new Zen reflected American values that these Japanese priests were drawn to—independence, creativity, iconoclasm, and personal experience—values that are indeed implied in traditional Zen literature but were not necessarily evidenced in Japan of that time, or anywhere else in Asia. In this sense, these men (for they were, sadly, all men) were indeed pioneers, Japanese Daniel Boones—frontiersmen not only of the Original Frontier but of cultural and historical frontiers as well.

Enter then the second Zen pioneer this book offers—Michael Elliston, its author. Like Rev. Matsuoka, Michael Elliston is perhaps typical of his generation, the generation of Americans that passionately and completely received Zen from the first Japanese teachers to come to the West. A lively and independent-minded person, searching for something beyond the traditional midwestern virtues in which he was raised, and, not incidentally, a creative person, a visual artist and designer by trade (it is astonishing how many of the first-generation American Zen students came from arts backgrounds; indeed, Zen was initially understood in the West as more art form than religion), he encountered Rev. Matsuoka while he was a design student in Chicago, and he never looked back.

I hope all this is enough to indicate why this book isn't exactly what it appears to be, a book about the Zen tradition for new or experienced students. Yes, it is that, but also, given its cultural matrices (post-Meiji Japan and 1960s America), it is more—a record of two generations of seekers in two different realms of modern upheaval, two individuals who saw in Zen a path toward their own unique authenticity and individual vision lived in response to uncertain times.

Although Michael wonders, in the introduction, why in the world anyone would want yet another Zen book, and why, even if there were no Zen books at all, one would even be necessary, since Zen is about simple, straightforward living—despite all this, The Original Frontier is full of useful ideas and reflections about what Zen is about and not about (I especially appreciated the wide-ranging sections on "Differentiating Zen Meditation" and "Deconstructing the Senses"). It's certainly the case that Zen, as Rev. Matsuoka and Michael Elliston transmit it, is not a doctrine or a cut-and-dried set of teachings or techniques (as other schools of Buddhism can tend to be). The paradox is that though there is nothing to say about Zen, this book is quite thoroughgoing and original, the thoughts and counterthoughts of a person who loves his teacher, loves his tradition, values it absolutely, and is willing to say so in as many ways as he can think of.

INTRODUCING THE
ORIGINAL FRONTIER

Welcome to yet another book about Zen. You may reasonably question why anyone would want to add to the vast body of Zen literature. Hasn't enough been written about Zen? Isn't everything that anyone might want to know about meditation—including Zen meditation (J. *zazen*)—already out there?

There are plenty of beginner books about Zen and its meditation. This book is not specifically for beginners, though anyone should be able to benefit from reading it. Other texts relate stories of Shakyamuni Buddha, and the ancestors of Zen. I quote their teachings, including some from my root teacher, Rev. Zengaku Soyu Matsuoka, Roshi (Japanese for "Venerable Teacher"). And particularly, those of Eihei Dogen, Zenji ("Zen Master"), who is recognized as the father of modern Soto Zen. I quote them liberally when needed to clarify a point. But it is important to recognize that for more than 2,500 years, throughout the countries of origin—India, China, Korea, and Japan—all teachers of Zen's ancestral lineage, from Buddha on down, speak with one voice. I hope to echo their message.

Some modern authors expound a personal philosophy based on Zen. The thrust of this work is not primarily philosophical but is meant to be useful in pursuing a Zen life. Zen is, first and foremost, practical. Its primary method, zazen, is especially appropriate to the way we live today. My intent is not to encourage you to read more about Zen, but rather to begin, or to continue, practicing its meditation.

Age of Anxiety Redux

Matsuoka Roshi would often refer to his era as the "age of anxiety," the title of a long poem by his famous contemporary W. H. Auden. Nowadays, we are even more likely to be filled with anxiety in a new age of uncertainty, driven by major shifts in societies around the world as well as right here at home. Ongoing intertribal strife, aggravated by climate change, is fostering record levels of global emigration: folks fleeing persecution, poverty, and famine. Uncertainty is the new bugaboo, roiling markets as well as political campaigns and giving new meaning to the adage that nothing can be said to be certain except death and taxes. An ancient Chinese curse says, "May you live in interesting times." The times, they certainly are interesting.

What is left of the middle class is assailed with a lack of progress on the economic front. Accelerating distribution of wealth to the upper class does not lend comfort to the hoi polloi. Those benefiting have their own reasons to feel uncertain, including resentment—verging on contempt—with which they are often regarded by those still struggling. But this is not merely class envy.

Adding to anxiety is the rise of attention merchants, those in the business of capturing eyeballs—and, in the digital age, clicks—clamoring for our attention. In the advertising and entertainment business, which these days includes the daily news cycle, eyeball bait and clickbait translate into dollars. And, in the political arena, power. The media dictate what is important, what we should be paying attention to.

Zen calls on us to redirect our attention away from the blandishments of the media—which after all are profiting from telling us what is important—to the wisdom of our own mind and body. Zen suggests that we begin reading our own breaking news, watching our own unique movie, and reading our own book, rather than following the outputs of others.

In these rather dire straits, I am somewhat ambivalent about adding to the babel of voices competing for attention. Especially in a saturated marketplace, in which new angles on Zen appear in publication frequently. But it is even more important, and necessary, to make the Zen worldview known, and to promote its process of meditation to the public, especially in times of great suffering.

In Zen, we address personal suffering, and social suffering, somewhat differently. We regard personal suffering rather stoically—as a consequence of our karma, if not of our immediate actions. But we do not regard the suffering of others cavalierly, as merely their karma. Suffering can be mitigated through social justice, but also through personal meditation.

We might dare hope that something as powerful as zazen, and capable of fostering personal transformation, would also have a ripple effect on the larger society, as it did in Zen's countries of origin. Especially in an era when truth itself is under assault, when controlling the narrative and the optics can be more important than the underlying, humble facts. When once-sober and relatively dignified national politics has now been exposed for the sleight-of-hand sideshow it has always been to some degree, now seemingly reaching its apogee. We yearn for good, old-fashioned verification of what is sometimes called empirical truth: What can I really believe, and believe in?

This is the inflection point that Zen takes aim at, from a cultural perspective. Positive changes to our national culture can, and indeed may, come about as a result of America's wider appreciation and adaptation of meditation. It is becoming more mainstream. But this is not my main objective, either. The revolution begins at home, with each of us.

I feel compelled to write what I know about Zen, from personal experience, simply because it has had a profoundly positive effect on my own life. And because I do not believe, in all humility, that anyone else writing about Zen today enjoys quite the same perspective that I have. I come at Zen from a background in creativity and design thinking, on top of significant time on the cushion. One notable exception is *The Zen of Creativity* by John Daido Loori, wherein the author introduces the idea that Zen is the key to unlocking creativity in all that we do:[1]

> The creative process, like a spiritual journey, is intuitive, nonlinear, and experiential. It points us toward our essential nature, which is a reflection of the boundless creativity of the universe.

While I am in complete accord with Master Loori's premise, this book is not about utilizing your creativity in all aspects of life, so much as it is about tapping the innate creative potential in zazen, which amounts to the same thing in the long run. Zazen is at the heart of creativity, in that it directly engages sensory consciousness as its medium. Zen offers a simple method of optimizing physical, mental, and emotional health through creative action. In this we can find at least a modicum of happiness, of a kind that is not dependent on our personal, or social, situation.

But I do not mean to suggest Zen as yet another regimen for

self-improvement. Nor do I tout Zen's worldview as a program for reforming society. Instead, I propose that Zen offers a deeply personal and practical way by which you, yourself, can undertake a voluntary reformation, engaging a process of personal, conscious transformation.

While I cannot claim that the material circumstances of my own life have been directly improved by Zen practice, I am certain that my attitude toward them has improved enormously. Having practiced Zen for several decades, I have come to accept, in a positive way, the limitations of my ability to mitigate the natural suffering in my own life.

You may, of course, realize many positive personal changes as side effects of your Zen practice, but they do not represent its fundamental purpose, which is impossible to define in words. You will find its deeper meaning in the experiential realm, not in verbal expression.

I do want to encourage you to do what Buddha did—to sit still enough, for long enough, to break through to your innate, creative potential. This is one of the simple secrets of Zen. I suggest eventually seeking out a teacher (J. *sensei*) or a group of meditators (S. *sangha*) when the opportunity arises, if you haven't already. In any case, I invite you to enter the original frontier.

Welcome to the Original Frontier

The original frontier I speak of is not restricted to any one place, and it does not abide in a specific, limited span of time. It is always here and now. Ready, willing, and able to meet and greet us, just where we are. It always has been, always will be. This is the point of no return we approach in Zen: the frontier of consciousness, itself. From the comfort zone of our familiar reality, we enter the strange territory discovered by Buddha, explored and settled by his descendants. After all, it has not gone anywhere. There is nowhere for it to go. Eihei Dogen (1200–1253), founder of Soto Zen in Japan, indicates where we are to find the entrance, in his early, written instructions on zazen:[2]

> The Way is completely present where you are, so of what use is practice or enlightenment? However, if there is the slightest difference in the beginning between you and the Way, the result will be a greater separation than between heaven and earth. If the slightest dualistic thinking arises, you will lose your buddha-mind.

The proper use of Zen practice, then, is precisely to overcome the seeming gap between you and the Great Way. Exaggerated as it is by dualistic thinking.

Another translation mentions the futility of pursuing enlightenment elsewhere, on pilgrimage. It has to be right here, if it is anywhere.

The frontier Buddha entered 2,500 years ago is still present today, still beckoning to all, just over the hill. Glimpsed from time to time, as it were, from the corner of your eye. But it is so close, so immediate and intimate, that it is unperceivable. This is beautifully illustrated by analogy to the moon and snow, in an ancient Zen teaching poem by Tozan Ryokai (807–869), founder of Soto Zen in China:[3]

> The dharma of thusness is intimately transmitted by buddhas and ancestors. Now you have it; preserve it well. A silver bowl filled with snow, a heron hidden in the moon. Taken as similar, they are not the same; not distinguished, their places are known.

The ostensible gap between our ordinary world and that of enlightenment is so subtle as to be virtually indistinguishable, like white on white. As long as we do not arbitrarily distinguish one from the other, they remain in their proper "dharma locations," or absolute positions, in spacetime.

Then suddenly, a pivot from the perceptual to the experiential:[4]

> The meaning does not reside in the words, but a pivotal moment brings it forth.

The "pivotal moment" is beyond words. But so slight a fine-tuning of awareness is easily overlooked:[5]

> So minute it enters where there is no gap, so vast it transcends dimension. A hairsbreadth's deviation, and you are out of tune.

Like the ocean to a fish, or the sky to a bird, the original frontier is vast, yet seamless. The water and air are too close, too intimate, to be an object of perception. But entering into this strange land radically changes perception, itself. Any and all willing pioneers, at any time and any place, can enter this original frontier, no matter their circumstances.

Like an old-fashioned radio dial, moving slightly to the left or right yields nothing but static. But what happens when we tune in to the exact frequency?[6]

> With his archer's skill, Yi hit the mark at a hundred paces. But when arrows meet head on, how could it be a matter of skill? The wooden man starts to

sing; the stone woman gets up dancing.

Hitting the bull's-eye is what we all want in daily life, with skills developed over the requisite 10,000 hours of training, which may also be said of Zen. But what Zen calls upon us to achieve can actually happen, but is nearly impossible, like arrowpoints meeting in midair. When and if it happens, everything springs to life. Including insentient beings, whether made of wood or stone.

This is the central message, and spiritual legacy, of Buddhism. It offers up the wish-fulfilling "Mani-jewel" of Indian legend. This gem is said to be hidden on each person, all unknown to the bearer. But we tend to look for it everywhere else. As did Buddha, until he discovered it in meditation.

This is a familiar syndrome, looking for love in all the wrong places. Searching everywhere, other than where what we are looking for is actually to be found. As my grandmother said, "Whatever you are looking for, you will find it in the last place you look."

The flip side is that we hope to escape those circumstances we imagine to be the problem. This is the issue Buddha confronted in his six-year quest: the universal problem (J. *koan*) of suffering. He tried everything to dispel it, but nothing had worked. Then, the story goes, he sat down in resolute meditation and found the Middle Way, the Path to the original frontier. He then laid out the map of the foreign territory for the rest of us to follow.

What Can This Book Do for You?

So, do we really need another book about Zen? Maybe not. But you, personally, may need a road map. A new way of thinking about, and a more creative attitude toward, Zen. And a manual to help you adopt its natural approach to meditation. Your exploration and enjoyment of zazen, as a practical method for coping, promises to simplify and enrich your life.

"'Tis the gift to be simple," as the song has it. Simplicity is one of the highest values in design, as well as in Zen. And equally difficult to achieve in each discipline. Classic examples in product design include the bobby pin and safety pin, and all the basic machines, such as the wheel, inclined plane, or the lever. To enter and explore the original frontier, you will need to pack some simple tools in your backpack.

This book is such a tool, meant for serious, modern seekers of Zen—experienced in meditation or not—ready and willing to give zazen—unguided, upright-seated meditation—a try. But it is not my intention to meet your expectations of what meditation is, or what you think it should be. That book would not be very useful to you. While other books encourage you to practice meditation, I want to do so via an approach that is down to earth, demystifying the process. Zazen is different from other styles of meditation. It is much simpler in concept, irreducibly simple. But it can be difficult in execution. We tend to overcomplicate matters.

Working with a living Zen teacher may be ideal, but they are in scarce supply. And not absolutely necessary, at least not in the beginning. It is enough, for now, to get started working on zazen. When the time comes, your teacher will appear, it is said. This text can provide some guidance, however inadequate to the task, until the real thing comes along.

If you are a novice, perhaps you will be encouraged to give Zen a try. If you are already practicing, some encouragement may persuade you to venture even further into the original frontier. Along the way, any remaining doubts you may have regarding Zen practice will, I hope, evaporate. If you have given up, are a lapsed meditator, or feel you have plateaued, I hope you will be convinced to try yet again, harder.

How to Read This Book

Wherever you happen to land on the experiential spectrum of meditation, you may find the most useful sections of this text to be those on how Zen and zazen actually work: "Differentiating Zen Meditation from All the Others" and "Finding Work-Arounds for Your Lousy Excuses." The long section on "Deconstructing Your Senses in the Most Natural Way" takes a deep dive into changes you may expect to validate during meditation, taken from my personal field notes. "Embracing Nonduality without Losing Your Grip on Reality" delves into the seemingly contradictory, dichotomous logic underlying Zen's worldview. "Applying Zen to Life by Applying Your Life to Zen" and "Benefiting from Zen in Every Way Imaginable" discuss some predictable and unpredictable benefits of Zen. "Following the Sages as Guides to the Frontier of Zen" revisits traditional teachings, in the light of all that has preceded. The few conclusions I draw in "Concluding Zen as If That Were Possible" place it in a broader perspective of the great American meme, the Frontier, as the gate to the "Original Frontier" of mind discovered by Buddha so long ago and recapped at the end of the text.

But any text on Zen, and especially on zazen, should be read intermittently—between meditation sessions—to be most effective. The utility of reading about Zen, as opposed to actually practicing zazen, may be regarded as analogous to documentation accompanying computer software.

Using the App

When it comes to finding balance in life, along with potential opportunity for spiritual growth, there's an app for that. It is called Zen. Its operative interface is zazen. If you are not actively practicing meditation, no amount of reading about it will be of much help. In zazen itself is where you will find the actionable answers you seek. The literature is merely the backup documentation.

Most software providers publish online manuals, training tutorials, and tech support. Such information is useless, however, unless you are actually using the application. But if you are and run into a glitch, troubleshooting tips can be a time-saver and lifesaver. There is no substitute for live coaching, of course, and the same may be said of Zen. Zen teachers provide technical support to those using the software of the mind.

If utilized in a similar manner, this text can function like the reference for a new operating system, or application. Unless you are actually using the application (zazen), the documentation (this book) will make little or no sense. But the text can provide a kind of user's manual for your zazen. One hopes that it will help you solve problems as they arise, and provide patches or work-arounds for any glitches you may encounter on the cushion.

I harbor no delusions that simply reading my comments about Zen, however cogent and well intended, will bring about any kind of transformative experience for you. Like most Zen teachers, I do not recommend reading too much about Zen. However, studying the extensive record of Zen's ancestors, as well as modern commentary, if pursued as an adjunct to zazen, can help clarify your own experience.

Beware of Book Knowledge

When I began training with Matsuoka Roshi in the 1960s, one could literally have read every book about Zen then published in English, which is unlikely today. But even then, my teacher warned against the dangers of what he termed "book knowledge": the conceit that reading everything available about Zen is tantamount to actually understanding Zen. I once mentioned Zen to a fellow professor at the School of the Art Institute of Chicago, and he responded, "Oh, I've read all the books about Zen; I know all about it."

In those days, Americans were just beginning to wake up to the practice of meditation and the message of Zen, forming initial impressions and speculations as to its meaning. And for some, realizing its implications for their lives. They were few and far between, however. Nowadays, meditation seems to be ubiquitous. Knowing our fickle culture, it may represent merely another passing fad. But Zen is designed for the long haul, a lifetime commitment.

The irony of concluding my introductory comments with a cautionary statement about reading books about Zen—in a book about Zen—is not lost on me. But especially in today's society, where publishing a tell-all book is the default response to any newsworthy event—such as the latest politician to resign or be fired—it is countercultural to suggest that reading about something may not be the best way to learn about it. But in the case of Zen, this is the case. The map is not the territory, as we say, and reading is like studying a map rather than actually exploring the original frontier. Exploration of new terrain is demanding, and often discouraging. Exploring Zen, a map is useful up to a certain point, but we reach a turning point—entering uncharted territory— where the map must be abandoned, as must most of the baggage we drag along with us on the journey.

Writing as Meditation

If you have ever written for publication, you are familiar with the old saw that writing is really rewriting. Unscrambling the word salad that we tossed on the pages of the first draft. But there is a limit to the patience we have for listening to our own voice, for revisiting our own musings. We really do tend to be our own worst critics. It is no different in Zen training.

You will be tempted to give up on the trail of Zen's frontier. Most Westerners do, all too soon. I have never wanted to give up on zazen, though I have gone on hiatus a few times. But I must admit that I have felt like giving up on this text from time to time. My process entails the usual steps: a first draft, reworking with suggestions from volunteer readers, submitting manuscripts, receiving rejection letters. Then reworking with editorial comments, reading aloud, redrafting with an ear to tone. And so on and on and on. Endlessly, it seems. You could continue to polish the same text for the rest of your life! Zen practice follows a similar, seemingly Sisyphean arc, as we will see.

All this is a long-winded way to say that Zen can work for anyone, including you. It is the ultimate in spiritual do-it-yourself: Zen = DIY. Even with a guiding teacher and a supportive community, you are still basically on your own on the cushion. But you are never really alone. All the buddhas and bodhisattvas of past, present, and future, "as innumerable as the sands of the Ganges," to borrow an old Indian expression, are practicing with you. At any given time somewhere on the planet, people are sitting in meditation. I hope my humble efforts inspire you to join them in the adventure. The original frontier is calling.

DESIGNING
A CREATIVE ZEN LIFE

My perspective on Zen training is informed by a background in training in creativity and design thinking. My mentors in design are complementary influences to my mentors in Zen. Design, as a profession, regards nearly everything in life as a problem, one subject to redesigning.

A classic example in product design is the chair, a traditional assignment for industrial-design students. Do we really need another chair? Aren't there enough chairs already? The conventional answers to these questions are no and yes, respectively. Most folks do not need yet another chair design. Yet, when a truly breakthrough design appears, buyers line up in droves.

In Zen, we typically sit on the floor, so the need for chairs in general comes into question. Chair sitting certainly has made a not-insignificant contribution to the general deterioration of fitness and flexibility in an aging American population. What began as a throne ends as a wheelchair.

Notable exceptions include when a chair is not just another chair but provides other functions. Such as adjustability, ergonomic support of the body, or relieving the stress of sitting at a desk all day. Or therapeutic features, such as massage and heat. Then there are multifunction transformers, such as the Franklin chair, which flips over to provide a stepladder.

A design student is called on to embrace all of these considerations in coming up with yet another iteration of "the chair." The challenge itself—in reinventing such a ubiquitous item—is the heart of innovation. How to come up with a meaningful improvement on the basic function of elevated seating?

Such training in basic problem-solving, in a variety of applied contexts—whether for the sake of a client or for the general public—fosters a generalist rather than a specialist attitude. In a similar sense, we are called on to reinvent Zen.

Design and Zen

Zen training, like design thinking, fosters a problem-solving approach to life's most intractable obstacles. Meditation in Zen allows us to contemplate the various issues in daily life, simultaneously with the deeper meaning of life itself. Much as the designer contemplates the potential for a new and useful chair, Zen invites us to contemplate the creative possibilities of our lives. Much as I contemplate the design, and content, of this book. Zen applies itself to everything, if you but allow it. This is one reason zazen is referred to as the "excellent method" by Dogen:[7]

> Those who attained enlightenment in India and China followed this way. It was done so because teachers and disciples personally transmitted this excellent method as the essence of the teaching.

One of the first things that convinced me that the Zen way would become my way is this emphasis on method, on taking action. There was actually something I could do! It wasn't about listening to someone preaching the gospel, but about gaining direct insight into the real problems of my own life. I do not mean to set up a false dichotomy between those who follow a teacher and those who take action, but to encourage you to at least try independent action in lieu of a teacher. Zen is a way of action. The apparent inaction on the cushion is, actually, the most we can do.

As a teenager training in the Bauhaus tradition of problem-solving, I came to view just about everything I encountered as a problem, the solution to which might be found in a different design approach. In order to produce a solution, such as a chair, in a material, such as wood, you need to understand how wood works: what it can and cannot do. Accumulating a sensory "vocabulary" of material behaviors through a process of manipulating various forming pro-cesses thus becomes the first order of business. The entire first year of design curriculum, called the "Foundation," is devoted to this kind of immersive training.

Zen meditation boils down to yet another process of immersion, but one in which the medium under investigation is consciousness itself.

The process of problem-solving is extendable to include all aspects of life. Your skill in defining a given problem you are facing—the ability to discern its hidden dimensions and anticipate any unintended consequences—determines how well the new approach is likely to work, and how soon you might have to revise it.

In design circles, we have a variation on the familiar joke: You couldn't design your way out of a paper bag! Especially if you're lacking the insight into how paper works. You cannot design your life without understanding the "givens" that are baked in, determining how life actually works. This does not imply a hidden designer, in the sense of creationism. Rather, it indicates that others who preceded you may have some inkling as to how all of this works. Experienced mentors, in design, become all-important. The ancestors of Zen are also design mentors. They have designed, and refined, Zen over a couple of millennia.

Discovering the Original Frontier in Chicago

Arriving in the late 1930s, Matsuoka Roshi was seminal in initiating a renaissance of sorts, placing the diligent practice of meditation at the heart of Zen, which had apparently fallen off in some monasteries and temples in Japan. As noted by one of his outstanding Zen contemporaries, Kosho Uchiyama Roshi, in the not-so-distant past, it was not necessarily the case that all Soto schools were assiduously propagating zazen: [8]

> The late Shibayama Zenei Roshi, the former abbot of Nanzenji, a monastery in the Rinzai school, once said to me, "Followers of Rinzai Zen practice zazen to attain satori. Satori is most important. On the contrary, in Soto Zen, zāzēn is most important. And yet, Rinzai practitioners, not Soto monks ārē the ones who have been practicing zazen consistently. Why has this happened?" In modern times in the Soto school, the first person who strongly advocated genuine shikantaza taught by Dogen Zenji was no one else but my late teacher Sawaki Kodo Roshi . . . Most Soto monks before Sawaki Roshi did not practice Dogen Zen. It is sad to say, but it's true.

The translator, Shohaku Okumura, Roshi, was a student of Uchiyama Roshi and is one of my formal teachers. He performed my transmission ceremony (J. *shiho*), entrusting me with the Dharma, in 2007. Matsuoka Roshi had done so informally in 1983.

Zen and WWII

Matsuoka Roshi was one of the generation of twenty-somethings, monks training under Kodo Sawaki Roshi at Komazawa University. Sawaki Roshi became a professor there, and was leading meditation, in 1935. Sensei later brought the same training to the US, where I was exposed to it in the 1960s. His efforts were foundational in introducing the original frontier to the country known for exploring frontiers.

Sensei must have practiced zazen under the great Master's supervision at the university. I was fortunate to meditate there during a recent trip to Japan, with a documentary film crew in tow. It was inspiring, to say the least. It felt like coming home, revisiting your ancient family homestead; closing the great circle of Zen (J. *enso*).

Matsuoka Roshi would sometimes say that Zen was "dead" in Japan, for similar reasons mentioned by Shibayama Roshi. In coming to America—bringing with him this great tradition of the centrality of zazen to Zen—he knew he was on a mission. Much as Dogen Zenji was, returning from China over seven hundred years earlier. Had Sensei stayed in Japan instead, he might eventually have been recognized as a reformer of Zen, in the mold of his mentor at Komazawa, known as "Homeless Kodo," since he never settled into a particular temple or monastery.

At that time, global rumblings of discontent and political fanaticism—fueled by the disastrous consequences to Germany of the First World War, and the developments of fascism that led to the arising of the Axis powers—were becoming louder. This must have given the propagation of Zen to the West a sense of urgency for Sensei. He said his mother told him to "Go die in America." Which is just what he ended up doing. First landing, and living, in California, then moving to the Midwest to found the Zen Buddhist Temple of Chicago (ZBTC) in 1949.

During this same period, Laszlo Moholy-Nagy, the founder of the "New Bauhaus"—which became the Institute of Design that I later attended—fled from Weimar Germany to come to Chicago during Hitler's rise to power. Shortly after my birth, these inchoate forces culminated in WWII, followed by the postwar reconstruction of Germany and Japan under the supervision of the victorious Western Allies and American occupying forces. This all happened in the early to mid-1940s, a rapid pace compared to modern wars. At or about this time, I was just becoming aware that there was a larger world outside the small farm in southern Illinois where I grew up. At seventeen, I left my hometown to attend college in Chicago, diving headlong into that larger world.

If you had visited the ZBTC in the 1960s, when I first did, you would have been handed a pamphlet titled *The Method of Zen*, featuring a concise, poetic description of the basics of zazen interwoven with Zen philosophy. Matsuoka Roshi is recognized as the first Soto Zen master in America to establish a meditation hall (J. *zendo*) for Westerners. This pamphlet may represent the first example of instructions for zazen published in English. Originally composed by Matsuoka Roshi, or quoted from unnamed sources, parts of it paraphrase Dogen's early tract on zazen quoted above, itself based on an earlier Chinese text. These instructions are still taught in modern Soto Zen monasteries and meditation centers, over eight centuries later. All such written instructions are meant to be ancillary to face-to-face teaching, of course.

Practical Poetry

The Method of Zen begins with an introductory poem, offering as good a summary of the aspiration to awakening Bodhi-mind as may be found, while teasing the long-term effects of Zen and zazen:[9]

INTRODUCTION
The thought of Zen is the flower—the mind is attracted by its beauty.
The art of Zen is the fruit—its savor comes home to one's heart.
The practice of Zen is the life—by it the body and mind become strong
    and continue to prosper for eternity.
The place of the practice of Zen is Zazen.
The ideal of Zazen is the seated figure of Buddha.
We love the flower of Zen.
We rejoice in the fruit of Zen.
We yearn for the life of Zen.

The first three lines express our innate attraction to Zen—its flower, its fruit, and its life. This attraction is to be found in the minds and hearts of all humans, including yours and mine. They also indicate that, with practice, the effects of Zen quickly begin to transform the body and mind, just as blossoms naturally morph into fruit under favorable conditions. Zen insists there is no separation of body and mind, a meme typical of Western thought. All such dualities are co-arisen. Mind arises out of body, which seems obvious. That body also arises out of mind is more challenging.

The next two lines introduce Zen's central method, Zazen, capitalized to emphasize the high regard in which it is held. And connecting it to Buddha's experience of spiritual awakening, while seated in meditation. We claim that our meditation is identical to his.

The last three lines express the aspiration to fully actualize the promise of Zen through loving, rejoicing, and yearning, recalling Buddhism's Three Minds (J. *sanshin*): the Magnanimous, Joyous, and Nurturing mind(s).

Zen in Three Parts

The simple way that zazen is outlined in the pamphlet stresses only what is most essential—posture, breathing, and attention, or mind—reflecting Sensei's grasp of the practical Western mindset. The complexities of Zen practice are distilled down to its essence, for ease of assimilation. For similar reasons, we were simply to call him "Sensei," meaning "teacher."

The following brief but eloquent description of the sitting posture captures the irreducible simplicity, and pragmatic physicality, of zazen—an approach to meditation that is suitable for everyone:[10]

DISPOSITION OF THE BODY

"Lotus form sitting" or sitting with folded legs is characteristic of an ideally
    seated figure of the Buddha.

The right leg is folded and placed on the thigh of the left leg.

Then the left leg is folded and placed on the thigh of the right leg.

It is permissible to reverse this order.

There are various kinds of seated figures of the Buddha.

It is sufficient so long as one folds one's legs and sits.

It does not matter if one cannot place one leg over the other.

It is also acceptable to sit on a chair and have the feet rest on the floor.

However, the feeling of stability that one experiences when one sits with
    his legs folded is so wonderful that one cannot help but wish to sit in
    this manner.

Once the disposition of the legs is completed to the best of one's ability,
    the hands should then be rested in front of the lower abdomen.

The palm of the right hand should be turned upward.

The palm of the left hand should also be turned upward and placed on
    the right palm.

The thumbs of both hands, the left lying on top of the right, are then raised, with the right thumb in contact with the left thumb.

The thumbs, which are raised, one in contact with the other, then face the palm of the hands and form a beautiful, gemlike ellipse.

Next is the disposition of the upper half of the body.

The lower abdomen (below the navel) is forcibly pushed forward.

The lower back becomes straight, and strength enters into the lower abdomen.

If strength should instead penetrate into the upper abdomen at this time, one should attempt this over and over again until the strength enters only into the lower abdomen.

A short and sweet description, but paying careful attention to the most salient details. Note the caveats on the sufficiency of sitting (no matter whether you can contort your body into the pretzel that is the full lotus), followed by the comment on the wonderful feeling of stability that accompanies the cross-legged posture. This occurs when we find the physical center of the body (J. *tanden*), the "sweet spot."

As a somewhat trivial historical detail, reversing the order of the legs is not found in Dogen's instructions, though it is mentioned in his Chinese teacher's written record.[11] Nor do we find the caveat about not being able to cross one's legs, or reference to sitting on a chair, which would have been highly unusual in Dogen's time. These may represent accommodations to Westerners and to older members of the Temple.

Floor Sitting versus Chair Sitting

In medieval Japan, chairs would have been relatively rare, since the cultural convention was to sit on the floor or a raised dais. One of the few contemporaneous portraits of Dogen shows him sitting cross-legged on an elegantly designed, bent-wood chair, the "high seat" from which he might have given dharma talks, a tradition that continues to this day. In the painting, his shoes are placed neatly on a footstool in front of the chair. A portrait of Hongzhi Zhengjue from about 100 years earlier in China has the identical composition, which cannot be coincidental. The former artist had to be familiar with the latter.

In the public meditation hall at Eiheiji, Dogen's monastery, I noted that the altar at the center of the room, with a seated wooden figure atop, featured a small shelf holding tiny wooden shoes. I presume that the statue represents Dogen, if not Manjusri, the figure traditionally represented in the zendo. In Japan, one removes one's shoes at the door.

Stomach Power

The last comment—on strength entering only into the lower abdomen—is an important point I have not found in other zazen instructions. Sensei also emphasized a physiological point, visualized a couple of inches down and in from the navel, called the tanden, in Japanese, the body's center of gravity. This is one reason we rest our hands in front of the lower abdomen, rather than bracing them on our knees, and do not lean on the back of a chair: the core muscles engage in holding us upright. Sensei often referred to this as developing "stomach power" (J. *hara*). They say an army marches on its stomach; likewise for zazen.

Another key point is found in the phrase "over and over again." Repetition, perseverance, and patience all pay off in Zen, reinforced by Sensei's frequent admonition: "Don't give up!" As with Dogen's earlier instructions, method and effect are woven together seamlessly, avoiding creation of future expectations, focusing on the present:[12]

> When strength has entered into the lower abdomen, one's posture will be as if he is lifting the ceiling with the vertex of his head.
> The neck will stretch with strength.
> The face will be cast downward just a fraction.
> When strength enters into the lower abdomen and one has established a posture as described above, then his upper body will assume a straight, poised appearance.
> His mind will be clear and refreshed.

When the body is straight and poised, just so is the mind. In due time. Note that usage of the male pronoun, today widely considered insensitive or incorrect, was customary at the time of this writing. Remember that Matsuoka Roshi was laboring under the constraints of what was, for him, a second language (English), while addressing an alien culture (America), as were all the early pioneers bringing Zen to the new frontier. Which we should take as evidencing their wisdom, dedication, and diligence, as well as their courage and compassion.

Some details of the posture, given verbally, are missing from the pamphlet, probably for sake of brevity. Notably, the fixed gaze: directed downward at 30–45 degrees; eyes open, not closed. Though when asked, he did not rule out closing the eyes occasionally. Also, the position of the tongue at rest, just touching the palate. These describe the natural state of repose. The best student strives to master the smallest details.

In zazen itself, method and effects also blend seamlessly. In teaching, encouragement is interwoven with instruction. Sensei repeatedly urged us to do everything to encourage ourselves, and conversely to avoid doing or saying anything discouraging to ourselves or to others. This neatly sums up the harmony essential to the Zen community (S. *sangha*). We practice together to encourage each other's practice.

Positive effects that we begin to notice build confidence in zazen. Crucially, we come to see, and believe, that Zen's stripped-down meditation does, indeed, work. Depending entirely on your investment in it. And not just quantitatively, in time, but qualitatively, in intensity.

Depends Upon

Sensei would often use condensed English phrases in order to express Zen concisely. One was "Depends upon." When you explained some obscure or complicated situation to him, he would say, "Oh, depends upon . . ." once he grasped the point. Zen depends upon you, and the effort you make in zazen.

Zazen works on a subliminal level. Its deeper effects are not directly noticeable, though even first-timers register an appreciable lowering of anxiety and other short-term, positive changes. Eventually, in retrospect, it becomes clear that Zen has changed our lives immensely.

Any identifiable effects claimed for zazen, including those you may experience, are of course impermanent, like everything else in life. For example, your mind may not always be clear and refreshed. But it is important to persist in the face of negative effects, particularly the distinct impression that you do not seem to be getting anywhere.

Plateauing may occur at beginning, intermediate, or advanced levels of practice. Sensei said this is a known issue, and there is a Japanese word that addresses it: *cho-da*. A bit like an "Aha!" or "Eureka!" moment, cho-da means "to fall up." We meditate for some time, sensing little or no progress. Then one day—cho-da! A fall-up! It may be small, or it may be huge. But the important thing is that we eventually fall up—to the next plateau. A plateau is, by nature, flat. So, once again, we continue with little or no sense of change, for some time. There are many plateaus in the original frontier.

The Breath of Life

The second essential focus of the zazen method—breathing—is treated succinctly:

DISPOSITION OF BREATHING
When the disposition of the body has been established, the next step is
   the disposition of the breathing.
Inhale the breath as much as possible through the nose.
One should inhale the breath—keeping in mind the thought of having it
   go deep into the bottom of the lower abdomen, filling it entirely.
The inhaled breath should then be let out through the nose in a thin stream,
   beginning quietly, lightly, and slowly.
Then the breath should be exhaled gradually in a thick stream, stronger
   and then rapidly, until it is all gone.
Inhaling breath deeply through the nose is known as *kyuki* or "drawing in
   breath."
Exhaling breath is known as *koki* or "expelling breath."

Breathing is given a great deal of attention in most styles of meditation. Paying close attention to the breath is an early instruction attributed to Buddha. But why would such a simple and obvious—seemingly inconsequential—focus be so basic to refining our awareness? Precisely because we are normally so unaware of our breath.

Unless we are engaged in strenuous activity such as running, are excited, or are otherwise emotionally aroused, we usually remain blissfully unaware of our breath. Paying strict attention to it—intentionally—is the beginning of heightened consciousness. It is something we can do anywhere and at any time, whether driving in rush hour or sitting in a boardroom.

Counting the breath was a regular part of verbal instructions. Not as a goal of zazen, but as a way of inducing attention to remain focused on the breath for extended periods. Eventually we may relinquish counting, simply observing the breath as it swings like a gate blowing in the breeze, one way and then the other. We are following the breath, not controlling it.

A visiting student once came into the interview (J. *dokusan*) room, bowed, announced his name, and declared that his practice was counting his breath. I asked him how long he had been counting his breath. He said, "About three years." I suggested he might want to stop counting his breath for a while. All such teaching techniques are provisional, not an end in themselves.

You Cannot Do Zen Wrong

Specific descriptions of methods, or their effects, can be problematic if taken too literally. Especially if they create further expectations. Counting is only a skillful means for focusing attention on the breath, which can be surprisingly difficult to sustain. But if we should, or must, always be counting our breath in zazen, it becomes a hindrance. There are countless such misinterpretations of "right," versus "wrong," practices of zazen.

Why breathe through the nose? Apart from the obvious noisome, and noisy, aspect of mouth breathing, air currents in nasal passages pass over sensitive nerve endings, soothing our nervous system. Initial emptying of the lungs through the mouth is recommended, however.

Another instruction suggests that deep, full breathing is naturally cleansing. The in breath (J. *kyuki*) provides refreshing oxygen, nourishing our energy level for sustaining zazen. The out breath (J. *koki*) expels impurities from the body. Breathing is our main source of energy and, absent air pollution, is naturally calming. Take a deep breath right now, and you will see for yourself.

These condensed instructions focus exclusively on the physical. They include no mental or visualization techniques. Dogen's instructions are also physical, with no mental techniques as such, as pointed out by Carl Bielefeldt in his exhaustive analysis *Dogen's Manuals of Zen Meditation* (the insertion is mine):[13]

Though the cultivation of meditation would seem to be the psychological practice par excellence, in Dogen's formulation of it, it seems to have to do with more the body than the mind. And, in fact, this is what he himself says. There are two ways, he says, to study the *buddha-marga* [buddha-path]— with the mind and with the body. To engage in seated meditation as the practice of the Buddha, without seeking to make a Buddha, is to study with the body.

As Matsuoka Roshi would often say, entwining his middle fingers and forefingers and holding them aloft, "In Zen, mind and body are just one; they cannot separate." So we train the body to sit, rather than try to train the mind directly. When the body becomes still, the mind must follow.

Body and Mind Cannot Separate

Even the third section in the pamphlet—on the proper disposition of our attention, or mind, while sitting—contains no explicit mental instructions. It focuses, instead, on your immediate experience—positive and negative—in zazen:[14]

DISPOSITION OF THE MIND
When Zazen is being practiced satisfactorily, one's mind is always quiet, peaceful, clear, and serene.
The mind then functions perfectly.
The intellect is crystal clear, without a cloud to dim it; the emotions and will are pure and strong.
When one is practicing Zazen, there are times when one becomes sleepy, when one's mind becomes cloudy and heavy; when one is restless like a monkey jumping from tree to tree.
Such conditions are due to an unsatisfactory Zazen practice.

The charming Zen characterization of the mind being like a monkey appears here, in what may be its first printed reference in the introduction of Zen to the West. This restlessness is only one of many barriers that you may expect to encounter in zazen. Also worthy of mention are the cloudy and heavy mind, and the barrier of sleepiness.

Sleepy Monkey

Physical discomfort has always been recognized as one of the main barriers to meditation. But as soon as zazen becomes comfortable, the barrier of sleep comes into play. Practicing with a Rinzai group in southern Japan in the late 1980s, the teacher told us, "You will overcome the pain in your legs. But you will not overcome sleep!"

The dividing line between asleep and awake states is very thin, as we discover in zazen. Between full alertness and deep sleep lie the middle ranges of cloudy and heavy mind, conditions affected by diet and exercise, or lack thereof.

The choice of the term "unsatisfactory" is worthy of comment. It is one definition of Buddhist suffering (S. *dukkha*). Only you can judge whether your meditation is unsatisfactory or not. Your teacher—even Buddha himself—would have a difficult time assessing your experience from the outside. If your zazen is not to your liking, coaching can help. But the call is yours alone to make. If it seems satisfactory, you may be drifting into complacency. But we never give up, sitting through good times and bad.

Ambivalence and vacillation do not constitute reasons to quit, but hurdles to overcome. Like agitations of the monkey, distractions are countered by returning our attention to our posture and breath. We cannot, by definition, know that zazen is not working, somehow, on a subliminal level. Suspending judgment, we do not gauge the quality of a particular session, but we can adjust as we go:[15]

> It is most effective to recompose one's body when you find that you are not doing Zazen satisfactorily.
> It is also traditional to ask to receive the *kyosaku*.

The *kyosaku* is a functionally designed, meter-long, flat stick, usually made of oak, used as an aid to correcting posture, the attendant placing it firmly against the spine. When the stick is gently pulled away, we feel a "ghost stick," telling us where true vertical is.

Blow of Compassion

The stick has rounded edges on one side, designed for striking the shoulders without bruising. This countercultural procedure—hitting someone with a stick—is highly recommended for enhancing zazen but is done upon request only, at least in Soto zendos. It is also greatly misunderstood in the West. Chronicled in one of Matsuoka Roshi's published talks, wherein he quotes a contemporaneous newspaper article titled *The Ordeal of the Oak Stave*, as reported by a Western journalist: [16]

> Just last week, in the *Chicago Sun-Times'* Sunday morning paper, there appeared an article about Zen Buddhism. Its title was "Zen Buddhism—Japanese Ordeal of the Oak Stave," and it had been written after the author's

visit to Engakuji Temple in Kamakura, Japan. The article told of a morning spent in meditation in the Temple. By this, the author meant to introduce what he saw of Zen Buddhism to those people who know Zen only as a name or as a cult joined by the neurotic or the discontented.

This is an early example of "fake news," a canard that has become widely believed. But the blow of the stick is not meant to punish, nor to impose discipline. It is instead a highly refined technique, similar in effect to shiatsu, a Japanese form of penetrating massage. The slap of the stick relieves strain in the shoulders, blowing thoughts out of the mind like an exhaust fan. The term *kyosaku* connotes "blow of compassion" and is sometimes called the "wake-up stick." Matsuoka Roshi would often say, with a mischievous gleam in his eye, "It will wake you up!" When I mentioned this to Okumura Roshi, whose lineage does not use the stick, he said, smiling, "That is your responsibility."

Many Zen centers do not take advantage of this compassionate technique. The stick has fallen into disuse, even disrepute, in some Zen communities. This apparently owes to misinterpretation, or the founding lineage teacher not recommending it. Or the notion that it smacks—no pun intended—of senseless and unnecessary violence in an overly violent age. If so, this is an unfortunate misunderstanding of an ancient Eastern tradition, colored by modern political and cultural correctness. Completely contrary to popular misconception, it is not a form of punishment, but startlingly refreshing.

Compassion versus Cruelty

Even posture correction, offered as needed, usually once per sitting period—through touch, rather than words—is avoided in some Zen centers. Perhaps because it intrudes upon the meditator's personal space. In our lineage, we consider correcting posture our responsibility, if someone clearly needs it. If the body is straight and upright, the mind has to follow. It is not compassionate to ignore someone sitting like a cashew.

Matsuoka Roshi had such great respect for the effectiveness of the kyosaku, referring to it as the "direct teaching," that he chose it as the title of his first published collection of talks, devoting two chapters to explaining its true meaning and import. He trained us diligently in its safe and effective use. He once said that his own father struck him many times with the stick as part of his Zen training in childhood. But he added that his father never struck him in anger. Contrast this with modern views of child abuse.

True compassion can sometimes look like cruelty, tough love. We apply the stick very carefully, and only if requested. When visiting Zen centers, it is prudent to inquire as to their approach to all protocols, including the use of the stick. Like most things in life, being struck with the stick can be understood only by experiencing it.

Finding Perfection

The summary stanza at the end of the pamphlet lists some of the short- and long-term benefits of Zen, in poetic but relatively specific terms:[17]

PERFECTION IN ZEN
When one is able to put into actual practice the disposition of the body, the disposition of breathing and the disposition of the mind, then one's Zazen is already in the stage of perfection.
Here are some of the effects that will appear when one's zazen is in the stage of perfection:
The body is filled with the feeling of good health and has the elasticity of a rubber ball.
The mind is clear and refreshed. Its functions are agile and quick.
One finds happiness in whatever one does.
One finds richness of life in everything one attempts.
One clearly knows one's life's direction and has no hesitancy.
One is calm, brave, and happy in thought, speech, and conduct.
One is openhearted, unsophisticated, and spontaneous.
One does not hide things from others.
One is in harmony with the surroundings into which one assimilates oneself.
One does everything with sincerity and initiative.

Note the phrase "When one is able to put into actual practice." This implies that we may believe we are doing zazen when, in actuality, we are not. We may lull ourselves into complacency very early in the game. Assuming that our posture is perfect, that we are breathing in the most natural manner, and that our mind is clear and focused. But we may be off just a tad. Similarly, one may presume that one is in "harmony with the surroundings into which one assimilates oneself," when, truth be told, one is the proverbial bull in the china shop.

We should also note that the term "perfection," here, is not meant to propose that we can actually perfect our Zen practice. It suggests, though, that
our zazen can become perfect at some point and will help us refine our lives,
an expression coined by Okumura Roshi's teacher, Uchiyama Roshi. Sensei
would often instruct us to just continuously "Aim at the perfect posture, never
imagining that you have achieved it." If we are not to expect perfection in
posture, how much more so should we abandon the idea of perfecting Zen
itself? Even Zen masters do not master Zen; Zen masters us.

Posture Paramita

The traditional Six Perfections of Buddhism—Charity, Morality (Precepts),
Patience, Endurance, Contemplation, and Wisdom—are called *paramita* in
Sanskrit. We regard them as processes of perfecting, rather than as fixed goals
to achieve. But they all begin with, and stem from, "posture paramita" in zazen.
Following the Buddhist Perfections is not an intellectual pursuit, but putting
them into action. Sitting in Zen is the greatest action we can take. It provides
the self-reflective mirror in which we begin to observe our own daily behavior.
Which is the first step toward coming into harmony with our surroundings.

On My Scout's Honor

If this part of the pamphlet is beginning to sound a bit like the Boy Scouts'
code of honor to you—without the God-and-my-country part—it is for good
reason. Matsuoka Roshi was completely convinced of the efficacy of Zen, from
his own personal experience, as was Master Dogen and as am I. He translated
that enthusiasm into language as colorful and effusive, as did the great thirteenth-century founder of Soto Zen, but in terms that modern Westerners
could readily understand.

Zen's promised benefits range from the development of personal well-being
to interpersonal harmony and cultural refinement, through attitudinal adjustments that we might reasonably expect from our efforts. Always with the caveat
that we do not become overly attached to outcomes. The issues and outcomes
that we can discuss are those that we have in common, to state the obvious.

But identifiable benefits are only the tip of the Zen iceberg. Sensei used
this metaphor to illustrate that the great power of Zen to transform our lives
is like the hidden part of an iceberg: most of it is invisible, just below the
surface of the ocean of awareness. But, like the Titanic, we will surely feel

its impact, eventually.

Meeting Buddha in Person

The quest for Zen may be considered a pursuit of the miraculous, but it is to be found in the ordinary. What was most miraculous about what I sought, and found, in Chicago was meeting Matsuoka Roshi, a genuine Zen master (J. *zenji*). His teaching of zazen as the essence of Zen, and its resultant spiritual confidence, was vintage Dogen. When a student asked him how he knew when he was doing zazen right, "Sitting-mountain feeling!" was his answer.

This phrase succinctly captures the undeniable experience of profound physical stability to be found in zazen, accompanied by mental clarity, emotional peace, and confidence in life. For me, at a time of turmoil in my life, it became a transformative experience. Which, by definition, cannot occur on a conceptual level. The rationale for devoting the requisite time to sitting still enough, for long enough, is to bring about just such a transformation. You have to push the envelope.

Two inescapable aspects of Zen have stuck with me since then: first—the simplicity of Zen's method, zazen; second—the character of the teacher-student relationship. These do not comprise two separate dynamics but are integrated in one holistic approach in Zen. Relying primarily on zazen relieves pressure on the relationship. The relationship of the Zen student to the teacher is a true collaboration, like that between a mother hen and a hatchling chick, both pecking at the same shell until it cracks, when the two suddenly find themselves in the same world. This is known as "coming to accord" and is accomplished through an apprentice mode of training. But you can get started meditating now and find your teacher later. When you need a guide to penetrate to the interior of the original frontier, you will find one.

DIFFERENTIATING ZEN MEDITATION FROM ALL THE OTHERS

Now that we have an overview of the method of Zen, and its provenance in my life, let's place zazen in the context of meditation in general. Zen offers a basic style of meditation, and a most appropriate philosophy for Americans in particular. As an entrée on the smorgasbord of various approaches on offer today, it is the simplest and most direct. The least encumbered with doctrine that must be assimilated, in order to start meditating and enjoying its halo effect on daily life. Zen is "jump in both feet," as my teacher would say. It is not really necessary to go through preliminary preparation, or extensive study, in order to begin benefiting from its practice of zazen. Other sects may disagree, but Zen places great trust in your original mind, and your ability to recover it on the cushion.

For a bit of the history of meditation in America, and to provide some background for your exploration of Zen's frontier, we turn to meditation historian Daniel Goleman:[18]

Meditation was new to the West some fifteen years ago when I wrote *The Varieties of the Meditative Experience*, which form the first three chapters of this book. To be sure, Eastern teachers such as Yogananda and D. T. Suzuki had come to America much earlier and had gained followers here and there. But during the late 1960s and early 1970s, there was a blossoming interest in meditation like none the West had witnessed before.

Matsuoka Roshi was one of the earliest pioneers of Zen in the West, arriving in America in 1939 at the tender age of twenty-seven. He was the first to recommend Zen meditation to his America students; his contemporaries apparently did not think that we were ready for it.

Many who seek out Zen today have read extensively about it and may have already discovered that there is something almost miraculous about its simple meditation. The testimony of Zen's ancestors—in the form of the written record of its transmission from Buddha in India to Bodhidharma, who brought it to China, and the great masters responsible for its transmission to the East through China, Korea, and Japan—is evidence that Zen has the power to transform lives. Many ancestors went to great lengths, even risking injury and death, to find the real Zen.

Of course, this kind of spiritual quest is not limited to Zen. But Zen has inspired its adherents to turn away from the blandishments and seductions of their predominant culture, taking up the search for that "something missing" in their lives. For many in Chicago in the 1960s, it took the form of exploring psychedelics and other drugs, experiments in nontraditional forms of community, and the inchoate blossoming interest in Zen.

My own practice of Zen began in the mid-'60s and so was a small part of this blossoming. In those days, from the numbers of people who came to the Temple on a regular basis, it seemed that Zen was catching on, but not on a very large scale. The zendo consisted of the living and dining rooms in the first-floor railroad apartment of a three-story brownstone walk-up on the Near North Side, leaving little room for a large congregation.

At that time, we had no access to the internet, no email, no handheld mobile smart devices, no digital social media at all. I was only marginally aware of the burgeoning of computer technology and had no inkling of the communications revolution it would bring. Which today certainly helps accelerate the propagation of Zen.

In spite of the dearth of connectivity, Dr. Goleman goes on to point out the rapid assimilation of meditation into the culture at large in the intervening years following his first publication:[19]

Now, more than a decade later, things have changed. Meditation has infiltrated our culture. Millions of Americans have tried meditation, and many have incorporated it into their busy lives. Meditation is now a standard tool used in medicine, psychology, education, and self-development. In addition, there are many old hands who are now well into their second decade as meditators.

As these meditators have taken their places in the ranks of business people, professionals, and academics, they have made meditation a part of the fabric of the culture. People meditate at work to enhance their effectiveness, psychotherapists and physicians teach it to their patients, and graduate students write theses about it.

Meditation has certainly become mainstream, perhaps one reason you are reading this book. Searching "meditation" online currently yields about 400,000,000 results. But Zen still has a long way to go to become a formative force in the culture. While meditation is increasingly common in America, the vast majority of its citizens still have no direct experience of Zen's approach, let alone the benefit of advanced training, especially with an experienced Zen teacher.

Some, including yourself, may have negative preconceptions of meditation—Zen or otherwise—as self-indulgent or a waste of time. Others may have a positive attitude toward meditation in general but have never experienced the deeper intensity of zazen. To begin illustrating the difference, we look to the onboard dictionary, which defines meditation as:[20]

1. the emptying of the mind of thoughts, or concentration of the mind on just one thing, in order to aid mental or spiritual development, contemplation, or relaxation
2. the act of thinking about something deeply and carefully, or an instance of such thinking
3. an extended and serious study of a particular topic

Workable enough definitions, given the conventional place of meditation in modern culture. However, here is where zazen begins to part company with meditation, as so defined. These characterizations are not typical of Zen's meditation, however much the descriptions may sound similar. The distinctions may be subtle, but they are crucial to the special place that zazen occupies in the panoply of meditation approaches on offer.

Where Zen Meditation Differs

Briefly, zazen is not about emptying the mind of thoughts, but getting beyond knee-jerk reliance on analytical thinking. Zen meditation is not concentration of the mind on one thing, but expanding awareness to embrace everything, optimizing inclusive consciousness. Zen's purpose is not limited to mental or spiritual development. Nor is contemplation the objective, in the ordinary sense of mulling over ideas or musing about reality. Relaxation is not a goal, as such, though greater calmness may be considered a side effect. And zazen is certainly not about thinking about something deeply, or the study of a particular topic. Intellectual ideation or speculation, however useful or entertaining, is not the purpose of zazen.

From this, you may grasp that it is easier to say what Zen meditation is not than what it is, exactly. If I had to say what zazen is, in contrast to meditation in general, I would say it comprises a backward step—Dogen's expression—turning our usual approach 180 degrees. Zazen reverses the usual grasping of the thinking mind, letting unfiltered experience flow to us, instead of chasing after enlightenment or any other preconceived benefit. Zazen is not a means to an end, as are other meditations, but an end in itself.

Not Your Daddy's Meditation

Zen meditation differs markedly from conventional meditation as defined by the dictionary. Emptying the mind of thoughts is not a practical approach to daily life and is not recommended while on the cushion. We observe thoughts dispassionately, just as we observe our breath and what is going on with our senses.

Not thinking actually proves impossible to achieve, at least by mere force of will. The cliché "Do not think of elephants!" illustrates this point dramatically. Our thoughts are usually running on autopilot. But they do not have to get in the way, as habitual or obsessive-compulsive rumination.

Discriminating mind (S. *citta*) can be stubbornly persistent, one reason it is called monkey mind. Like the archetypal, greedy monkey with its fist stuck in the cookie jar—stubbornly clutching too many cookies to fit through the opening—the grasping mind is unaware that it is getting in its own way. But it will not let go without a fight. The monkey will not be satisfied with a few cookies, let alone one. It is intent on indulging its cravings and entertaining itself. It seeks out as much distraction as it can manage to conjure up. Especially when confronted with a blank wall, typical of Soto Zen meditation.

Any attempt to suppress the natural process of clinging thought also amounts to a form of thinking. We assume a position of simply observing thoughts: watching them arise, without judging. Without giving them too much importance, but not ignoring them entirely. They could be leading somewhere important, after all.

Obsessive thinking naturally, but gradually, comes to play a less central role. Eventually, the monkey settles down and takes a nap, like a worn-out kitten or puppy. This allows the emergence of Wisdom Mind (S. *bodhi*), original mind. Deep intuition, beyond, or underlying, thinking.

We do not concentrate on any one thing but, instead, pay full attention to everything. Everything is always changing. Like driving on a busy expressway, where so much is happening simultaneously and at a deceptively rapid rate of change that there is no time to think. The difference is that we are sitting still, on a cushion. But everything is still changing continuously, if subtly, below the threshold of normal awareness.

Thinking versus Nonthinking

The second definition above, "the act of thinking about something deeply and carefully," is the flip side of emptying the mind of all thoughts. This is the usual definition of concentration and is culturally synonymous with meditation. These two polar definitions contrast with the middle way of zazen, in that it is neither thinking nor not thinking, but somewhere in between. What Master Dogen referred to as "nonthinking."

Thinking deeply, along with the third definition, "an extended and serious study of a particular topic," is more germane to scholarly pursuits than to Zen. They have little or nothing to do with zazen. However, extended periods of not thinking—or nonthinking, as our new normal frame of mind—prepares us for intensive bouts of thinking, when it is demanded. Like resting up before running a marathon.

Thinking is the exercise of the brain. Like any muscle, it occasionally needs a break. Extended study usually entails assimilation of knowledge, via fact-gathering and analysis. Gaining knowledge is, in a way, virtually the opposite of zazen, which is more accurately defined as a process of unlearning.

Zazen is personal application of the K.I.S.S. (Keep It Stupid Simple) principle. Keeping our practice stupid-simple means avoiding meditating on any specific subject in particular. Sensory experience in zazen is, itself, the direct teaching of the dharma.

We do not meditate on any particular teaching or doctrine, to assimilate its content or to realize its implications. Nor do we use any specific, external object as the focus of concentration. Contemplating any identifiable thing at all necessarily divides reality into subject and object. Eventually, zazen becomes objectless (J. *shikantaza*). It is not meditation, in the technical sense. When the mind no longer has an object, likewise there can be no subject. You cannot get any simpler than that.

Concentration, Relaxation, Contemplation

Zen practice certainly does aid mental or spiritual development, and it fosters concentration, relaxation, and contemplation. But concentration in Zen is not merely restricting attention to one object or subject matter. Instead, a state of intense concentration accumulates over time. Like a supersaturated saltwater solution, crystallized by zazen practice.

This explains the mysterious, sudden insight of a monk sweeping the sidewalk, triggered by the sound of a stone striking the bamboo. Or being enlightened by the sound of a frog jumping into a pond. When ripe and ready, any ordinary everyday event can turn the trick.

Relaxation is often overemphasized in meditation. It is not an attribute, or a goal, of zazen. Zazen may be regarded as the opposite of relaxation in the conventional sense. Zen's sitting posture is very rigorous, not at all like normal sitting. It is more like a cobra rising off the floor, ready to strike. Or a lion ready to pounce.

The relaxation found in Zen functions on a deeper level, not subject to control. Over time, our body develops a balanced muscular tension—equilibrium, or equipoise—and the nervous system relaxes in response. This depends on surrendering our usual defensive reflexes, as well as mental resistance. The self-centered, frenetic monkey mind is difficult to cajole into relaxing. It is hardwired to be ever alert to threats to its survival. And Zen is definitely a threat to the survival of the ego. You can expect your personal monkey to put up a terrific fight. More like a 600-pound gorilla. Don't fight back.

Contemplation is a traditional form of meditation, the terms often being used interchangeably. Let's clarify its unconventional meaning in Zen.

Zazen versus Contemplation

A venerable meditation technique, translated from Sanskrit as "contemplation" (S. *dhyana*), entails focusing attention upon an object, external or internal, for extended periods of time. This fosters a mode of awareness eventually transcending thought, reducing interaction to raw observation. Contemplating any object—say a plumb blossom on a branch—will eventually exhaust any and all thoughts about it. What is left is contemplation, unfiltered awareness. Extended to the environment, contemplation becomes total absorption.

When pundits in China would come to quiz Bodhidharma, the story goes, he would turn his back on them, facing the wall. They interpreted this as "wall-gazing Zen," presuming he was using the mountain wall of his cave as an object of contemplation (C. *ch'an*). But the Twenty-Eighth Patriarch in India, the first Zen ancestor in China, was not demonstrating contemplation. He was "just precisely sitting" (J. *shikantaza*), in which there is no object of contemplation. Thus "Zen," phonetic Japanese for *ch'an*, turns out to be something of a misnomer.

Zazen may be regarded as contemplation of a totally different order. No specific object selected from Nature. No sutras, or an assigned riddle, or koan, as in Rinzai Zen. We do not even contemplate the blank wall we are facing. You could say that we contemplate reality itself. Or its salient aspects, such as impermanence. But more simply, "Sit until you forget there is someone sitting," as Sensei suggested.

In Soto Zen, we do not rely on thinking and study, let alone thinking about something deeply and carefully. Of course we are encouraged to study the written record diligently, but only in concert with meditation. We are admonished to thoroughly examine buddha-dharma in practice, not to substitute our own standards. But meditation comes first; study, second. If pursued in a balanced manner, this sets priorities, reinforcing and mutually informing both.

Forgetting the Self

The initial object of contemplation in Soto Zen is your own "self." More expansively, your self-centered worldview—which we are challenged to examine, deeply and honestly. This includes scrutinizing your self-identity, with a growing, healthy skepticism as to its validity. Which, understandably, makes anyone uncomfortable. Sustained study of the self, informed by Zen's teachings regarding nonduality of self and other, becomes the primary focus. The separation is more apparent than actual, as indicated by Dogen in a famous passage from the first fascicle of his written masterwork, the *Shobogenzo*:[21]

> To study the Buddha Way is to study the self. To study the self is to forget the self. To forget the self is to be verified by all things. To be verified by all things is to let the body and mind of the self and the body and mind of others

drop off. There is a trace of realization that cannot be grasped. We endlessly express this ungraspable trace of realization.

What appears at first blush to be self-centered navel gazing—studying the self—evolves and expands with the maturing of practice to embrace not-self. The first significant turning point is forgetting the self, after which meditation is no longer only, or all, about yourself. Forgetting the self is not willful self-sacrifice, or naiveté, but a mark of spiritual growth. We turn from intense absorption in the self, necessary to beginning Zen practice, to attention to other—primarily the sufferings of other humans, but also all sentient beings. Body and mind of the self cannot drop off—without the body and mind of others dropping off. And vice versa. The two are "not-two," an ancient expression of nonduality, from Chinese Zen.

Of course, many seekers first come to Zen to deal with a personal crisis, social suffering, or a generalized, existential angst. For some time, this remains the focus of their Zen practice. But in time, we come to forget the self, through identifying with the original nature we share with all beings. Which, in turn, becomes the verification of our Zen practice.

A wider embrace emerges, a more complete worldview, in which other merges with self. Master Dogen assures us that once our awakening to the preexistent reality of all things becomes thoroughgoing and complete—traceless—it is forever. There is no turning back, but there is also no detectable trace of any such change to be found. This is the deeper meaning of "leaving no traces," expressed in ordinary daily activities such as cleaning (J. *soji*).

In Goleman's estimable book, he clarifies, in some detail, differences and similarities inhering in a broad range of meditation approaches, including Hindu Bhakti, Jewish Kabbalah, Christian Hesychasm, Sufism, Transcendental Meditation, Patanjali's Ashtanga Yoga, Indian Tantra and Kundalini Yoga, Tibetan Buddhism, Zen, Gurdjieff's Fourth Way, and, finally, Krishnamurti's Choiceless Awareness. Goleman laments that the original raison d'être for meditation, in all these instances, is often lost in translation to future generations:[22]

All too often, religious institutions and theologies outlive the transmission of the original transcendental states that generated them. Without these living experiences, the institutions of religion become pointless, and their theologies appear empty. In my view, the modern crisis of established religions is caused by the scarcity of the personal experience of these transcendental states—the living spirit at the common core of all religions. And that spirit unites the diversity of meditative forms.

Zen may be the exception that proves the rule. Its lineage ancestors, down to the present day, are presumed to have personal insight. Otherwise, they would be nothing but pretenders. Matsuoka Roshi constantly insisted on the primacy of "living Zen."

While we may be sure that each of these approaches to meditation has something to offer, we believe zazen to be the most directly accessible of all, deceptive in its simplicity. Importantly in today's climate of religious ambivalence, zazen is free of overlays of belief systems. Anyone, of any belief or worldview, is welcome and able to practice Zen meditation, though it may result in challenging their beliefs or rebooting their worldview.

Today, more than another couple of decades later, the list of meditation styles itself would likely fill a large volume, comprising evermore variations on the theme. Introducing his survey of meditations, Goleman declares:[23]

Experience is the forerunner of all spiritual teachings, but the same experience can be expressed differently. In any given tradition, the map of meditative states set down is to some degree arbitrary. The map is not the territory, and the terrain traversed in meditation is nebulous to begin with. It is little wonder that maps of meditative states seem so different from one another.

This distinction between the experience and the expression of it is crucial to understanding Zen's teachings. Personal emphasis is on experience, expression being more or less a matter of social necessity. Experience comes first; expression, second. We may safely assume that this holds true for all categories of meditation, and for any resultant spiritual insight. It must be experiential, in essence. Whether any two people's experience can be defined as the same, however, is questionable.

Experience versus Expression

The experience and expression of the insights of Buddha and the revelations of Jesus were very different. Both spent time in the wilderness, both ascended and descended the mountain, and both sat in the garden. And neither ever wrote a word, apparently. Goleman seems to assert that their experience was at least similar. But we can be sure that it was necessarily informed by, and framed within, the idioms of their disparate cultures: that of India some 2,500 years ago, versus that of the Middle East 500 years later, respectively.

In retrospect, for us living today, the half millennium separating the inception of these two great world religions shrinks in proportion to the two millennia transpiring since. Some authors have made the case that the founders' original teachings are, in many ways, similar, when translated correctly. This debate I gladly leave to the scholars. Let's pay it forward.

Exploring any new frontier—boots on the ground—precedes reporting back to others. In exploring Zen, experience is first in importance, as well as in time. Reporting necessarily follows. Intellectual analysis occupies an even more remote third position in priority. And speculative flights of fancy, dead last. Wishful thinking can be deadly on the wild frontier.

First-person experience being the sine qua non of Zen—and, one hopes, deepening with time—humility dictates that we resist the temptation to indulge expression of premature insights. Talking about ourselves is an endlessly fascinating preoccupation: witness ubiquitous talk shows, the selfies craze, and the me-me-me mania of social media. But Zen is not up for debate and is not a suitable topic for casual discussion (e.g., at a cocktail party). Following dharma talks, or dialogue with your teacher (J. *sanzen* or *dokusan*), is encouraged. But it is best not to talk too much, publicly, about your Zen practice.

There are several reasons for this circumspection. "Insight" means "seeing into" in Zen. Seeing into the truths that Buddha pointed to. Which takes some time. Your first insights are likely to be relatively trivial. Better to wait until they comport with buddha-dharma.

And it is not that Zen values secrecy: Buddha's truth is said to be open and accessible to all. But it is difficult to discuss Zen without causing confusion, creating "flowers in air." Talking excessively about one's experience—especially following an intense retreat, for example—tends to dilute its effect. Casual conversation amounts to a kind of dissipation, particularly as regards Zen's deeper meaning.

We also want to avoid creating an impression that Zen teachers should be telling others what they should be experiencing, and what it means, in meditation. This is one reason Zen does not stress guided meditation. Reasonable exceptions include dispensing simple instructions, and occasional, inspirational exhortations to meditators (J. *teisho*).

Emphasizing experience over expression is a cautionary tale for our times, as it has been throughout generations of Zen. Expression is, nevertheless, an important dimension in Zen, but given a twist by Dogen:[24]

All Buddhas and ancestors are expressions. Thus, when buddha ancestors intend to select buddha ancestors, they always ask, "Do you have your expression?" This question is asked with the mind and with the body.

There it is again, the nonseparation of body and mind. Dogen appreciates both linguistic and nonlinguistic manifestations of buddha-nature. Zen masters express the Way through verbal as well as nonverbal behavior. Their very being is, itself, an expression of awakened nature. All beings share buddha-nature but are not necessarily awake to it.

Dogen insisted that Dharma is a universal expression, to be found in Nature, in the works of humankind, in our direct experience, and even in the written record. It follows that we can apprehend it directly, if we have the eyes to hear and the ears to see. Eyes, or seeing, traditionally symbolize intellectual understanding, whereas hearing, ears, represent intuition. We want to see intuitively and to hear with discernment.

But in our approach to our personal practice, we may be distracted from unfiltered experience, engaged in the more entertaining activity of translating our every insight, however trivial, into words. This is getting the cart before the horse, or ox, so to speak. Dogen expands on the transcendental meaning of expression via mixed analogies regarding firewood and ash, birth and death, winter and spring:[25]

Firewood becomes ash and does not become firewood again. Yet, do not suppose that the ash is future and the firewood past. Firewood abides in the phenomenal expression of firewood, which fully includes past and future and is independent of past and future. Ash abides in the phenomenal expression of ash, which fully includes future and past. Just as firewood does not become firewood again after it is ash, you do not return to birth after death.

This being so, it is an established way in buddha-dharma to deny that birth turns into death. Accordingly, birth is understood as no-birth. It is an unshakable teaching in Buddha's discourse that death does not turn into birth. Accordingly, death is understood as no-death.

Birth is an expression complete this moment. Death is an expression complete this moment. They are like winter and spring. You do not call winter the beginning of spring, nor summer the end of spring.

A lengthy quote, but all of a piece. And sufficient to illustrate the multidimensional meaning of "expression" in Zen. The analogy utilizes an everyday reference—at a time when your HVAC system consisted of firewood in the winter, shade and a cool breeze in the summer—to get at the highly fraught issue of birth and death. Note that he does not set up death in opposition to life, but instead to birth. These two events—though clearly different from our self-interested perspective—in a neutral sense belong to the same class: major turning points, necessary to the natural progression of life itself.

The phrase "the phenomenal expression" of firewood or ash begs the question: Who or what is expressing this? Ordinarily, we take expression to be the activity of someone, or something. In this case, we may assume Nature to be the agent, for sake of argument. But Dogen is not directly imputing the expression of firewood, or ash, to any other source, but to the firewood and ash itself: as self-expressions, necessary and sufficient manifestations in time.

When he takes the abrupt turn to address birth and death in the same breath, the shock tactic creates a kind of whiplash. Suddenly this abstract dissertation has turned very personal. That both birth and death are regarded as "expressions complete this moment" again begs the question: Expressions of what, exactly?

Again, one may assume Life, itself, to be the culprit. Birth is an expression of life; death is an expression of life. They are part of a continuum that is not a respecter of persons. Just as winter, summer, and spring, as well as the unmentioned fall, are well-known concepts that we differentiate as "seasons." At one and the same time, they do not exist as separate entities and yet do not become each other, with the passage of time. This is the nature of time itself. Past, future, and present are inseparable, in what my teacher referred to as the "eternal moment," the present reality. Dogen succeeds in neatly conflating human expression with that of Nature in this marvelous passage.

Experience First, Expression Second

From its inception, the history of Buddhism separates these two parallel tracks, for the sake of clarity: the experience of insight versus its expression, in whatever media. Experience is essential. Expression is a matter of skillful or expedient means, which vary greatly from person to person. Even some of Buddha's disciples were said to "have it, but not the use of it." "It" indicates the possibility that they—or you, or I—may experience deep insight. But we may have little or no ability, or even any inclination, to express it. And that is okay, as we say—better than the alternative: lots of expression, with precious little experience.

Some may have more natural ability to express their experience, but it doesn't help much, in lieu of any real depth of experience. Dogen did not hesitate to criticize such teachers in his time. This latter group also includes contemporary teachers you may have come across, some self-anointed. As well as earnest, but overzealous, meditators. Sensei cautioned against this in our time as well (insertion is mine):[26]

> In critically examining the Zen sects, you will find a range of teachers in each of the three sects [Soto, Rinzai, and Obaku] that runs from priests and Roshis with little realization who are but selfishly incompetent impersonators, to lay instructors and Zenjis—or great Zen teachers of complete Samadhi—who have great effectiveness in teaching.
>
> I warn you not to rely only on a particular human tradition, or a name alone, as an emblem of true transmission of wisdom. There are lazy, self-important, and self-indulgent priests who do possess the "right" credentials, not because they have penetrated to the core of life and death, but because they are clever in a worldly sense. Absolutely, you cannot trust them.

This may also help explain the glut of published material available on Zen and meditation. And one reason I feel some ambivalence about contributing to the glut. Zen does not hold smooth talkers in high regard. Nor those, smooth or not, who insist on endlessly talking about Zen. We do not casually promote Zen, nor do we use it for self-promotion.

However, we live in a society in which expression clearly takes precedence over experience, where all opinions are considered equal and the loudest voices get the most attention. A familiar example is the seemingly endless parade of pundits offering the latest and greatest self-help nostrum on television. Another is seen in the false prophets and preachers—supposed leaders—who talk the talk but do not walk the walk. Zen is not immune to this particular disease, unfortunately. This is why finding a true teacher can be an arduous process.

The main point I am trying to make here is that the natural impulse to express our understanding of Zen—in speaking or writing about it to others, or even to ourselves—should take a back seat to the actuality of experiencing Zen. Some contemporaries seem to rush into print with their take on any current fad, including meditation, stoking the publish-or-perish syndrome. The worst-case scenario may be that of influential professional writers, who, immediately upon experiencing their first retreat, cannot resist the impulse to write yet another bestseller about it. Consequently, they can end up misleading a lot of gullible people. On the other hand, some meditation may be better than none, and all meditations eventually lead to Zen, or so I believe. Any meditation that works has something of Zen in it.

Grazing the Spiritual Smorgasbord

Americans tend to approach meditation as a smorgasbord of entrées, grazing through a feast of varying flavors, aromas, and textures and selecting a bit of this and a bit of that. In the context of this moveable feast, Soto Zen is a lot like drinking water: refreshing and nourishing, yes, but relatively tasteless. Zazen is the ultimate reduction, distilled down to utterly irreducible simplicity. And like water, necessary to sustain a Zen life.

The great classical guitarist Andrés Segovia spoke of the guitar in an similar way. Paraphrasing freely, he declared that the guitar is not the full orchestra, with all its voices—but the distillation of the orchestra into a single, all-encompassing voice. Zen is like this.

Being in the Moment

This is not to say that we should smugly keep our mouths shut when something needs to be said, no matter how fraught. Or to be blissfully lost in what is happening in the present moment, no matter how compelling. This latter is a popular interpretation of mindfulness. But just being in the moment is called the "Zen sickness of falling into the moment." It induces us to ignore karmic causality in the Three Times: past, future, and present. If Zen were only about staying in the moment, it wouldn't have lasted 2,500 years!

Addressing just such a misconception, and the danger of thereby getting stuck in our present fixation—a hypnotic state of absorption in meditation—Goleman goes on to quote an admonition from the venerable D. T. Suzuki:[27]

Suzuki warns (1958: p. 135): "When this state of great fixation is held as final, there will be no upturning, no outburst of satori, no penetration, no insight into Reality, no severing the bonds of birth and death." Deep absorptions are not enough. They are necessary but not sufficient steps toward enlightenment. The wisdom of insight follows after and flows from Samadhi.

Note the emphasis on penetrating to the core, or severing the bonds, of birth and death, also mentioned by Sensei. Matsuoka Roshi studied with D. T. Suzuki at Columbia University, so they must have come to some sort of accord, though they hailed from differing influences: Soto and Rinzai, respectively. They would probably have agreed on this point.

Here we find two central terms of Zen jargon: "satori" in Japanese; "Samadhi" in Sanskrit. They recall the two-step formula of stilling the mind (S. *samatha*) and insight (S. *vipassana*) in most meditation techniques. Another Japanese term, *shikan*, has the meaning of "stopping and seeing." In most cases, the former is seen as setting the stage for the latter.

Samadhi, the stillness cultivated in zazen, is important enough to zazen, and how it works, to try to clarify it. As Suzuki warns, in meditation you might find yourself stuck in a false Samadhi, mistaking it for the real thing, prematurely supposing that you have achieved the pinnacle of Zen. This "great fixation," then, must be a compelling and unusual experience. This illustrates the power of the discriminating mind to bring about a state of self-delusion, akin to self-hypnosis. It is a known issue in the history of Zen, found in the "Warning to Practisers: The Fifty False States Caused by the Five Aggregates," an appendix to *The Surangama Sutra*, addressed to one of Buddha's major disciples:[28]

> Ananda, in this profound and clear state of your penetrating mind, the four elements cease to hinder you, and after a little, your body will be free from all hindrance. This is your clear mind spreading to its objects and shows the effectiveness of your meditation, the temporary achievement of which does not mean that you are a saint. If you do not regard it as such, it is an excellent progressive stage, but if you do, you will succumb to demons.

In this set of warnings, Buddha cautions against interpreting transcendent experiences that may come about for anyone who persists sufficiently in meditation. Ten warnings are connected to each of the Five Skandhas, or Aggregates of Clinging: Form, Sensation, Perception, Impulse, and Consciousness, totaling fifty.

The clear and present danger is that upon having extraordinary experience—such as hearing a voice eloquently expounding the dharma, or engaging in dialogue with the creator god Ishvara—one may presume oneself to be fully awakened. Buddha does not deny the validity of such experiences but warns that we can get stuck at a preliminary way station on the path to full realization.

According to Buddha himself, then, Dr. Suzuki's point is well taken. We should not presume that our present experience in meditation, no matter how seemingly profound, is the end of the Path. All such interpretations should be set aside. After all, our ideas about spiritual awakening are just that: just ideas.

True versus False Samadhi

The suggestion that we may experience a false Samadhi is very interesting. But it may come to prey upon the mind of a lot of meditators. How do we know whether our experience on the cushion is genuine Samadhi, or not? Even if there is really no way to be sure, simply accepting the possibility—that we are laboring under a fallacy—may be helpful. Matsuoka Roshi would often say that whatever happens in your meditation, it is the product of your own mind. So we should not give any discovery too much importance, nor should we discount it entirely. He would often say, "Just keep cutting through, like the razor's edge."

It is also worth remembering that if Samadhi is real, it is already present. Our practice of meditation does not create it. All beings must be in natural Samadhi to some degree, including chickens, dogs, cats, and cows. Even plants and insentient beings, Dogen asserts, are all vitally engaged in "buddha activity:"[29]

> Because earth, grass, trees, walls, tiles, and pebbles all engage in buddha activity, those who receive the benefit of wind and water caused by them are inconceivably helped by the buddha's guidance, splendid and unthinkable, and awaken intimately to themselves.

If we do not get stuck in a shallow experience of false Samadhi, it cannot deter us from experiencing deeper Samadhi, awakening intimately to ourselves. Whatever genuine Samadhi is, its meaning cannot be fully captured in words, as the earliest Ch'an poem *Verses on the Faith Mind* assures us (insertion is mine):[30]

> When such dualities [e.g., stillness in motion, motion in stillness] cease to exist, Oneness itself cannot exist. To this ultimate finality no law or description applies.

In light of this ancient Master's conclusion, it is best not to look for a conclusion to Zen practice. Its ultimate finality defies definition. Changes coming about in awareness in zazen can be dramatic, but highly subject to misinterpretation. The best way to avoid misinterpreting is to avoid interpreting in the first place.

Indulging in speculation is yet another step beyond mere interpretation. We must relinquish any preconceptions regarding goals, or final stages, that we may harbor, however attractive they may be. It is better to presume that there is no endpoint. Resolving to continue meditating before, during, and after any realization, however deep and complete it appears. If we do finally reach the end of the original frontier, we will know it for sure.

Contrasting Zen Sects

It may be helpful to note some differences represented by Zen's distinct sects. The two main schools, Rinzai and Soto, are named after their Chinese founders, Master Rinzai (C. *Linchi*), and Master Tozan (C. *Dongshan*), respectively. Thoroughgoing expositions of these sects are available online; a brief overview will suffice for our purposes.

If you yearn for structure, clear stages of progress in practice, you may share a bias of the scholar, as distinct from the open-ended mindset of a simple practitioner. D. T. Suzuki was an eminent scholar and influential writer, instrumental in introducing Buddhism and Zen to America. But his training was in the Rinzai tradition. As was that of Alan Watts, the most famous of D. T. Suzuki's American students. Western impressions of Zen were initially skewed toward the Rinzai worldview and may yet be today. Soto Zen was little known at that time in America.

Rinzai = Koan Practice

Matsuoka Roshi, D. T. Suzuki's student at Columbia University, accompanied him on speaking engagements. Sensei always emphasized the sameness between these two schools, rather than superficial differences, exemplifying the bias of Zen toward inclusiveness. Full disclosure: I have been trained only in the Soto way, qualifying any comments regarding Rinzai.

You may be familiar with this approach associated with Rinzai Zen, known as koan study or word-based Zen (J. *kanna Zen*). An illogical riddle assigned by your teacher provides the object of contemplation while sitting in zazen, as well as during daily activities. While practicing with a Rinzai temple in southern Japan in 1987, we were told that the guiding teacher had just passed over a hundred koans with his teacher. One such koan, coined by Rinzai Master Ekaku Hakuin, a staunch advocate of zazen in eighteenth-century Japan, goes something like "You know the sound of two hands clapping; what is the sound of one hand?"

This question cannot be understood, let alone answered, through logic. The purpose, as I understand it, is to frustrate our habitual analytical processes, so that eventually, ordinary logic is abandoned in favor of a more fundamental, intuitive faculty of mind.

Both sects agree that establishing genuine zazen Samadhi—in simple terms, a profound level of centered and balanced stillness—is a prerequisite for penetrating insight. But the views of meditation itself are distinctly different. Rinzai pedagogy is more inclined to look upon meditation as a means to an end, rather than as an end in itself. Sitting upright, while contemplating your koan, is seen as a vehicle for attaining insight.

This develops at progressively deeper levels, guided by a teacher with whom you have to "pass" a series of selected koans. This would appear to posit a definite cause-and-effect relationship between the contemplation of the koan during sitting and the resultant insight. It also reinforces a dependent relationship with the teacher. The intensity of the relationship, and the combined techniques of sitting meditation and koan study, may be a means to a worthy end, and an aggressive way of countering the monkey mind. But it requires great skill on the part of the teacher.

Soto = Zazen Practice

In Soto Zen, meditation is not merely a posture for contemplating a koan, or a vehicle to achieve a goal, even one as worthy as enlightenment. Zazen is not a means to an end, but the full expression of enlightenment. We are sitting smack dab in the middle of the primordial koan.

This illustrates the true meaning of "expression" in Zen. We fully express the essence of Buddhism in zazen, if all unknown to ourselves. But when it becomes what Sensei called the "real zazen"—when posture, breath, and attention all come together in a unified way—you will know it for sure. This is not yet awakening, but we reach a turning point, in single-pointed awareness, that is beyond conceptual expression. At this point, we are ready and able to "hear the true Dharma" (Dogen), which is manifestly expressed in the working of Nature as well as in the works of humankind, though the majority of human beings are deaf and blind to it.

Soto Zen regards upright sitting itself as the central, indispensable method. It is revered as the full expression of enlightenment in the present, rather than as a means to achieve enlightenment in the future. In this context, a koan would be considered superfluous. And, like any other object, a distraction from the existential koan of reality itself.

We focus our attention on the present reality, the real and present riddle, in the midst of which we are sitting. Rather than on a koan assigned by our teacher, hoping for a future result, triggered by penetrating a series of insights. Right before your face is the living koan, actualizing the fundamental point (J. *genjokoan*).

I do not mean to critique the koan method as ineffective or counterproductive, since I have no training in it. However, it seems complicated, stress inducing, and overly dependent on the teacher-student relationship. To an extent, the approach best suited to you depends upon your individual temperament. But in Soto Zen, we feel that we already have plenty of things to think about. An assigned koan may simply amount to just one more intellectual distraction.

Bringing Zen Home

In the next section we will zoom in on some of the glitches we run into in meditation, and propose some work-arounds that may work for you. Zazen is not your daddy's meditation, as mentioned. Actually, in more and more cases these days, it is. We are now beginning to see twenty- and thirty-somethings whose parents were into Zen in the 1960s and later. We are witness to the second—in a few cases, third—generation of American Zen.

However, the vast majority of parents of today's newcomers to Zen have never studied, let alone practiced, Zen. They may do some other form of meditation, such as yoga, or the trendy mindfulness meditation. But it is important to distinguish where and how Buddha's meditation differed, and how zazen carries on that distinction today.

FINDING
WORK-AROUNDS FOR YOUR
LOUSY EXCUSES

In this section, we will consider some popular notions about meditation, especially those that may discourage us from continuing with the Middle Way method of Zen. Zazen means "just sitting." Contemplating, yes. But nothing in particular. I suggest breaking that rule, temporarily, with some suggestions for dealing with negative attitudes.

When using an application on the computer, we may run into glitches, situations we do not know how to handle, in order to proceed. We turn to the documentation, go online to chat rooms, and, one hopes, find a wizard who can help us with what turns out to be a known issue. They have often been there and done that and can provide work-arounds to get past the problem. Same, or at least similar, for zazen.

Zazen is simple, but no one would say it is easy. Like any method, such as aerobics, Zen cannot work itself but must be worked. Most of the difficulty arises not from zazen itself, but from our resistance to it. Resistance stems from preconceived ideas and expectations about how meditation is supposed to work, and what it is supposed to do for us.

There are many variations on this theme, too many to recount here. But if you see yourself in the pictures painted below, try the "try this" exercise that follows each example.

Most of what you are called on to consider in this section amounts to an attitude adjustment regarding meditation, and your resistance to it. But resistance to the way things work—and disappointment when they stubbornly resist working the way we want them to—is not limited to time on the cushion. Take one example from real life.

The Horse You Rode In On

On the small farm where I spent my formative years, we had a barn and about 20 acres of fenced-in pasture, later planted in soybeans. We boarded horses and would ride them in the spring, after they had wintered in the barn. A stallion that had been captured wild and was then tamed would occasionally kick a hole in the barn wall. Followed by the mare, followed by our gelding; the trio would run a merry race around the grounds of the golf course next door, paying special attention to the greens and occasionally trampling the flags. They did not endear us to the small-town country-club set. The golfers would return the favor by trampling our crops, looking for lost golf balls.

One spring, my older sister was all gussied up in bright white shorts and top for a fashion photography session with my dad. Upon mounting the gelding, just as her leg was slinging up over the saddle he bucked, sending her flying through a graceful arc above him, straight into the mud pond behind the barn. Obviously, he did not appreciate being saddled, let alone ridden. All he wanted to do was to frolic in newfound freedom, after a long winter of confinement. Understandable from an equine point of view. Not so much from my sister's perspective, though she laughed uproariously. Nor my dad's, who did not find it funny.

Zazen is like riding a horse along the unknown trails of the original frontier. It is literally the horse you ride in on. Like my sister, or a cowboy on a cattle drive, you and your horse may not get along very well at first. You may want to go this way, but the horse wants to go that way. Horses have personalities, wills of their own, and they can be mighty stubborn. You may develop some saddle sores in the process.

But if horse and rider, together, are going to finally bring the cattle safely to the end of the drive, every day you have no choice but to get back in the saddle again. Fortunately, after a while, you and the horse begin coming to accord. Eventually, it is as if you are both thinking, and moving, with one mind. But it is still a long way to the end of the drive.

Attitude Adjustment

Certain attitudes that you may harbor—about meditation in general, and zazen in particular—may not reflect simple negativity, reasons why you may feel you cannot do Zen. Instead, they may be misconceptions, leading to disappointed expectations.

Others amount to "must-dos," convictions about "right" versus "wrong" ways to meditate, which are not necessarily true and end up discouraging further efforts. Sometimes we are not happy with what comes up in our meditation. We revisit painful memories and feel anxiety about the future, compulsively planning for imagined, worst-case scenarios.

Take another analogy: you may regard zazen as a key to unlocking the gate to the original frontier. But the lock may be rusty; the key may not turn easily. The dharma gate may be heavy, narrow, or ablaze. In any case, the resistance is mainly in your own mind.

But how zazen can begin to work for you—on the drive, or penetrating the gate—may present less of a mystery than how Zen works overall. It begins with the simple act of sitting down to face the wall. First, let's dispose of some of the top reasons—not to say excuses—that you may feel Zen's unique meditation may not work for you.

Damn Your Lousy Excuses

While consulting in retail design, I came into contact with a Canadian company called DYLEX, which turned out to be an acronym for—I am not making this up—Damn Your Lousy Excuses. Driven by contemporaneous definitions of success in business, they did not admit making excuses for failure. In Zen, however, success is preceded by failure, no excuses.

During my tenure practicing Zen and propagating it to others, this phrase came to take on more relevance. It is so easy to find reasons why we cannot, or will not, do what we secretly know we need, and want, to do. Some of the more common ones, and tricks you may want to try to work around them, follow. They are all interconnected, variations on the same theme.

"I DON'T HAVE TIME FOR MEDITATION."

This is probably the number one reason most modern people claim they cannot do meditation. They imagine that the ancients had plenty of time on their hands, in spite of having none of the technological time-savers we enjoy today. But this was a known issue, even in the early days of Zen in China. Then as now, it can be attributed to limited views:[31]

To live in the Great Way is neither easy not difficult. But those with limited views are fearful and irresolute; the faster they hurry, the slower they go.

This last charming expression may be a historical precursor to the more current "The hurrier I go, the behinder I get" from *Alice in Wonderland*, by Zen Master Lewis Carroll. It is true that most of us seem to have little or no spare time these days. But Zen meditation will repay your investment in it, with interest. By spending time in repose, you tend to be more rested; ready, willing, and able to do the right thing, at the right time. And you tend to do it right. You save time that otherwise you would waste, going off half-cocked, or second-guessing yourself. In exploring any frontier, you have to bivouac once in a while, to conserve your energy for the next portage.

Matsuoka Roshi used to say, "Five minutes zazen: five minutes buddha! Half-hour zazen: half-hour buddha! But wouldn't you rather be buddha all day?" Just sitting in the posture is already enlightenment, as Dogen emphasized, over and over again. It does not really require sitting for long periods of time. A little bit of Zen is better than nothing.

TRY THIS:

See if you can get yourself to squeeze in Your Minute of Zen (apologies to Jon Stewart) on a daily basis, for however long. In short order, it will begin to work its magic. Most find it reasonable to sit a bit after waking, and just before sleeping. If you do so for a month or two, you will detect a definite difference in your daily attitude. Others will notice too.

Since the duration does not matter that much, you do not have to assign yourself a certain period that you must sit, otherwise feeling that you have failed. You cannot get this wrong. It will be interesting to see how long you can stand to sit there in the morning, before giving in to the anxiety and hitting the panic button.

When and if you begin to freak out, just give up sitting for now, and go about your morning routine. After all, you can sit again tonight, just before you lie down to sleep. Or maybe a bit over lunch. So, no big deal. Even if you can sit for only a minute or two. Or fifteen. Give yourself a break on this.

Then at night, same thing. Watch and observe what happens when you just sit there for a while, instead of immediately lying down to sleep. Or instead of whatever you usually do—watching TV or reading—which, by the way, sleep experts recommend avoiding altogether.

Next time you get ready for bed, or the next time you wake up, just sit on the side of the bed for a few minutes. No cushion, no crossed legs, no incense burning; nothing special. Just give yourself a few minutes for your body to assume the posture, and for your breath to slow down. Your mind will soon follow, becoming calmer before you go to sleep, mitigating any insomnia you may suffer owing to stress. In the morning, it will serve to tamp down any anxiety you may feel regarding the things you have to get done that day.

Each day you can keep track, morning and evening, and see what happens. Keep a journal if you like. You may find that in the beginning, it is difficult to just sit there for more than a few minutes. But if you don't make a mountain out of this particular molehill, you may find that next time, you can be a little more patient. You may even find that you prefer sitting to lying down, after a while. And that your issues around sleep begin to diminish. You may find yourself moving your sitting spot to a permanent location, and sitting longer. A half hour, say.

"MEDITATION IS TOO PAINFUL FOR ME."

This is probably the second-most-common complaint, after the time thing. And it is true that there is physical resistance to the posture, sometimes extreme, that sets in, right away. As well as mental and emotional resistance, a kind of intangible pain. Then there is always social pain, when family and friends are not into Zen and may ask impolite or even impudent questions or make insolent remarks. As to this last kind of pain, the medicine is simply not making an issue of your practice in public, or at home. And continuing long enough that you develop confidence in Zen. The best way to rationalize Zen to others is through your behavior. But here, let us focus on the more obvious kind of physical discomfort.

Time will not necessarily heal all wounds. Make sure any chronic pain is not coming from an actual physical disorder, by checking with your doctor or chiropractor. If that turns up nothing of consequence, then you may have to work it out, in zazen. In this case, time—and correct posture—will win out. And, of course, the usual roster of exercises—walking, biking, swimming, stair climbing—that works the leg joints also prepares you for zazen.

TRY THIS:

Next time you have physical pain, allow yourself to sink into it beyond your usual comfort zone. If adjusting your posture does not help for long, take a more aggressive approach. In your mind, go to the center of the pain, whether a headache or in one of your joints. Imagine that you are at the very pinpoint source of the pain. Then try to make it worse. Turn up the intensity knob. You may find that if you take this "give me your best shot" approach, the pain will not know what to do about it and will give up, before you do.

Another approach is to breathe into the pain. You can feel the rhythm of the breath in the vibration of the pain. You can feel your pulse in the throbbing. Go with it. If you regard the pain as heat, it will take on the property of heat, which is to disperse. When all else fails, move. Zen meditation has the reputation that you must sit stock-still. Ideal, but movement is permitted. Try moving for one whole period, allowing your hips to subtly pulse forward and backward. Then, when you are feeling little or no pain, settle into deeper stillness.

"MY LIFE IS TOO COMPLICATED FOR MEDITATION."

This one is a variation on the not-enough-time theme. If you are like me, your life is, indeed, too complicated. But how you might simplify it should become more obvious in zazen. Often, we overlook the many ways in which we are making things worse, in our hurry to meet our goals and expectations.

Owing to the many difficulties entailed in sustaining a Zen practice, and in the face of the complex lives we live today, the many prescriptions for zazen reduce to a final distillation: Just sit! This is different from your parents' admonition to "Sit down and shut up!" Zen's version is "Sit up and shut down!" And more importantly, "Don't give up!"

Beginning Zen meditation with our ordinary thinking mind (S. *citta),* and progressively giving it less and less to think about, our intuitive mind (S. *bodhi)* can come to the fore. This rebalancing shift in awareness is inevitable, if you are committed to your practice and don't give up too soon. Our self-centered ideas of the world, and of our place in it, eventually have to give way under the relentless, dispassionate observation of zazen. The complete mind (S. *bodhicitta)* can then be realized as our new normal, and natural, fully functioning state of mind.

TRY THIS:

The next time you find yourself in the rush hour of traffic, hurrying somewhere on foot, or engaging in a lively exchange with friends or coworkers, remember to remember what it was like the last time you sat in zazen. See if your motor-muscle memory does not kick in. Finding yourself breathing more slowly and deeply, and sitting up straighter.

In turn, when you find yourself sitting in formal meditation again, remember to remember the frenzy and frantic nature of the prior situation, comparing and contrasting it, on a gut level, with sitting. You make the assessment—you make the choice. We need to be able to come to a full stop from time to time, if only to know the difference. Buddha, it is said, stopped the sun in the sky.

"MEDITATION IS WAY TOO COMPLICATED."

Another concern is that meditation is itself a complicated affair, requiring endless study of techniques and texts or exhaustive training under a guiding teacher, as well as an inordinate investment of time, to bring it to fruition. The overwhelming mass of literature on meditation reinforces this concern, documenting findings, conclusions, and recommendations of thousands of predecessors on the basis of their practice/experience, accumulated over millennia.

Some texts of this corpus explore potential political implications for society of the Zen movement, which can lead to the slippery slope of taking sides in ideological debates of the day. Which may complicate the embrace of Zen even more for the neophyte seeker.

Zen may be complex in execution, but only because we human beings are complicated. Zazen is extremely simple in principle, but tricky to sustain in practice. This owes primarily to the unrelenting anxiety and evasiveness of our monkey mind. Fortunately, the monkey cannot escape the scrutiny of Zen. It has to surrender, eventually.

TRY THIS:

Regard zazen as a minivacation, as one of my teachers suggests (Okumura). Everything else we do in life is output; zazen is input. We spend most of our lives working, generating output. In zazen, we can take a break from everything, soaking in the input of our senses, the wisdom of our body, and the delight of our mind. Don't overcomplicate matters. Enjoy.

"I DON'T WANT TO HAVE TO JOIN A GROUP."

Many people try meditation at home first, following one of the many self-help books available, or those online instructions and mobile apps that the digital age has wrought. Eventually, they seek out a group, realizing that they have gotten only so far with the lone-ranger approach. This brings up the value of Zen Sangha, or community.

Zen meditation goes beyond the limited goals for personal development of ordinary meditation. Another dimension of complexity is added to the pursuit of the real Zen: having to join a group. Since Zen professes that it is the simplest of activities, this is seemingly contradictory.

But Zen practice is not an either-or proposition, but a both-and one. Its full expression includes all three Treasures, or Jewels, of Buddhism: buddha and dharma, as well as sangha. If you can find a group that meets close enough to you, with a competent teacher, you should join them. But you do not have to stress yourself out by commuting every day. Strike a reasonable balance between practicing at home on a daily basis, and less frequently in a more formal setting.

TRY THIS:

Sit by yourself, but also try sitting with others on a temporary, test basis. When and where you can fit it in—on the way home from work, perhaps—find a sitting group in your area. It doesn't matter much if they are Zen based or not. Or start a group, if there is none available. Affiliate yourself with a recognized teacher—online if necessary—who can help you over some of the inevitable hurdles you will encounter. Keep it simple. You will find the commitment to a group encouraging, like any book club or other support group.

"I DON'T HAVE ENOUGH SELF-DISCIPLINE."

Another way of saying this is that I don't have the patience for it. But this is a cop-out in the context of the real world, which tries our patience on a daily basis. If you find that zazen is testing your patience—and your patience is losing—you may want to deflect your attention to the bigger picture. Consider your meditation as part of a more general approach to Zen, as a different attitude and lifestyle. Give it a window of opportunity, say six months.

Zen teachers suggest not trying to do meditation the way you do everything else in life. Go against type. If you are fairly rigid in your daily regimen, loosen up in Zen. If you are relatively sloppy in your daily life, tighten up in meditation. Encourage yourself in this way.

The Zen life, especially zazen itself, is best conducted as an open-ended experiment. We are, after all, exploring a new frontier, the oldest one in existence. Like the scientific method, Zen meditation is an individual path of exploration and observation, combined with an apprentice-based process of training and discovery, if you are lucky enough to have a guide.

Unlike the scientific method, however, the results are not strictly measurable.

Returning to sitting, each time we reenter the laboratory of our own mind, mounting the bench test once again. In this sense, Zen's method is empirical, though not strictly limited only to data accessible through the senses, or reasoning, the traditional definition of empiricism. Zen transcends the senses, primarily through sensory adaptation.

TRY THIS:

If you tend to enforce strict constraints on your sitting practice—such as fixed duration, frequency, and regularity—try approaching it on a more spontaneous basis. Instead of insisting on meditating at the same time each and every day, and for the same length of time, change things up. When the urge strikes you out of the blue, just go and sit. If you happen to be at the office, take a few minutes to drop everything and just sit there. No one will notice. If you are driving on the expressway and the impulse hits, sit up straighter and breathe more deeply. Or take the off-ramp and find a quiet spot to sit behind the wheel for a bit. Then you can get back on the road with a brand-new outlook.

"I CAN NEVER STOP THINKING LONG ENOUGH TO MEDITATE."

Zen meditation is an empirical form of learning from observation through the senses, more so than from analytical thinking. But we can apply scientific observation to thinking itself. Let us go into the weeds a bit, clarifying the more technical meaning of "empirical." Empiricists have long allowed that empirical data also derive from internal observation—as well as from external sources, via the sense realms—involving reflection on what one is feeling and thinking at any given time:[32]

Second, the other fountain from which experience furnisheth the understanding with ideas is the perception of the operations of our own minds within us, as it is employed about the ideas it has gotten . . . which could not be had from things without. . . . But as I call the other sensation, so I call this REFLECTION, the ideas it affords being such only as the mind gets by reflecting on its own operations within itself.

The term *furnisheth*," being "olde" English, is a dead giveaway as to the antiquated provenance of this quote. It is from John Locke, one of the most influential thinkers of the Enlightenment in the seventeenth century.

Ironically, Dogen is also sometimes referred to as the greatest thinker in the history of Japan. Ironic because what he taught was not thinking, but "nonthinking": neither thinking nor not thinking. The Middle Way, on a strictly mental level.

The functioning of the thinking mind—that which furnishes our understanding with ideas—is the self-reflective awareness of the operations of our own mind. This sounds similar to Buddhist expressions of the nature of inmost consciousness and validates the value of introspection to the philosophical endeavor. But Zen is not a philosophical endeavor.

The kind of empirical experience pointed to in Zen transcends the apparent separation of within and without. While the argument may seem to devolve into mere semantics, reflection in Zen implies not the reflection of the mind upon the workings of mentation—but a merging of mind and object. Thus, zazen cannot remain in the realm of traditional empiricism. This is clarified in an ancient Ch'an poem: [33]

Although it is not constructed, it is not beyond words. Like facing a precious mirror, form and reflection behold each other.

The fundamental reality of our consciousness is not constructed—as are our ideas, our native tongue, and our perception. Nonetheless, it can be pointed to with words. The emotive term here is "precious." What is so precious about this mirror? This conjures an image, not exactly a thought. Intuiting the presence of this mirror is not simply an intellectual exercise. It is a direct, and precious, insight—into the nondual reality of the apparent duality of self and other. Of form—appearance—and its reflection in our awareness.

TRY THIS:

Next time you are sitting, see if you do not sense this Zen mirror in the back of your mind, so to speak. It is something like suspecting that the objects of your vision are somehow looking back at you. As if what you are hearing is listening to you. Or what you are feeling is touching you back. A bit eerie, perhaps, but bridging the gap between self and other. Dogen touches on this more than once in another tract:[34]

> At this time all things realize correct awakening; myriad objects partake of the buddha body, and sitting upright, a king under the Bodhi tree, you immediately leap beyond the boundary of awakening.

And further:[35]

> Hundreds of things all manifest original practice from the original face; it is impossible to measure.

While this may sound a bit mystical, as well as eerie, it is only the natural state of things. Things, and you, are not separate from buddha (awakened) nature, which pervades the universe. But this is not to be confused with, or construed as, animism, or as evidence of an independently existing spirit or god. Which are only further constructions of the mind, whether true or not. Then, see if this mirror does not go with you when you leave the cushion.

"MEDITATION BRINGS UP BAD MEMORIES AND WORRIES ABOUT THE FUTURE."

When we sit still enough for long enough, everything will come up in consciousness, like bubbles on a pond. Including what are perhaps long-suppressed, or forgotten, memories. Some of these do not flatter us. We all have things we can't explain, as well as things we are not proud of, in our past.

I find it useful to regard these memories as real, in a particular sense, and not real, in another. If we regard the brain as a recording device with massive storage capacity, we can see why old memories that we would rather forget keep hanging on, long past their relevancy. In this analogy, the recording is real enough. But it is just a recording, not the real thing.

When we hear live music, there is a real person, or a group of people, playing instruments and singing. The result can be emotionally moving. The same principle obtains with nonmusical events in our lives, especially if they are traumatic. Both leave indelible impressions, like the recording grooves of the old-time vinyl records or the digital etching of sounds on a microchip. Unless we destroy the record or erase the file, the recording can be played back again, over and over. Same for memories, stored in the monkey mind. And the monkey loves to replay our collection of greatest hits.

While the karmic consequences of our actions are real and natural, obsessive ruminating over them is not. We are listening to recordings from the past, not the present. Like an archived television show or an old movie, they are shadows of what was definitely real at one time. They may have had dispositive and determinative effects on ourselves and others, traces of which still remain. But they are not real in the present moment, though they may have the same vibrancy. In cases of PTSD, as an extreme example, traces remain in the neurological record, ready to play back at any moment. But they cannot harm you.

TRY THIS:

Next time you are harassed and harried by regrettable memories—anxiety associated with their implications, such as what they might mean about your character, or the pain and suffering yet to follow from them—remember that you are listening to a recording. Without trying to change the channel, take a step back and take in the full context. Recognize that the memory is the movie playing on the inner screen. Look around at the real environment, the theater. It is also like a movie, of course. But it is more real than the memory.

"I CAN MEDITATE IN THE MIDST OF EVERYDAY ACTIVITY, WITHOUT HAVING TO SIT STILL."

Some think they can do meditation while totally disregarding the idea of taking up a specific physical form. They may define meditation as getting into the flow of running, or other exercises such as yogic stretching, or just paying hyperattention to everyday activities. Going with the flow.

I have met adherents of Dzogchen (Tibetan, meaning "great perfection") who claim that this is why they do not practice any discipline such as seated meditation. Instead, they simply engage with every emerging event as the focus of their practice. This is appealing in its simplicity and relieving of the burden of a regimen.

This is close to the connotation of "practice" in Bodhidharma's time, I have heard: intently observing the behavior of oneself and others—the Three Actions of body, speech, and mind—as well as noting underlying motivations. Witnessing whether or not they conform to the Buddhist Precepts, for example. Seated meditation, by contrast, comprised a kind of "analysis," observing whether or not one's direct experience evidenced the tenets of Buddhism, such as that of Emptiness (S. *shunyatta*).

Those who prefer to follow this way of nonmeditating may think they are practicing the Samadhi of action rather than that of repose, I suppose. Some in the martial arts claim that the "Samadhi of action" is a hundred, a thousand, a million times more effective than the Samadhi of repose found in zazen. I say, more power to them.

But zazen stands in stark contrast to what many presume it to be (i.e., primarily mental effort, and unnecessarily demanding physically). If Zen meditation were merely mental, then indeed it could be readily exercised while immersed in the hurly-burly of life.

But because body and mind cannot separate, we cannot really practice zazen without fully engaging the body. The Samadhi of action is built on the Samadhi of repose. Sitting upright, and still, reduces the clamor of activity to a dull roar, for a time. But if we try to force this, we run up against a contradiction:[36]

> When you try to stop activity to achieve passivity, your very effort fills you with activity. As long as you remain in one extreme of the other, you will never know Oneness.

Wholehearted zazen certainly has a halo effect on our daily activities. We examine the Three Actions in zazen, but not necessarily by thinking about them. Simply observing will do.

We begin by thoroughly examining the senses, the focus of the next section. The sixth of which—thinking itself—is seen as mainly, and merely, the pedestrian output of the brain. Thought itself becomes an object—not the instrument—of investigation. Thinking is not aimed at analyzing other phenomena, the usual form of studying anything.

Of course, we may spend a lot of time thinking about thinking itself, leading to some interesting conclusions. Or resulting in an endless regress, a dog chasing its own tail. Our focus in Zen is beyond thought, and prior to its momentary arising. Thinking functions, usually, as an impediment to tapping into the Zen mind. So we turn to the body as our starting point. Dogen captures the physical-logical orientation of zazen in an analogy, quoting a famous exchange between a Ch'an master and student: [37]

> Nan-yueh replied, "When a man is driving a cart, if the cart doesn't go, should he beat the cart or beat the ox? In the world, there is no method of beating the cart, but . . . on the path of Buddha there is a method of beating the cart, and this is the very eye of [Buddhist] study. And even though the method of beating the ox is common in the world, we should go on to study the beating of the ox on the path of the Buddha.

This is a distant relative to today's idiom of "putting the cart before the horse." Making the body sit (the cart), the mind has to follow (the ox). The ox is tethered to the cart just as tightly as the cart is tethered to the ox. For the vehicle to go where we need it to go, we should just simply sit. The rest will follow. However, we do not exclude training the mind on the path of Buddha. Body and mind cannot separate in Zen, but the body is more direct of access. We do not need to overthink this.

TRY THIS:

Go ahead and take a week off, or even just a day, from sitting meditation. During which, diligently focus your attention on your actions, all day long. Or pay strict attention to the actions of others instead. Or both. However you direct your attention, notice any difficulties you have. Again, keep a journal if you like, to document the experiment.

At the end of the day, or the week, sit in meditation again and observe the difference. You will probably find that zazen is like a clearing house, where whatever confusion has accumulated during the day can be dissipated if not completely cleared up.

"YOU HAVE TO GO THROUGH SO MANY STAGES IN MEDITATION."

This is a variation on the theme of overwhelming complexity. And our penchant for incremental gain. Most learning processes we go though are logically divided into stages: beginner–intermediate–advanced;

apprentice–journeyman–master. Approaching practice in this way tempers expectations, fostering patience with going through the drill, hoping to eventually achieve some level of accomplishment. Much like practicing the scales in order to play the piano.

But Zen is a kind of unlearning process. We have to be careful about setting up neat and tidy steps in order to get from here to enlightenment. As Dogen reminds us:[38]

> Zazen is not "step-by-step meditation." Rather it is simply the easy and pleasant practice of a Buddha, the realization of the Buddha's wisdom.

Here, the first Buddha might be rendered with a lowercase "b," representing anyone—including you or me—who practices zazen, potentially realizing wisdom. Buddha with a capital "B" usually represents Shakyamuni himself. The idea is that the wisdom we realize in our meditation is fundamentally the same that he realized in his. But in order to penetrate to the heart of Zen, we must set aside expectations of linear, stepwise, stage-by-stage development leading up to final realization.

Assuming that there are stages to be passed through makes looking forward to the next step, or anticipating the final stage, all but irresistible. This causes us to miss what is directly in front of our face.

TRY THIS:

When you next find yourself in meditation, take another look at this idea of proceeding in stages. What stage are you in at this moment? What stage were you in last time you sat in zazen? How about last week? Last year? Or before you even began practicing meditation? When you were a child? Before you were born? This last is a classic Zen koan. Carrying an idea to its logical extreme can reveal the underlying absurdity of the proposition.

"I GET ENOUGH OUT OF READING ABOUT ZEN WITHOUT MEDITATING."

This attitude characterizes what some have referred to as "bedtime Buddhists." The tendency to treat Zen as something interesting to read about, to study rather than practice, or to take up as another leisure activity. Like a good summer read or joining a book club.

There is no harm in this. Tapping into the vast literature now available is how a majority of people come to be exposed to Zen in the first place. It will, one hopes, lead to a more serious pursuit, in the form of pursuing meditation, at a later time. But it can also become what I term a "substitution effect." Talking the talk is a lot easier, more entertaining, and less demanding than walking the walk. Or, more literally, sitting the sit.

The tendency to read about Zen, instead of practicing it, may be reinforced by any number of cultural influences, such as responding to the latest post of someone you are following on social media. Or as a natural outgrowth of society's overweening emphasis on intellectual knowledge.

Matsuoka Roshi repeatedly warned about substituting "book knowledge" for direct, sensory learning in meditation. Intellectual prowess takes a back seat to humble experience on the cushion. Reading, as well as watching documentaries and movies, can be appealing and entertaining, keeping the monkey happy.

But if we settle for getting what we can secondhand, we miss out on the true potential and meaning of Zen for our lives. On a more sophisticated level, scholarly study of Zen and Buddhism can consume a lifetime and become a total substitute for any real practice. Especially in any profession where publish or perish is the operative catchphrase.

The mind that clings to erudition is the same mind that clings to youth, or to anything else that it may hold dear. Clinging itself is, in fact, the hallmark of the survival-oriented, discriminating mind. Such obsessions mask our fear of aging, sickness, and death. They can comprise the underpinnings of our beliefs and fuel our fantasies. Losing yourself in erudition may be a way of hoping to find an escape, or at least a temporary reprise, from the inevitable decline and decay of life. "What do you do till the doctor comes?" as a design mentor of mine used to ask.

But studying Zen by reading what others write about it is a bit like lapping up leftovers. Counting the treasures of others is a maxim that transcends Zen. The idea that somehow, something may be gained more quickly and readily from efforts made and insight gleaned by somebody else, is justly ridiculed. Received wisdom may offer clarification and guidance along our personal path, but resolution of the crucial issues of life and death come only from direct experience. This is not to lobby against study of buddha-dharma, but only to beware the substitution effect of bedside Zen: reading about it instead of practicing it.

TRY THIS:

For the present, read only what is inspiring, and when it is encouraging. If you find yourself reading instead of sitting, put the book down for a while. You can always get back to it. It's a book.

Next time you meditate, you might bring this into sharper focus. Consider something that you have recently read about meditation, or its implications. Then examine whether or not you actually find anything like that in your own experience. This is the type of analytical meditation practiced in the time of Bodhidharma. Like focusing on a koan, it is not recommended for the long term. Eventually, drop the analysis and get back to just sitting.

"THE PURPOSE OF MEDITATION IS TO CHANGE MY MIND."

For several years running, I gave talks at "Change Your Mind Day" at MABA, the Mid-America Buddhist Association, outside St. Louis, Missouri. One year my talk was titled "You Can't Change Your Mind."

A prevalent attitude is that meditation is mental, all up in the head. If only we can get our mind right, everything will fall into place. But zazen is more physical than mental, or perhaps equally both. This is both its personal strength and its social weakness. Zazen is accessible: just sit. But it takes time to overcome physical, emotional, and mental resistance. Many find it difficult to begin and, even more so, to continue.

Because zazen's method is mainly physical, its effects on awareness stem from natural and familiar processes, such as sensory adaptation. We do not try to make the mind behave; we make the body behave. Eventually the body adapts, along with the mind. But Zazen should be the comfortable way, more like a refreshing stretch of the body than a muscular exercise. Likewise, breathing should be more like a sigh than a belabored effort.

TRY THIS:

Keep a notebook where you sit. When you find yourself lost in thought, whether during meditation or not, make a note of what you have been thinking about, so as not to forget it. Then, setting the note aside, redirect your attention to what is happening in the environment around you. Get outside your head for a moment, feeling the pulse of activity all around. Breathe with it. After a few minutes, return to the train of thought that was so preoccupying you. What does it look and feel like now?

"YOU HAVE TO BE AN EXPERT TO REALLY DO MEDITATION."

Another convention suggests that the deeper meaning of meditation can be taught to you by those in the know. But the secrets of Zen will be revealed only through your zazen, rather than in any text, however enlightened the author and however brilliant their descriptive powers. Even Buddha could not verbalize his experience directly to others.

Shunryu Suzuki Roshi, an outstanding pioneer in establishing American Zen, said this:[39]

In the beginner's mind there are many possibilities, but in the expert's there are few.

The expression "beginner's mind" (J. *shoshin*), made famous as the title of the first collection of Suzuki Roshi's informal talks published in 1970, implies just this. He makes the point that while the mind of the expert is full to overflowing, with no room for anything new, it is not so for the beginner.

This is not to deny that senior practitioners may have some wisdom to share. Zen is probably one of the last bastions in which seniority garners due respect. But expertise in Zen is the opposite of having a narrow, specialist focus. Zen is a broadening experience.

If you are a first-time practitioner, your zazen is essentially identical to that of the most experienced Zen master. Both have the same final purpose— liberation through spiritual insight. Both have beginner's mind. The only difference is in accumulated experience, and maturity in practice. We begin afresh with each sitting session—like a beginner, as opposed to an expert—with an open, inquiring mind.

If Zen could be taught, one way would be through descriptive narration. But most writers about Zen are leery of sharing descriptive accounts of their own personal experience. Notable exceptions include the *Surangama Sutra*, attributed to Buddha, and writings of Hakuin Zenji, the famous eighteenth-century Rinzai Zen master.

The reasons for this hesitancy include a recognition that while much of their experience might be reflected in yours, it is far better discovering it on your own rather than having it laid out for you. Doing so would deprive you of the impact of your own insights and, to that extent, spoil it for you. Describing the experience of the ineffable can also be dangerous, in that words cannot capture it and are likely to be misleading.

My efforts at description are not meant to capture the breadth and depth of Zen, but instead to demystify meditation itself. I confine my remarks to changes I have witnessed from sitting still enough for long enough. I outline the process and progress of sensory immersion, as I know it from personal experience. But this approach is not meant to preempt your natural path, leading you by the nose via secondhand scenarios or suggesting artificial stages of progress. Descriptions of the frontier are bound to fall far short of the actual experience.

TRY THIS:

In that notebook next to where you sit, occasionally jot down major changes in awareness that you notice. Your powers of descriptive writing will be challenged, so don't make this too onerous a process. Just think of your notebook as your short-term memory for the moment. After a week or so, go back and check your earlier entries. Note any evolution from the earliest notations to the most recent. Remember this is an expedient means, intended just to get you over the hump. Zazen is not a means of providing fodder for writing. It is a temporary way of polishing your Zen mirror and keeping your beginner's mind fresh.

"I TRY TO MEDITATE, BUT IT JUST MAKES ME SLEEPY."

You are not alone. Issues with sleeping, and their effects on health and happiness, are a growing area of concern in this age of uncertainty. Sleep is one of the traditional barriers we overcome in zazen. Once sitting in Zen becomes comfortable, drowsiness sets in, erecting yet another barrier. Just when the zazen is getting good, up pops another hurdle.

At this point there arises a fuzzy boundary awareness, like stumbling about, half asleep. You may find yourself drifting in and out of sleep, including startling dreams. Our natural temptation to surrender to slumber is resisted in zazen, just as when driving on the expressway at night. But falling asleep is not dangerous on the cushion, nor is it an insurmountable barrier. Paying strict attention to the boundary between sleeping and waking—a deceptively thin line—is not just another diversion, but a point of departure.

Comparison with sleep offers an apt analogy to Zen. Zen posits no absolute separation of physical and spiritual, or of sleeping and waking. What we normally consider being physically awake is actually a kind of dream state, spiritually asleep. Normal waking is analogous to spiritual awakening. But Buddha's awakening transpires while we are already awake. We are all relatively awake or asleep, both physically and spiritually. The two are an interdependent modality, points on a sliding scale.

A simplified way of framing Buddhism's premise, and promise of fully awakening, derives from this analogy. We were all asleep last night; we all woke up this morning. And we certainly know the difference. Zen suggests that we are still asleep to a significant degree, and that we can wake up from this state as well. If and when we do experience awakening, we will definitely know the difference, as surely as we know the difference between normal sleeping and waking. Both differences are actually very small, a mere quantum leap.

Zazen, then, may appropriately be described as falling asleep but staying awake. The same process we experience when drifting off to sleep, or when slowly waking up, comes into play in zazen. You have probably experienced some odd sensations while falling asleep in bed. Lying in a half-awake, half-asleep limbo, you may feel that your arms and legs are in a certain position. But on closer examination, it becomes clear that they are not. You think your leg is over here, but actually it is over there. If you attempt to move your leg, or arm, it may feel impossibly heavy. Or you suddenly jerk with a violent start, as if you unexpectedly tripped and stumbled. We are startled awake by a panicky feeling of vertigo, falling through space, even though we are still just lying there, safe in our bed.

While falling asleep, the area of our awake brain, ordinarily receiving motor impulses and sense data from the body, turns off. An internal switch is thrown. Sometimes it occurs before we completely lose consciousness. These disorienting impressions are triggered in half-awake, half-asleep states. We enter boundary zones just before we lose consciousness, and just as we regain it. These fluid states are recognized as important to creativity and have been explored by artists, authors, and scientists. Utilizing these gray areas of awareness in creative problem-solving and innovation has been the subject of extensive research:[40]

Although popular wisdom associates trances with seers and yogis and hypnotists, we all experience several varieties of trance state every morning and night. The threshold awareness that often comes upon awakening—called the *hypnopompic* state by modern psychologists—is one of these periods. The twilight state that happens right before the conscious mind drifts off to sleep—called the *hypnagogic* state—is another.

These kinds of awareness, halfway between sleeping and waking, also occur in zazen. In this twilight zone of consciousness, the mind is remarkably uninhibited, which is one reason that zazen may be regarded as the heart of creativity, and critical to problem-solving in everyday life.

Even after we arise from bed and are going through our usual morning routine, it often becomes obvious—from the absentminded things that we do, or forget to do—that we are still half asleep, though we may feel wide awake. This is a truism in Buddhism: We are actually sleepwalking through life. Zen offers a way to wake up completely, like Buddha: this Sanskrit term denotes "the fully awakened one."

TRY THIS:

In zazen, when you are dozy, discrete adjustments to posture can be helpful, such as stretching your neck more vigorously or slowly pumping your chin up and down, like jacking up a car. If you find yourself yawning, breathe more deeply. Occasionally hold your breath, especially the out breath.

When you first lie down in bed, instead of tossing and turning, lie as still as possible, in whatever posture you find yourself in, as long as it is not uncomfortable. Let your attention wander to every part of your body, feeling the weight of your limbs and trunk, but without adjusting your position. Then expand your awareness to include all of your body at once. See if you can feel the whole mass of your being simultaneously, floating in gravity. If you stay in this awareness long enough, you will begin to feel tingling in your extremities. Numbness will set in, which is the beginning of adaptation, entering the hypnagogic segue into sleep.

In the morning, see if you can hold still just after you wake up, breathing deeply, again examining the position of your body, an awareness known as proprioception. If you are in the hypnopompic transition, you will not be fully awake and may find the experience illuminating.

Then, next time you sit in meditation, understand that the same processes will set in. Pay strict attention to the tactile sensations of your body as it adapts to the deep stillness of zazen. Fall asleep, but stay awake while it happens.

"MEDITATION IS TOO LAID BACK TO COPE WITH THE CHALLENGES IN LIFE."

If you are a newcomer to Zen, you may think of zazen as the opposite of action: sitting still, or calming the mind. Our Zen mind is calm, of course, but it is capable of great action. This is illustrated by an example Matsuoka Roshi often used to make the point. Driving on the interstate at full speed, you suddenly veer off the road, for reasons beyond your control. Somehow managing to miss all the trees, you bring the vehicle to a safe stop. This is the real Zen mind in action, he would say. The Zen mind moves faster than anything. It is not dependent on calm circumstances.

Something like this once happened to me, long before I met Sensei. Passing a tractor-trailer rig on a two-lane highway, an oncoming car suddenly emerged from a dip in the road, heading right at me. My choices were to brake and attempt to pull in behind the truck I was passing, or pull off the left side of the highway, into the ditch. I chose the latter. Time seemed to stop, everything moving in slow motion. I was eerily calm. The car slid down the slope of the deep ditch but fortunately did not roll over. We came to a stop, safe and sound but shaken up. That I was driving my future father-in-law's Karmann Ghia—with his daughter, my future wife, onboard—made the incident even more fraught with potential bad karma.

Zen mind is not always calm. But the intermittent, surface disturbances of ordinary awareness are increasingly set against a background of relative equanimity. Like a deep current underlying the rapids of a rolling river. Or the stillness in the depths of the ocean, far removed from the typhoon roiling the rippling surface overhead. Our original mind remains calm and undisturbed beneath the surface.

TRY THIS:

When you are driving—or engaged in any other fast-moving enterprise—without taking your eye off the road, let your awareness take a backward step for a moment, engaging the big picture. This could be as simple as including the interior of the vehicle in your field of attention—while maintaining contact with the world outside the windshield! Remember your peripheral vision while focusing intently on the moving parts in front of your face. You can walk and chew gum at the same time. Tunnel vision, having blinders on, can have survival value but may also work against you. Pay attention to everything, not only to one area of consciousness at the expense of others. Expand to include the sound-surround, and tactile sensation. Be safe at the speed limit, or under. Most drivers are either on the road or in the car in their attention. Be both.

"I CAN'T STAND THE INNER DIALOGUE."

No wonder we long to be free of thinking, when most of our thinking is in words. We are badgered by constant chatter, the urges and self-doubt of the judgmental monkey mind. But longing for the end of thought is like longing for the end of breathing. Both are automatic, autonomic functions of a sentient being. The problem is our attitude, not the thinking itself.

Intuitive mind, or *bodhi*, may be regarded as playing a background role, while *citta*, discriminating mind, occupies the foreground. This is a useful construct by Richard Baker Roshi, successor to Suzuki Roshi. The two minds eventually merge as not-two, *bodhicitta*.

Foreground mind is usually engaged in high-frequency, erratic vacillation, moving like a school of fish near the surface of the ocean. Background mind moves in low-frequency, smooth waves, like whales deep in the depths. The two harmonize in a complementary, synchronous polyrhythm, as *bodhicitta*. Foreground and background merge in mental and emotional Samadhi, the balanced state of complete wisdom: heart-mind (J. *shin*; C. *hsin*). In Zen, total mind encompasses mental and emotional—both heart and brain—intuitive and analytical functioning, in synergistic synchronicity.

Zen practice entails withdrawing from foreground obsessions of the monkey mind, the tendency of the ox to wander off in search of greener pastures. We take refuge in something new, yet at the same time strangely familiar, in deep background. Nothing is more familiar than our own consciousness. So when our own awareness changes in a fundamental way, the effect can be surpassingly strange.

TRY THIS:

When you find the monkey incessantly jabbering away, with nonsensical random thoughts, or obsessively carping and criticizing yourself or others, take a deep breath and hold it for a count of four or so. This is akin to the old adage of counting to ten when upset. But notice that while you are holding your breath, the internal dialogue stops for just a moment. Then, after exhaling, let your lungs remain empty for a count of eight. These periods of relative quiet expand in time, becoming your new normal. Far less or no more chatter.

"I DON'T WANT TO, BUT I KNOW I HAVE TO MEDITATE."

In one sense, this is true, depending on what you mean by meditation. Complete this sentence: "I have to meditate in order to:_____" (fill in the blank). Then complete "I have to (whatever you filled in) in order to:_____." Repeat. This is an endless regress.

Everyone is doing some form of Zen practice, however poorly. Everyone is on some sort of spiritual path, whether they know it or not. But when we cast meditation in the mold of things that must be pursued—in order to achieve some predetermined goal—we have gone too far. This is connected to the notion that we have to do meditation "right."

That we must do meditation for some outside reason, any reason, casts an unnatural pall over zazen. We should never sit because we feel we have to, but only because we really want to. Or because, right now, we get to. Otherwise, we are not really doing zazen; we are only pretending to do zazen. In the back of our mind, we are meditating for one or more of all the wrong reasons—responding to outside influences—rather than inner motivation or personal prerogative. We have to be careful of this in our own practice. We don't have to sit. We get to sit.

Sitting in zazen, still enough for long enough, nothing can prevent its having a profound effect on our reality. But we may have good reason to wonder whether we are doing zazen right or not.

Sensei declared that the "real zazen" occurs when the three dispositions—upright body posture, natural deep breathing, and comprehensive, undifferentiated attention—all come together in a unified way. When this occurs, any remaining confusion, pretension, or illusions about Zen will fall away of themselves.

TRY THIS:

Next time you meditate, remind yourself that you do not really have to sit right now, but, fortunately, you get to. With this in mind, pay close attention to your posture, then your breath, then to what you are paying attention to—your thoughts, and all six senses. Do this in turn, one after the other. Then try paying attention to all three dispositions or all six senses (or both) simultaneously. See what happens.

"MEDITATION CAN DO LITTLE TO HELP IN MY CASE."

This is a form of insidious doubt: self-doubt, or doubt in the efficacy of zazen to help with personal or social problems. Known benefits of meditation—such as lowered stress levels and greater self-confidence—have been measured scientifically and will become evident in your experience. But the complete footprint of zazen is impossible to measure, as Dogen reminds us in his teaching on "Self-Fulfilling Samadhi":[41]

> Hundreds of things all manifest original practice from the original face; it is impossible to measure. Know that even if all buddhas of the ten directions, as innumerable as the sands of the Ganges, exert their strength and with the buddhas' wisdom try to measure the merit of one person's zazen, they will not be able to fully comprehend it.

From this, one effect of Zen training is that we come to see that even all insentient things, not just sentient beings, are part of it. Every object is manifesting the dharma, without error. While you may not be able to measure such effects or prove them to others, you can come to know them intimately.

Of course, overall effects of Zen on your personality will be shaped by psychological and social conditions unique to you. Zen is not a cookie-cutter approach, one size fits all. But it is up to you to custom-design it for your needs.

Zazen provides a dependable sanctuary, a necessary redoubt for regrouping, on the original frontier. Like a freshwater well, to which we return frequently for refreshment, it never goes dry. But zazen is more than a sanctuary and is not to be pursued as an escape from the strife of life.

TRY THIS:

When you find yourself becoming frustrated, angry—or just discontented with the way things are going—go ahead and sit with that feeling for a while. Like filing papers, which no one wants to do, limit the time to five or ten minutes. See if the unpleasant feeling is really that unpleasant after all. If you associate unpleasantness with another person or persons, instead of rationalizing or suppressing your emotions, give full vent to them on the cushion while visualizing their imputed source. Stop short of fantasizing revenge, however tempting.

"MEDITATION IS SUPPOSED TO IMPROVE MY LIFE."

Self-improvement is such an obsession in America that it is its own genre. Many people want to apply Zen to their life in some beneficial way, and preferably right away. But in Zen, meditation comes first; application to daily life, later. It is important to be clear, and patient, on this point.

You may feel that the purpose of Zen is to help you become a better person, happier and healthier, better able to cope with daily life. This attitude is to be expected in a culture saturated with self-improvement philosophies and programs, relentlessly hawking products that supposedly guarantee success.

But it may be premature and is definitely ill advised to intentionally try to apply Zen to your daily life. Just apply yourself to zazen, and not to worry—it will apply itself to your life, in a natural way. If you attempt to apply Zen in an intentional way, it will probably not work. "Try this" exercises are not really applications, but self-reflective work-arounds.

Introducing Zen to newcomers, we always strive to meet them where they are. We do not ask you to entirely discard reasonable expectations you may bring to Zen. Because in fact, practicing Zen usually produces positive results attributed to meditation. Greater calmness, patience, and mental clarity are desirable side effects of Zen practice. But they fall far short of the deeper purpose. Dogen insists that our loftiest goals must be set aside in meditation:[42]

> Setting everything aside, think of neither good nor evil, right nor wrong. Thus, having stopped the various functions of your mind, give up even the idea of becoming a Buddha. This holds true not only for zazen but for all your daily actions.

As a result of "setting aside all everyday concerns," as another translation has it, our attention shifts away from goal-seeking activity, including even any aspiration to buddhahood. The cushion becomes our safe place, where various functions of our mind—impulses to judge ourselves and others—may be suspended for a time. Normal distinctions—good and evil, right and wrong—cannot get in the way. Zen opens up to a less conventional view. Not that good and evil, right and wrong, are not real choices that we have to make every day. Just not while we are on the cushion.

But this in no way suggests that we should substitute another goal, no matter how worthy—such as becoming a buddha—for more pedestrian goals. Buddhahood is based on conjecture, which may get in the way of realizing our actual buddha-mind.

Awakening does not imply that we literally become Buddha, in the sense of channeling Shakyamuni. Nor some kind of magical transmogrification into something better, some exalted state, that is not already real and present. "Buddha" signifies one who is fully awake to the present reality—not to secret, inside information. The implication is that we can likewise wake up, fully. But nothing else really changes.

If you are too eager to find immediate benefits in daily life from Zen, or to morph into some imagined saint or sage, you are sure to be disappointed. Becoming discouraged and quitting—before the longer-term effects of Zen can begin to sink in—is the likely result.

In Dogen's time, as in ours, the higher functions of intellect generally trump direct experience. For example, such talents as erudition are taken as evidence of wisdom. Dogen counters this tendency with a single-minded emphasis on the direct approach:[43]

In the authentic tradition of our teaching, it is said that this directly transmitted, straightforward buddha-dharma is the unsurpassable of the unsurpassable.

Receiving this transmission requires giving up our attachment to the intellect, to any dependency on ritual and protocols, and even to physical well-being, as exemplified by America's notorious worship of youth. Aging is a fact of life and is embraced with humility in Zen. Yet, my teacher would unabashedly claim that "Zen keeps the men younger and the women more beautiful!" He was a shameless promoter of Zen. As am I.

TRY THIS:

Make a list of all the improvements you can imagine coming about in your life. The list should not be too long for this exercise, maybe the top three or, at most, the top ten. Then when meditating, after settling into the posture and breath, take up one of the items on the list. Turn it over in your mind, without attempting to analyze or judge it. As if you found it on someone else's list. If you find yourself chuckling internally, move on to the next item. Do not regularly use zazen for this kind of exercise. Finally, discard the list.

"MEDITATION SHOULD HELP ACHIEVE MY GOALS IN LIFE."

A variation on improving my life. The open-ended mindset nurtured in zazen begins to affect self-striving in all areas of life. Goals are not necessarily a negative, in and of themselves. Pursued with a mind open to surprise, goals can even bring about a kind of secular liberation.

Freedom to pursue goals comes into balance with freedom from goals. We can be more creative by being open to unanticipated options emerging in daily life. Missing one goal makes room for another. This idea is captured in a question from Taoism: "Which is more destructive, success or failure?"

Success in achieving any specific goal destroys, or at least restricts, opportunities to pursue others. Which might have proven more important in the long run. Failure reboots our definition of a particular goal. There is no success without failure.

Creativity of mind, enhanced by liberation from slavish devotion to fixed goals, is a dynamic aspect of Zen mind. We begin and rebegin each day, each hour, each moment, open to change. Followers of Zen must reinvent it for themselves, on a daily, moment-by-moment basis. This requires a flexible mindset.

First, flexibility of mind to imitate our Zen teachers, then flexibility of mind to innovate, in collaboration with others and within the constraints of our community. Flexibility and creativity of mind are required to integrate Zen practice with lay life.

Zen helps bring about a balanced, creative engagement in all aspects of life. This is the exercise of social Samadhi. But any and all effects of Zen—including a sense of serenity, or immediacy—appear, disappear, and reappear with changes in circumstance. Goal-oriented effects of Zen depend at least partly on circumstance, including inherited temperament and learned character traits. But we should not become overly attached to Zen's effects, however welcome. Zen practice enables, and ultimately requires, going beyond expectations and goals.

TRY THIS:

Examine thoroughly, in practice, whether you may harbor expectations underlying your practice. While sitting, observe what is transpiring at the present moment. See if, indeed, you do look forward to something different happening in the next moment. Or perhaps at the end of the day, or tomorrow, owing to your practicing meditation now. Ask yourself whether that expectation, however subtle, cannot happen in the present. If it cannot, how can it happen in the future?

"MEDITATION SHOULD MAKE ME HAPPY."

Meditation itself does not change anything in the material world. But it may help make the necessary attitude adjustments toward circumstances in your life, so that you can stop making yourself unnecessarily miserable.

Operational, positive mental attitude of Zen, expressed by Sensei as "Every day is a good day; every day is a happy day," is attributed to the founder of the Yunmen school, a ninth-century Ch'an master. However, Zen's happiness is not dependent on happy circumstances. The everyday "good" of Zen's good day is not the result of good fortune.

In Zen, we practice happiness—just as we practice patience—regardless of immediate circumstances. This is reminiscent of the Native American warrior's attitude going into battle: "It is a good day to die." Even our final day, when we find ourselves facing death, is a good day. Beginner's mind, in good times or bad, is the first and last mindset in Zen.

TRY THIS:

Consider the things you feel are making you unhappy. Take the most salient one at the moment and ask yourself, What is it about that, exactly, that I am unhappy about? Further, what can you do about it, really? If something occurs to you, upon which you can, indeed, take action—make a note. Then get back to meditation. See whether you are not actually pretty happy, if not deliriously so, just to confront whatever is bumming you out.

"WHEN I AM SITTING, I AM MEDITATING; WHEN NOT, I AM NOT."

Actually, when you are sitting, you may not be meditating. It is important to distinguish between the appearance of zazen and the reality of zazen. Merely mimicking the posture—meanwhile spending the whole time scheming, daydreaming, or ruminating—we can waste our whole life posing, as it were, in pretend zazen. This is not likely to last for long but is a known issue, especially in the short term.

We have all found ourselves going through the motions, in elementary or middle school, for example, when we were supposed to sit still and at least appear to be paying attention to the teacher. Or in other situations where we were not really comfortable, but peer group or other social pressure forced us to go along to get along, say at the junior prom. It is also possible to try this approach with Zen, particularly if we want to impress others with our sincerity, which, we secretly know, is not very strong.

Residents in a Zen community, for example, are often required to attend so many meditation sessions per week in order to qualify for residency. This is a reasonable requirement. The students may wish they were anywhere else, doing anything else, other than zazen. But there they are, facing the wall, like good soldiers who do not really want to be at the front line.

This is a conventional mode of discipline, imposed from the outside. But in Zen—as in athletics, even the arts and sciences—true discipline is self-imposed. If we sit for other, outside reasons, it taints the meaning and dilutes the effectiveness of the meditation.

This places us squarely on the horns of a dilemma. We cannot depend on just sitting—in the sense of going through the motions—as a panacea. Meanwhile, our world is crumbling around us from neglect. But we also cannot really avoid zazen either. Of course, we can stop doing zazen. But when we do, we find out why we do zazen. Our world crumbles much more quickly around our feet.

TRY THIS:

If you find that you are trying to use your meditation as an escape, or as a "good thing to do," while lots of bad things are happening in your world, take one of the worst-case scenarios and sit with it for a while. Like some other tedious chore, give it a time limit, so that you engage with it intensely. See if taking the time to consider one of your most grievous areas of neglect does not do something to your view of it. And inform your sense of what you might do differently to manage it. Make a note. Then act on the note, but after zazen.

"I MEDITATE BECAUSE I AM BUDDHIST."

Zen Buddhists do not believe they are Buddhists, as such. Buddha was not a Buddhist any more than Christ was a Christian. If we self-identify in this way, it is actually contrary to the teachings of Buddhism. We are simply applying another label, rather than penetrating to the emptiness of all such labels when applied to the true self. Zen repeatedly points to the inadequacy of language and concepts. Anyone, of any faith, can practice meditation. It is not the exclusive property of Buddhism, or Zen.

But Zen is not separable from Buddhism, whose teachings are, arguably, some of the clearest and most pointed verbalizations about reality ever spoken or committed to writing. Confidence in the Dharma is buttressed by the evidence of our own experience.

Of course, it is entirely possible that we may misconstrue our own experience to conform to our deepest wishes or beliefs. No one is immune to this. But if we did not have some conventional belief or trust—that is, that the Dharma is true—we would not likely be motivated enough to make the necessary effort to prove them out to ourselves.

TRY THIS:

Conjure up all the traits you identify as yourself: age, gender, ethnicity, family lineage, faith, and so on. Consider them one at a time, with a mind to determining whether they are genuinely central to your sense of being. Or on the other hand, peripheral: circumstance, if not exactly mere. In the midst of this self-identity exam, see if you can find the "true person of no status," a phrase attributed to Master Rinzai. Not "Who am I?"—but "What am I?"

"MEDITATION SHOULD HELP ME BE MORE COMPASSIONATE."

Zen does not foster a mystical "belief" in compassion. We find compassion inherent in life, particularly in its original meaning of "to suffer with." When we come to realize that we are largely the recipients of compassion—from our parents, our peers, and from the Universe itself—by dint of its providing the means of existence—we find we have all the compassion that there is to be had. And we can share it freely.

But we do not believe in the value of compassion blindly, and without evidence. Compassion is a finding, a conclusion, stemming from practice. Like any scientific research, findings must be translated into recommendations in order to be useful to ourselves, or to others. Practicing compassion is a recommendation. We "practice" compassion in order to wake up to the reality of compassion.

The Buddhist canon consists largely of such research on the nature of the mind as tripartite: magnanimous, nurturing, and joyous. The work of meditation is mainly disabusing ourselves of erroneous beliefs or misconceptions, including those concerning the meaning of Dharma, "compassionate teachings." We find the supporting evidence in our own experience. As a Ch'an poem promises:[44]

Indeed, it is due to our choosing to accept or reject that we do not see the true nature of things. Be serene in the oneness of things, and such erroneous views will disappear by themselves.

The "oneness of things" does not assert that all is one. Because we tend to err on the side of the obvious differences, Zen tends to emphasize the other side, underlying sameness. But not as an assertion of absolute truth. The most we can say is not one, but "not-two":[45]

To come directly into harmony with this reality, just simply say, when doubt arises, "Not-two." In this "not-two," nothing is separate, nothing is excluded. No matter when or where, enlightenment means entering this truth.

The buddha-way is inclusive of both the one and the many, complementary dyads in nondual reality.

TRY THIS:

Instead of thinking of yourself as practicing compassion—whether on the cushion or in service to others—consider the situation from the other side. Examine the ways in which you are the recipient of compassion, its direct beneficiary. Let me count the ways.

"MEDITATION SHOULD LEAD TO ENLIGHTENMENT."

No one can claim that zazen is the sole cause of the effects of Zen, up to and including spiritual awakening. No one can even make the case that it is necessary to do zazen in order to experience original mind. There is no provable cause-effect relationship there. This point was made long ago by Bodhidharma himself:[46]

> But Bodhidharma's approach to Zen was unique. As he says in these sermons, "Seeing your nature is zen. . . . Not thinking about anything is zen. . . . Everything you do is zen." While others viewed zen as purification of the mind or as a stage on the way to buddhahood, Bodhidharma equated zen with buddhahood—and buddhahood with mind, the everyday mind.

This suggests that Zen's insight is everyday, not dependent on zazen. Although, the "wall-gazing Zen" attributed to Bodhidharma was, indisputably, not Dhyana, contemplation, but objectless meditation (J. *shikantaza*).

In spite of the lack of causal connection, zazen seems entirely necessary for most people to fully appreciate Zen. Its primary function is to overcome ingrained impediments to insight. Which is why Zen requires such an investment of time. We carry a lot of baggage.

I was once asked by a Catholic prison chaplain what Zen meditation might do for him, to add to his religious practice. I told him that it might not add anything, but it might take something away. This raised his eyebrows. The process in Zen is more one of subtraction than addition. We see through—and delete—erroneous notions and confusions as they arise.

It is crucial to appreciate the central place, and indispensable value, of this "mountain-still" meditation to the power of Zen. My teacher would say, "If you can put your whole self into this simple act of sitting, you gain the power to put your whole self into everything you do." But this is not a gaining idea. We already have the power. The only thing is to apply it.

It may seem incredible that something as simple as zazen—just sitting still enough, long enough—could be so effective. We are blindest to our own strengths and weaknesses but are also our own worst critics. Zen employs an intuitive work-around, a kind of mental jujitsu, circumventing the source of self-doubt: the discriminating, recriminating, judgmental, and self-loathing monkey. This psychological trick is simple in principle, but difficult in execution.

TRY THIS:

When you find yourself dwelling on the idea of enlightenment, especially while sitting in meditation, ask yourself what it must be like. How would it look? How would it feel? How would it sound? Taste? As to how it would smell, an old saying sums it up: "For the enlightened, all odors are perfumes."

Or, what is the "thought of enlightenment"? If there were such a thing as an enlightened person, could enlightenment really exist for that person? Then return your attention to your present, unenlightened self.

Incidentally, sitting cross-legged with the right leg on top is referred to as the "pose of the unenlightened." The left leg on top is the "pose of the enlightened." The former has long been my preference, which I find highly appropriate. As one of my teachers remarked (Okumura), Soto Zen is the "no-enlightenment school."

In Zen, we do not pursue such goals. We are interested in returning to our natural awareness, in which nothing is gained. Other than a more grounded outlook.

"DO YOU BELIEVE IN MEDITATION
(OR WORSHIP BUDDHA)?"

These are examples of the kinds of socially uncomfortable situations that arise when practicing Zen, when others find out about it. Which may end up becoming yet another reason, or excuse, not to do Zen. The question is a "tell." That this person is a faith-based believer and does not know much about Zen, which is not based on beliefs.

Believing in meditation is not the same as believing in its effectiveness. The latter is a conventional belief, based on evidence. The former is blind faith. Believing in something, anything, is the quintessential meme of ideology, theology, or magical thinking in general. But meditation is not magical. Our confidence in it is not in lieu of evidence. Zen does not magically change anything other than our attitude.

It may seem disingenuous to suggest that there are no beliefs in Zen. We believe that all sentient beings share buddha-nature. And that all human beings are capable of waking up spiritually, as Buddha did. In particular, we do not harbor any beliefs about Zen itself. We do not "believe" in Emptiness (S. shunyatta), for example. We do not believe that all is empty, a teaching of Buddhism. If you assert this, I will twist your nose, as an ancient Master once did. If all is empty, where does the pain come from?

But we do experience the reality of emptiness in our meditation, which strains the meaning of "experience" itself. Zen practice may challenge some of your core beliefs, which, after all, are only deeper goals.

TRY THIS:

When you are in meditation, ask yourself if you are nurturing any unconscious beliefs about it, positive or negative. Such as that it is a good thing to do. Or that it will lead to enlightenment or make you a better person. Have you substituted true self, Buddha, and enlightenment for the soul, God, and salvation, unconsciously? If you find any inkling of such underlying ideas, see if you can entertain the opposite belief, that zazen is not necessarily good and may be a waste of time. Or that you are getting nowhere in terms of salvation. Keep your doubts at a keen edge. Holding both in mind simultaneously, don't give up.

JUST SIT—BUT STILL ENOUGH, AND FOR LONG ENOUGH

Zazen starts with physical stillness: finding more comfort in sitting. Which, in turn, leads to mental stillness: more clarity, less confusion. And to emotional stillness: more calmness, less reactivity to the ups and downs on the roller-coaster of life.

Samadhi—centering balance, prerequisite for insight, according to Dr. Suzuki—begins with posture, including fixed gaze and slow breathing. This engenders emotional and mental Samadhi. Accumulation of concentrated stillness, over time, begets social Samadhi, the ability to maintain balance even in complex relational situations.

For you, a sense of comfort, clarity, and calmness may arise right away, the first time you sit. It may seem that you have already tasted the fruit of Zen. But this may be an instance of the false fixation Suzuki warns against. If so, it can lead to a smug complacency. Or perhaps disappointment, leaving you asking, Is that all there is?

In any case, this sense of stillness in the early going will likely prove to be only a preliminary calming of the nervous system, brought on by the relative stillness of zazen. A deeper cycle of anxiety, or frustration, may follow on its heels, forming a natural cycle. We penetrate to the depths of Zen in phases, like drilling deep into the ground for water.

To foster stillness, sensory stimulus is tuned to relatively constant, moderate levels in the Zen environment. But zazen gradually becomes transsensory, obviating the need to control exterior stimulation. Fully aware of our surroundings, intensely engaged with senses—sitting still enough, for long enough—our awareness shifts to sensation itself. And beyond sensation, to perception itself, then beyond perception. Rather than perceiving objects through the senses, we engage the senses directly. Sensory adaptation sets in as a prelude to total, transsensory immersion. Entering a neutral, balanced state of pure (nondual) attention, sinking deep into zazen Samadhi. It begins with deconstructing the senses.

DECONSTRUCTING YOUR SENSES IN THE MOST NATURAL WAY

Owing to their interactive, overlapping functions and complex nature—of which we count six in Buddhism, remember, including the thinking brain—this section is lengthy. We take a deep dive into sensory change as it unfolds in zazen, involving all six. We look at each in some detail, a profound process of sensory adaptation setting in when we sit still enough, long enough. Sections on each sense are divided into subheadings, to allow you to digest the text in small bites between bouts of meditation. Your senses are the jumping-off point for exploring the original frontier.

Sometimes referred to as the Six Thieves, they can steal our birthright: spiritual insight. In its place, they offer the seductive distraction of sensory pleasures. Though we engage the senses intensively in Zen, it is in order to transcend them, ultimately. The aforementioned Bodhidharma has this to say about that:[47]

> Cultivating the paramitas means purifying the six senses by overcoming the six thieves. Casting out the thief of the eye by abandoning the visual world is charity. Keeping out the thief of the ear by not listening to sounds is morality. Humbling of the thief of the nose by equating all smells as neutral is patience.

Controlling the thief of the mouth by conquering desires to taste, praise, and explain is devotion. Quelling the thief of the body by remaining unmoved by sensations of touch is meditation. And taming the thief of the mind by not yielding to delusions but practicing wakefulness is wisdom. These six paramitas are transports. Like boats or rafts, they transport beings to the other shore. Hence they're called ferries.

The rather contentious relationship with the senses—subduing the band of thieves by frustrating their nefarious activities—may be a bit overwrought for the newcomer to Zen. We emphasize a more relaxed, gradual adaptation process, one that values collaboration over confrontation. Sensory learning, or unlearning, comes into play.

Direct sensory learning plays an important role in training both for Zen and design. I was exposed to the Bauhaus method while earning a BS at the Institute of Design. It began with a first-year "foundation," immersion in a broad range of materials, media, tools, and processes. Later, while pursuing graduate work toward an MS, I began practicing Zen. I soon recognized zazen as yet another process of immersion, in which the medium is consciousness.

Our study of consciousness begins with the senses. A famous Ch'an teaching states this:[48]

All the objects of the senses transpose and do not transpose. Transposing, they are linked together; not transposing, each keeps its place.

This startling comment from ancient China sounds a bit like modern neuroscience. The author is speaking from personal experience, however, rather than reporting findings from a scientific experiment utilizing sophisticated instruments such as brain-scanning technology. The human brain is still the most sophisticated instrument we have at our disposal. But in order to fully utilize it in Zen, we have to go beyond our normal interpretation of sensory input.

Description versus Experience

Most Zen literature does not indulge in descriptive passages on the experience and effects of meditation. This is probably in order to avoid spoiler alerts, killing some of the joy of personal discovery. Having no advance reconnaissance provided by others enhances the impact of direct experience, without the bias of preconceptions, on the frontier.

My descriptions are not meant to predict your findings in Zen but provide some inkling of where zazen may take you, if you stick with it long enough. Beyond the initial resistance of body and mind, and acceptance of lowered expectations, through the process of adaptation, zazen has some surprises in store. Beginning with the senses, Zen's purview expands, eventually embracing all dimensions of our existence.

The traditional sequence of the six sense realms (S. *dhatu*) or Sense Bases (S. *sadayatana*) in Buddhism is eyes, ears, nose, tongue, body, and mind. Sight, the most diaphanous and information rich, comes first of the five conventional senses, and touch, the most grossly physical and primordial, comes last. Finally we come to thinking—at once the most complex and ephemeral—as the sixth, overriding sense. The brain is its organ, the objects of which include the other five through cognition and conceptualization. Not only do we see, hear, and feel, we also think about seeing, hearing, and feeling.

But in zazen, we confront each of these realms in a different sequence—determined, I argue, by their degree of resistance. And given moderate, ambient conditions of the zendo.

Sequence of Senses in Meditation

Our senses operate simultaneously, but our attention can be captured by only one at a time, like the squeaky wheel getting the grease. Let us reorder them, in the sequence in which they usually command our attention, on the cushion. The traditional order aligns them as follows, by Organ versus Faculty:

A. Eyes/Seeing	B. Ears/Hearing	C. Nose/Smelling
D. Tongue/Tasting	E. Body/Touching	F. Mind/Thinking

But in meditation, in order of commanding attention and confronting resistance:

A. Body/Touching	B. Mind/Thinking	C. Eyes/Seeing
D. Ears/Hearing	E. Nose/Smelling	F. Tongue/Tasting

I place nose/smelling and tongue/tasting last—since they are virtually subsumed, early on, into body/touching, as minor forms of sensation with a chemical component. They usually adapt rapidly to the lack of stimulation in the moderate environment of the zendo and, so, ordinarily put up little or no resistance in meditation.

Confronting the Resistance

Each sense faculty examined in zazen consists of a tripartite "sense realm" (S. *dhatu*), as defined in Buddhism—comprising the organ, its object, and the field in which it functions. In modern parlance, they may be regarded as occupying different points on the electromagnetic spectrum (e.g., seeing captures high-frequency light, hearing registers lower-frequency sound waves, and so on).

TOUCH

Sensory immersion, and accompanying degrees of resistance, begins with touch, tactile sensation. Tactility is understood as sensation triggered by and filtered through the organs of skin, flesh, and bones, moving through the field of gravity. In the relative stillness of zazen, most encounter body sensations right away, reacting to the unusual posture, particularly in the legs and lower back. Monkey mind leaps into action, putting up mental and emotional resistance to the physical demands of sitting still enough for long enough.

THOUGHT

Thinking is the ordinary output of the brain, with concepts as its objects, usually verbalized as trains of thought—the inner dialogue. After body resistance is overcome, discriminating mind (S. *citta*) emerges as the next level of difficulty most persistent and most likely to recur, for most practitioners. Citta is a double-edged sword: simultaneously our best tool, but also our greatest source of distraction.

Thinking takes longer to quiet down, another probable reason it is traditionally listed last in Buddhism's hierarchy. But in zazen, it raises its head early on, as "the Resistance."

In the beginning, our attention typically vacillates between body and mind, as if they are separate. We learn that they are not actually separate, but co-arisen, intricately interrelated. Mind arises from body, which seems self-evident.

But body also arises from mind, which seems counterintuitive. Eventually, we experience a merging of body and mind. We no longer have to think about which comes first.

SIGHT AND SOUND

Seeing and hearing, come into play as the third and fourth major senses in sequence. Seeing puts up more resistance than hearing, owing to its relative acuteness compared to the fuzziness of hearing. Seeing and hearing take longer to adapt than body sensation, perhaps because the visual and auditory are more specific, more attuned to detecting threat, and higher on the electromagnetic spectrum.

SIGHT

Light, passing through the organs of the eyes, renders a complex realm of reflected objects, third in level of resistance. For others, sight may be the last to succumb to the deconstruction of zazen, rather than taking third place, as it does for myself. This may be partially owing to my extensive training in the visual arts.

SOUND

Compressed air waves impacting the eardrum, their object being internal and external sounds, put up less resistance. Yielding up no apparent boundary between inside and out, and relatively amorphous, it may take longer to come into play in your awareness, unless you are a musician. My exposure to music from an early age, my father and brother both being professional jazz musicians, may make for an unusual emphasis on hearing on my part. But most forms of meditation make deep listening a focus of attention.

SMELL AND TASTE

Least resistant of all is smell—with its organ, the nose, and its objects, aromas or scents floating in the air. Then finally, taste, the province of the mouth, detecting flavors floating in food and drink. These two seem deceptively simple, combining forces in chemical-based roles. Speed of adaptation is inversely proportional to the resistance engendered, in the absence of strong stimulus.

Both usually adapt quickly in zazen.

No Sense in Emptiness

Of course, your results may vary, depending on your physiology and sensory makeup. For most, progressive confrontation with sensory resistance will likely follow a similar sequence. Whatever your specific experience, with repetition all six will finally adapt, merging into original balance. You will begin to understand this line in the Heart Sutra:[49]

Given emptiness, no eye, no ear, no nose, no tongue, no body, no mind

Challenging common sense, this assertion, like all of Zen's teachings, cannot be explained but requires experience to make sense of it, no pun intended. It does not insist that the five senses are completely delusional, and that thinking is merely madness. But it does imply that there is something missing in our usual take on the senses—all six of them—in concert or individually.

The other side of the story is that all sense data we receive through the five organs—our primary interface with reality—are impermanent, imperfect, and insubstantial, three hallmarks of all phenomena. Following direct sensation, what the thinking mind does—to organize sensory input into perceptual/conceptual reality—does not make things any clearer, or easier, in apprehending the emptiness at their core. Instead, ordinary mind reinforces delusions of substantiality, perfection, and permanence.

Noumena and phenomena (shout-out to Immanuel Kant) coexist in a convincing way, but both outer and inner realities are ever changing. None of the senses exist as separate and apart, self-existent entities. But let's take a closer look, give a listen, and get a feel for each of them anyway. Perhaps we can penetrate beyond the projection screen.

The list of sensory experiences and references to the testimony of others recounted below is by no means exhaustive. Not surprisingly, the sections on thinking, feeling, seeing, and hearing, the big four, are longer and more detailed than those on smelling and tasting, which, in the absence of stimulus, adapt very quickly in zazen.

Some of the personal anecdotes are from early childhood, long before I had any exposure to Zen. Others are more recent and ongoing. I hope to present enough of a range and variety that you may find something that resonates with you, perhaps recalling boundary events in your perceptual history. Their relevance to Zen may seem a bit of a stretch, but Zen is all inclusive. The smallest detail may have hidden meaning. We say that God is in the details. Perhaps Buddha is to be found there as well.

A. TOUCHING: SKIN, FLESH, BONES & FEELINGS

It may seem odd, or at least arbitrary, to place the body's sense of tactility first. Especially for those readers who may not have spent much time sitting in meditation. But posture comes first in the instructions for zazen, for good reason. Training the body to sit, patiently, develops patience of the mind. Just as body and mind cannot be separated, nor can the body and its tactile sense.

In Zen, birth as a human being—that is, the body—is considered a necessary, but insufficient, pivot point (J. *yoki*), the essential condition for waking up to underlying buddha-nature. Other animals share buddha-nature, but not our potential for insight:[50]

> You have already had the good fortune to be born with a precious [human] body, so do not waste your time meaninglessly.

Touch is biologically important (e.g., to comforting the newborn, embraced by Mom, as well as for geriatric folks in our declining years). Touch conveys a subtle message that the other senses do not. When we correct posture in zazen, it is done through touch, not with words. Touch is not always a source of pleasure. It includes pain. But pain is considered a great teacher in Zen.

Getting in Touch

Touch may be considered the grossest, or lowest, of the senses. The body registers external material and energetic forces—primarily gravity—through contact with outer and inner layers of skin, flesh, and bone. You may not think of these as sense organs. We detect tactile sensation holistically, throughout the system, including stress and pain in musculature and organs as well as joints and bones. But touch is also a quality of the other senses.

On a molecular level, touch includes smell and taste, triggering chemical reactions. Seeing and hearing are a step removed, providing a less direct interface. But they can be felt, even painful, under extreme conditions, such as a loud sound or a bright light.

Thinking is even more indirect, with several layers of filters between subject and object. We speak of being deeply touched by an experience, even if vicarious. Thought is not usually something felt in a tangible way, but it happens, as with a strong "Aha!" moment. Or when we are "thunderstruck," "gobsmacked," horrified, or taken aback. Some thoughts make us nauseated, an absolutely visceral form of mental touch.

Touch is the most direct and the most intimate, ubiquitous, and down to earth of the senses. Yet, at the same time, the most diffuse, the fuzziest of focus. Tactility includes a wide range of sensations from pleasurable to painful, registering primarily through the skin, the largest organ, but also through underlying flesh and connective tissue. We feel pain, pressure, or tension throughout the body. And even in the eyes, ears, nose, and tongue, if the stimulus is strong enough. Wherever there are viable nerve endings, there is some degree of tactility.

In meditation, you may find that touch is the earliest to adapt of the three predominant realms: seeing, hearing, and feeling. Tactile adaptation begins when resistance abates, with numbness setting in, leading to an absence of feeling altogether, as when drifting off to sleep.

Honoring the Body

One of the first five Precepts in Buddhism is to honor the body, not to engage in sexual or other misconduct that may be harmful to oneself or others. Sexual intercourse is one of the most pleasurable of activities for most people and, at the same time, can be a source of immense suffering, both on personal and social levels; from cases of rape and the abortion debate to serious birth defects, as well as complications of parental relations. Doing justice to reproductive, gender dimensions of the body would be impossible at less than book length, requiring a sophistication and purpose that is beyond the scope of this text.

Where attraction and aversion are greatest, as in human sexuality, the danger of delusion is commensurate. Romantic and erotic love are inextricably intertwined. Suffice it to say that Zen, with its notable history of celibacy, would tend to agree with theories of science and some philosophers. That as regards reproduction, exerting our will in the pursuit of pleasure is actually following the dictates, or will, of the species. Opposites attract when selecting a mate. Our urges are biased in favor of progeny. Nature prefers hybrids, for evolutionary reasons. We are deluded to think, or feel, otherwise.

Where my teacher cautioned against falling for deceptions gleaned from history—such as that Dogen was the one and only outstanding Zen master of his time—biology is also a great deceiver. We are in thrall to its addictions. We go through gradual withdrawal in zazen.

The body is inconceivably complex, consisting of hundreds of muscles and bones, attaching ligaments and tendons, and metabolic and reproductive organs, as well as the six senses. It is also host to hundreds of symbiotic and parasitic organisms. Any regimen of diet and exercise must be custom-tailored, taking this unique complexity into account, to be optimally effective. Likewise, how you and your body engage zazen will be unique to you in its particulars. However, it is not irreducibly complex. We find irreducible simplicity in Zen.

Inherited physical attributes, as well as your present state of health and well-being, influence your body's capacity for flexibility and your consequent level of comfort in zazen. Zazen is said to be the "comfortable way." But for most, it is anything but, especially in the beginning. Your distress level is dependent on physical conditioning, to a degree. But people in great shape report a surprising amount of resistance to zazen. On the other hand, folks with minor infirmities find that they are not significant hindrances to sitting still.

One Size Fits All

Zen meditation offers essentially the same simple method for everyone. One size does fit all, in concept. But the devil is in the details. Specifics of your sitting posture, the frequency and duration of each of your sessions of meditation, and so on, can be tailored to your capacity and needs, like any other physical regimen. Zazen is for everyone, in that it can be practiced just about anywhere and under nearly any conditions. But it is uniquely different for everyone as well. And not everyone may be ready for zazen.

Zen proclaims the principle of nonduality, including the physical and mental and, by extension, the corporeal and spiritual. This is a testament to Zen's high regard for the human body as essential for awakening to insight. The preciousness of our body is not just a product of this life, but of our ancient karmic heritage, according to Buddhism.

The body includes the mind; the mind includes the body. Notable anomalies, such as ravages of dementia and Alzheimer's or worst-case vegetative states, illustrate the downside. These biological examples of Buddha's teaching—of innate imperfection, impermanence, and insubstantiality—become undeniable in our declining years. The body is our vehicle for practicing Zen.

Body Puts Up a Fight

Nearly everyone who sits in zazen expresses surprise, and some dismay, at the degree of physical resistance the posture soon triggers. Physical discomfort becomes the first barrier to the comfortable way.

Most of the stress, or distress—particularly in the knees, ankles, and hips, but also the lower back, shoulders, and neck—comes, yes, from our lack of flexibility, but also a lack of familiarity with Zen's strenuous, upright posture. It immediately stretches tendons and muscles in unaccustomed ways, and we hold them for a long time. When your posture becomes painful, move. Zazen is not an endurance contest.

Ordinarily, we tend to overreact, moving at the first sign of distress, adjusting our posture to reestablish a comfort level. In Zen meditation, however, we sit as still as possible for as long as possible. The body, through the medium of pain, throws up the first barrier. We adapt and adjust, becoming more comfortable in due time.

Getting Comfortable

Sensations registered through touch include weight, temperature, contact, pressure, and friction. Each of these can be pleasurable but may become painful at an extreme. In some cases, repetition is not a good thing. Scratching an itchy rash is the familiar example.

Resistance to zazen usually arises first in the form of physical discomfort (e.g., distress in the legs, hips, or back). But this obviously cannot stem from repetition or overexertion. It may be a symptom of a malady, if it persists. Your degree of discomfort may surprise you. Simply adjust your posture, if it is too stressful. You have my permission to move.

But this is also where you may notice the first encouraging signs of progress, even in your first session, as the posture becomes more comfortable. As we surrender to a higher threshold of discomfort, our body adapts and resistance abates, allowing necessary stretching in joints, muscles, and tendons to take place. Massaging the resistant muscles and joints (e.g., the knees and Achilles tendon) can speed the process of adaptation.

It turns out that most discomfort, and even pain, is a result of our own holding back, as with most things in life. When we find that we can sit for longer periods in relative comfort, say a half hour or so, we are greatly encouraged.

As a result of feeling better physically, the effects of zazen become more pronounced, in a positive feedback loop. From physical comfort comes emotional and mental comfort. Like most disciplined activities, what we get out of zazen is a function of what we put into it. Many people give up too soon, giving in to the resistance. Or they stop sitting because they conclude, prematurely, that what they have already experienced is all that there is to Zen.

When your physical posture becomes truly comfortable and completely balanced, it can lead to physical disorientation. A disconnect in proprioception—subliminal awareness of the disposition of our body in space—causes us to literally lose touch with where we are. Being lost in space, we are lost in time as well. Profoundly out of touch, no pun. But no worries; you can return to normal sensation in a trice.

Feeling Change

If only you sit still enough, for long enough, everything changes. Everything in awareness neutralizes as your senses adapt, more and more completely. Soon, tactile sensations level out. We literally feel ourselves settling into deep stillness, physical Samadhi: evermore centered, balanced, and evermore still, on deeper levels.

Awareness of your own body adapts to the extreme stillness of your posture, much as your skin adapts to the weight of your clothing: you stop feeling it. The same natural, neurological process neutralizes any and all normal sensations, given sufficient time and repetition. Eventually, a lack of sensation—nonsensation, or "off-sensation," as John Daido Loori[51] expresses it—sets in:

> Developing the power of concentration, we reach a point where we develop an off-sensation of the body during long periods of meditation. This experience can be very disquieting for some. It's similar to what happened during the seventies in sensory-deprivation-tank experiments. People immersed in water that perfectly matched the temperature of their body would lose any sense of physical boundaries. For many, this was an intolerable experience.

But we are all familiar with this lack of sensation: it is what we felt in the womb. It is neither feeling nor not feeling. It is nonfeeling, somewhere in between. Sensory attenuation sets in. The attention switch moves to the "off" position.

A negative corollary to what can be a pleasant lack of sensation is found in extreme cases of unbalanced sufferers, called "cutters." This dissociative disorder drives victims to literally cut themselves in order to feel something, anything. Apparently, existential pain imposes a complete shutdown of their nervous system. The positive approach of Zen—regarding a lack of sensation as familiar, normal, and even healthy—might help overcome this neurosis. Or maybe not. Zen is not a panacea. But it is generally good for what ails you.

Sensing Nonsense

Comparing Zen's positive connotation of off-sensation to the conventional pejorative term "nonsense," you begin to appreciate the countercultural character of Zen. Floating in and out of sensation—much as when falling asleep, or waking up—we stay alert, allowing everything else to shut down. We literally go out of our senses.

A traditional metaphor describes the penultimate state of Zen meditation as perching atop a 100-foot pole, a very precarious place to be. Climbing the pole, inch by inch, represents the long and arduous journey of Zen practice, sometimes slipping backward when we hit a slick spot. Getting there is half the fun, as we say. But once we have achieved the pinnacle, perched on all fours, there is still one more step to be taken.

Touch then becomes the final, last toehold on the pole. Our last grasp, and the last gasp, of the known. Zazen provides the opportunity of "stepping off the 100-foot pole." Losing our grip on the familiar and leaping into the abyss of the unknown frontier.

Zazen works via sensing beyond sensation. Touching the sensation of emptiness. Feeling the emptiness of sensation. Getting in touch with the heart of the Dharma.

Natural Posture, Natural Breath, Natural Mind

Remember, the way zazen works its magic is primarily physical. Sitting upright, the body begins to approximate the natural posture. Following the breath begins to reveal the natural breath. Listening to thoughts, we begin to go beyond attachment to, and dependence on, thinking. We penetrate to the natural state of mind. Zazen becomes your natural teacher. Fortunately, it is always accessible, unlike human teachers.

But zazen can be a difficult taskmaster. My teacher would often say, "You have to work your way through every bone in your body." And there are lots of bones in your body. My senior dharma brother, Kongo Roshi, at ZBTC, titled one of his recorded talks *Sitting with Muscle and Bone*. A popular book from the early days of Zen in America is titled *Zen Flesh, Zen Bones*.[52] Zazen is a visceral, intimate, gut-level practice, not merely a mind game.

You may have heard an anecdote about Master Bodhidharma, when he decided to return home to India from China. This incident may have inspired the phrase "Zen flesh, Zen bones":[53]

> Before departing, he called his disciples to him in order to test their realization. The first disciple he questioned answered, "The way I understand it, if we want to realize the truth we should neither depend entirely on words nor entirely do away with words; rather we should use them as a tool on the Way. Bodhidharma answered him, "You have grasped my skin." The next to come forward was a nun, who said, "As I understand it, the truth is an auspicious display of the buddha-paradise; one sees it once, then never again." To her Bodhidharma replied, "You have grasped my flesh." The next disciple said, "The four great elements are empty and the five skandhas are nonexistent. There is in fact nothing to grasp." To this Bodhidharma responded, "You have grasped my bones." Finally it was Hui-ko's turn. He, however, said nothing, only bowed to the master in silence. To him Bodhidharma said, "You have grasped my marrow."

The fourth student turned out to be Bodhidharma's lineage successor, Master Huike (J. *Eka*). This is sometimes interpreted that the use of "marrow" indicates a deeper level of understanding compared to skin, flesh, or bones. However, we should not be too hasty. Skin, flesh, bones, and marrow are all interdependent parts of the same body. Absent any one of them, the living being cannot survive. Skin and flesh, then, are equivalent to bones and marrow in their necessity. Skin is not shallower than flesh, notwithstanding the expression "Beauty is only skin deep." Nor is flesh shallower than bones. Marrow may be at the center of each bone, but it is not the center of the body itself.

Leading Cause of Death

Clinging or craving—in extreme forms of greed, hate, and delusion—comes with the territory of life. In this sense, our delusions are not totally our own fault. But slavish attachment to this "stinking skin sack"—an ancient Ch'an phrase expressing corporeality in starkly unsentimental terms—drives most human behavior. Blind pursuit of self-gratification often leads to unintended, and unfortunate, consequences. But inevitably, this body to which we cling carries the seeds of its own destruction. Birth is the leading cause of death.

But these facts do not relieve us of responsibility for our body, or for the consequences of its behavior. The only person who can really take care of your body, or temper its excesses, is the person reading this text. A Ch'an poem quoted by Dogen makes this point:[54]

> Those who in past lives were not enlightened will now be enlightened.
> In this life, save the body, which is the fruit of many lives.
> Before buddhas were enlightened, they were the same as we.
> Enlightened people of today are exactly as those of old.

The human body is the pivot point necessary to Zen insight. But Ch'an Master Lung-Ya reminds us that it embodies karmic inheritance as well. From DNA to parentage, it comprises our physical birthright, as well as determinative causes and conditions of the constructed self. In Zen, we recognize the limits of our control over reality, even over our own body. The body has its own mind, so to say, and in Zen, we listen to its wisdom.

Take breathing, for example. In zazen, we simply observe the breath; we do not attempt to control it. The body actually does the breathing. If you pass out, your body will keep breathing. The body also does the living, and eventually it will do the dying. There is not a lot that we can do about this, certainly not much to prevent it, ultimately. In that sense, we are merely along for the ride, definitely not in the driver's seat.

Zen teaches that it is best to wake up to this reality, before it is too late. The wake-up call is impermanence. The alarm bell is Zen. We ring it in zazen.

B. THINKING: Brain & Concepts

Thinking is the second-most-resistant sense realm encountered in zazen, mostly in the form of monkey mind, compulsive-obsessive thinking. It re-emerges in full force shortly after we have overcome discomfort of the body. In the traditional order of Buddhism's Six Sense Realms, thought is positioned last for logically rational reasons, such as its relative complexity. In order to do justice to that reality, this section is a bit long.

The thinking mind is the sense realm least amenable to unraveling, being the most gnarly and resistant to change. We largely ignore the monkey for the present, like fast-forwarding through commercials on television, paying strict attention to the other senses, our posture, and our breathing. In zazen, thinking is not of much use, but not much of a hindrance either. We mitigate its usual, deleterious effect of running interference by focusing outward. We become transfixed on the unvarnished, present sense-surround, rather than indulging in conceptual fantasy.

You may presume that thought would come first in zazen, what with the rarefied stratum it occupies in the West, where thinking is revered as deep meditation. But in Zen, intellectualizing is regarded as limiting, though highly useful in other areas of endeavor. The discriminating function of the brain is not generally regarded as part of sensory awareness. But as the sixth sense in Buddhism, it lords over, and distorts, the other five.

Thought, being the function of an organ, the brain responding to stimulus—as seeing and hearing are functions of eyes and ears—argues for inclusion as just another sense realm, the main distinction being that the brain is relatively isolated from direct interface with the outside world, unlike the other sense organs. It makes contact through them.

The sense organs provide direct interface with external stimuli, as well as internal sensations. Data processing begins with the five conventional senses but immediately engages thinking. The knee-jerk resistance of Citta seems to take forever to break down.

The Fab Four

Thinking is one of four dominant areas of activity commanding our attention in zazen, along with feeling, seeing, and hearing. Smelling and tasting quickly recede into irrelevance. Thinking is most associated with the third major area covered in zazen instructions, after posture and breath—attention or mind. Paying attention to attention itself. Attention in Zen transcends thinking. It embraces intuition, along with the five senses, and what they tell us about what is happening in our environment. But attention must eventually surpass ordinary sensory perception to get to the bottom of things.

The brain may be regarded as a second, the go-to guy, for each other sense. It receives, reviews, and feeds back data from engaged senses. This dynamic dialogue confirms, or refutes, initial impressions, triggered by any change in perception. This is the built-in double-take. To that degree, thinking is not a direct sense but indirectly registers information in the encapsulated brain, from our primary organ interface.

But there is also a great deal of sense data constantly originating in the body itself. Each of the five sense organs might be logically regarded as extensions of the central nervous system, distant early-warning systems—the DEW line—of the brain.

Categorizing the brain's discriminatory function as analogous to senses is sensible. It is constantly processing data filtered through the other disparate organs, integrating into a holistic whole: our worldview, including our place in it. But like any sense, it can be fooled.

I Think Not—Therefore I Am Not

Apologies to Descartes notwithstanding, embracing thinking as an automatic function relieves us of a certain amount of responsibility. Lusting in the heart is not identical to lust in action. In order to penetrate to a more concrete and complete worldview, we must somehow slip past our proclivity to overthink everything. We must go beyond thinking altogether.

Going beyond thinking may appear a hopeless ideal. As long as we view thinking as essential to awareness, to our self-identity, it will remain so. But thought ranks dead last in priority in Zen. This argues against its first positioning in Western society, repositioning it as the catchall caboose at the end of the train of awareness. It also suggests that consciousness is not at all dependent on thinking.

It becomes clear that, like breathing, we are not really doing the thinking, at least not all of it. The brain will continue thinking whether you want to or not. It is only marginally under our control. Thought is the most recalcitrant of the senses, capable of leaping out of control at any moment, like a crazed monkey. The other senses are relatively compliant, constrained as they are by the hyperbusy interface between inside and outside.

But monkey mind is not easily fooled and will not be ignored. Attempts to suppress thinking just encourage it and amount to thinking in another guise. So the very act of trying not to think fills our head with thinking, a kind of perverse Catch-22, as the Ch'an poem quoted above reminds us: "Trying to stop activity . . . your very effort fills you with activity."[55]

This comes into sharp focus under the microscope of meditation. Rather than methodically restricting attention—via conventional concentration on any one thing—Zen prescribes paying attention to anything and everything, without discrimination.

Throughout the evolution of anyone's meditation, from rank beginner to advanced practitioner, the persistent monkey will continue to chime in from time to time, demanding our attention for the moment. No matter whether the body is comfortable or not. So get used to it. But it cannot forever have its way with us.

This inclination of the monkey—to create even more chaos in the pursuit of order—is a given in Zen. Employing thinking—in order to discuss thinking—some confusion is inevitable. Using concepts—to discuss concepts—is an inescapably circular process, inherently contradictory. From a Ch'an poem:[56]

To seek Mind with discriminating mind is the greatest of all mistakes.

Thinking does not rule. At least not in Zen. Deep meaning is not accessible to analysis. Thought is extraneous to zazen, though it can be useful. Learning how to suspend thought—sitting without relying on thinking—we begin to appreciate sensory learning, direct knowing. As a bonus, we become more adept at applying reasoning ability, when and where it is needed.

Through flexing its muscles, the brain may be strengthened. But thinking has to be given a rest, in order that the brain may be refreshed. Just as the muscles of the body cannot function in permanent contraction, constant thinking causes the mind to seize up, brain lock.

As goes the body, so goes the mind, and vice versa. Ease of access to our own body makes it the logical starting point for Zen. We know exactly where it lives. Taking on the mind directly, instead, would require some sort of metaphysical approach—beginning at, or looking for, an unknown locus of the mind. Regarding an undefined dimension of some project, a former design colleague, an architect, would sardonically say, "It is slopendicular to an unknown axis." The axis of the mind cannot be found. Fortunately, that of the body can. It runs from the crown of your head straight down through your spine.

But the Zen mind is "round and rolling, slippery and slick," to use one of my teacher's expressions. Like a wet bar of soap, the more frantically we try to grasp it, the more it pops out of our grip. Better to approach the mind through its natural abode, the body.

Unraveling Mind

The thinking mind, as our sixth sense, necessarily undergoes adaptation and transformation in zazen, along with the other five conventional senses. Functioning as a kind of ombudsman—operating secretly behind the curtain, like the Wizard of Oz—with its tendrils penetrating the other senses, discriminating mind takes longer to unravel.

The process of sensory transformation we undergo in meditation is likened to untying knots in a scarf:[57]

> The Buddha . . . took from the teapot a piece of beautiful cloth. . . . Then in the presence of the assembly, he tied a knot and showed it to Ananda. . . . Buddha tied another knot. . . . The Buddha tied four more knots, showing it to Ananda. . . . The Buddha said: "Ananda, originally there was only one piece of cloth, but when I tied it six times, there were six knots." The Buddha said: "These six knots are different but come from one length of cloth, and you cannot reverse the order. It is the same with your six sense organs, which, though coming from the same (source), are manifestly different." Ananda asked: "How can one untie these knots created by trouble and confusion?" The Buddha said: "Correct, Ananda, correct. A knot should be untied from its heart. Therefore, Ananda, choose one organ from the six, and if its knot is untied, all objects of sense will vanish of themselves. When all illusions disappear, if this is not Reality, what more do you expect? Ananda, tell me now if the six knots of this cloth can be untied simultaneously." Ananda replied: "No, World Honored One, because they were originally tied one after the other and should be untied in the same order. Although they are in the same piece of cloth, they were not tied simultaneously; how can they now be untied all at once?" The Buddha said, "Your six organs should be disengaged in the same way. When you begin to disentangle them, you will realize that the ego is void."

A long quote, but important to the premise that zazen is largely a process of profound sensory adaptation. As a starting point, one sense must be more amenable to unraveling than the others, depending on the individual. Otherwise, we would be forever refocusing our attention from one sense to the other, like the proverbial monkey jumping from limb to limb of the sensory tree. Buddha's disciples report on their first sensory breakthrough, with several citing hearing as their first. Which of the six do you find most amenable?

This analogy recalls the story of the Gordian Knot, which Alexander the Great of Macedonia legendarily untied with a single stroke of his sword. The Sword of Manjusri, represented in Zen meditation halls by a central statue, is similar. Held aloft, the bodhisattva's sword is ever at the ready, to cut through all delusion. Our discriminating mind is like this massive knot, hopelessly entangled with the five other sense realms. Zazen is the sword.

Taming the Ox

In addition to the monkey mind, Zen uses another potent symbol, the ox, most famously in the "Ox-Herding Pictures," or "Ten Bulls,"[58] a set of classic ink paintings (J. *sumi-e*) by Kakuan (1100–1200). You may be familiar with these; if not, you may want to look them up. They illustrate various stages in the pursuit of Zen. As such, they stand as an apt analogy for the process of zazen as well. Discovering the first hint of Zen parallels the ox herd finding its footprints. Pursuing zazen is illustrated by catching a glimpse of the ox, engaging in the struggle to tame it, and, finally, peacefully riding it home. Compared to the monkey, the ox offers a more muscular metaphor for the mind, and our struggle with it.

Beginning with an illustration of the young ox herd finding hoofprints in the soil, which look like calligraphy—indicating the presence of something so far unseen, the first inkling of the existence of the ox—the series culminates in both ox and ox herd disappearing in the empty circle of Zen (J. *enso*). Finally, reality reemerges, and the ox herd, transformed into a living bodhisattva, reenters the public marketplace of the village, helping all others with bliss-bestowing hands.

The paintings illustrate the arc of Zen practice, both on the cushion and off, with the emphasis, in Soto Zen, being on the cushion. Eventually, sitting upright in zazen—sitting still enough for long enough—the ox becomes tame. All conflict between the ox and you, the ox herd, is overcome, like the analogy of the cowboy and his horse on the cattle drive. The ride home is effortless, the ox no longer attempting to go its own way.

Whereas the monkey is a symbol of hyperactivity, anxiety, and the constant, frenetic search for instant gratification, the ox may be taken as representing plodding stubbornness of will, but also great strength and perseverance. The ox herd represents the inquiring, striving mind—looking for, catching, and trying to tame the ox—which, of course, has a mind of its own. The ox-herd parable visualizes Zen in action.

Boredom = Poverty of Imagination

Alternatively, we may take it that the ox represents the body-mind; the ox herd, the self or person, meaning you or I, the sense of self. The comfort, and discomfort, we experience in zazen is very much like taming the ox, a sometimes arduous process.

Like the ox in the paintings, the mind wants to wander off into greener pastures. And who can blame it? Zazen is the ultimate in boring. In zazen, however, we come to recognize boredom as our own poverty of imagination. If you think you can afford to be bored, you simply do not realize the gravity of the situation you are in. Life is, after all, life-threatening.

Fighting off boredom becomes a second barrier, after overcoming initial, physical resistance to the posture. By the time we become comfortable with sitting, the novelty may have worn off. But there is no time to waste on boredom or any other self-indulgent distraction. Time is literally the essence, not simply of the essence.

Thoughts can quickly go off on a tangent, as an evasive maneuver to escape terminal boredom, physical or emotional discomfort, or thoughts of mortality. A popular therapy recommends conjuring pleasant thoughts to replace unpleasant ones. Daydreaming, rerunning the past, and fantasizing about the future are entertaining, as we can all attest. This mindlessness can be gradually mastered via diligent application of mindfulness. By redirecting attention to the breath, posture, and the exercise of bare attention, we tame the ox. This may come across as just another diversionary tactic. But it quells the nattering internal dialogue, if only for the moment. Those moments then become longer, your new normal.

That discriminating mind can focus on only one thing at a time, we assume to be true. We can use this trait to our advantage. As distracting trains of thought arise, we simply turn to the other five senses. Focus on feeling the stillness of the posture, following the movement of the breath, witnessing inner and outer radiance of vision, listening to sounds emanating from within and without. We employ a kind of sensory foil against distracting thought—a mental jujitsu—turning the ox mind's own energy back on itself and returning to the present. Literally coming to our senses.

Observing Thought

Conventionally, thinking is not considered a sense, as it is in Zen's model of the mind. But thinking is not the whole of the Zen mind, or even its greatest or most important faculty. In zazen, we observe our thoughts as dispassionately as we observe our breath, sensations, and external phenomena. Thoughts arise as automatic output of the brain, but also as reactions to incoming sense data. Just as sights, sounds, smells, tastes, and feelings are automatic responses of sense organs interacting with their objects, just so the mind interacts with thought objects. This interdependency is illustrated in the earliest Ch'an writing:[59]

> Things are objects because there is a subject or mind, and the mind is a subject because there are objects. Understand the relativity of these two and the basic reality: the unity of Emptiness. In this Emptiness the two are indistinguishable, and each contains in itself the whole world.

Remarkable. They had an expression for "relativity" 1,500 years ago. Speaking of relativity, the "thought experiments" of Albert Einstein illustrate another mode of cognition, one that is not derived from immediate physical stimulus. These were not exactly normal thinking, from the great man's description of them as "visceral." Some sort of gut-level imagination is in play, similar to Zen mind.[60] This is not to generalize that all ordinary orders of thought are automatic, or mere reactions to stimuli.

Studying any subject matter involves intentional modes of thought. Applying conventional techniques—research methods, deductive and inductive reasoning, etc.—we develop findings, conclusions, and recommendations for further study. To some degree, we can apply this standard to Buddhism's teachings, often articulated as formulae or models. However, Zen does not rely on analytical modes or models. They are found to be lacking compared to intuitive, experiential testing. Both approaches are complementary, in praxis.

Focused thought—intentional, or artificial—may be seen as a second-level order of awareness. It follows on unfocused thought—unintentional or natural—as first-level order. Reacting to a stimulus such as hunger, the thought of hunger follows registration of sensation in the stomach. Second-level processes determine a course of action: eat something or resolve to bear with the hunger, for the sake of losing weight, for example.

Intentional versus Natural Thought

Concepts such as losing weight may be seen as third-level objects of the mind.

They follow on intentional thought, which follows on initial, natural thought, or instinct, in immediate reaction to perception. Parsing thoughts into intentional, versus natural, is useful in dealing with them. Intentional thoughts are usually self-serving and reactionary, the source of most of our troubles. Natural thoughts come with the territory of sentience and are relatively harmless, unless we overreact. The time lag between natural thought arising and intention-driven decision-making may seem negligible. Modern brain science is hot on the trail of this gap, measured in milliseconds. But over time in zazen the gap widens, muting our reactionary response. This is the area of awareness Dogen termed "nonthinking":[61]

> Once you have adjusted your posture, take a breath and exhale fully, rock your body right and left, and settle into steady, immovable sitting. Think of not thinking. What kind of thinking is that? Nonthinking. This is the essential art of zazen.

Raw physical sensation precedes perception. Stimuli register before being discriminated as to sensory origin. Sensations quickly translate into categories: pleasant, unpleasant, or neutral, even harmful or life threatening. Percepts are then first-level transactions of discriminating mind (S. *citta*) in its function of sorting raw sense data (S. *manas*). Concepts follow, organizing percepts into dyads: attraction or aversion. Reactionary concepts then color our future perception of sensations. Perception becomes a back formation of conception.

Interpretation of sense data leads to perception-cum-conception, conditioned by circumstance. Concepts arise necessarily as a form of thought, though not necessarily in the form of language. They may appear as images in the visual arts. Or as sounds in musical composition. A raw concept may be neither lingual, visual, nor acoustical, but kinetic, as in choreography. It may arise from a gut-level instinct, a fuzzy felt need, calling for response. Or as a numerical formulation in the language of math, at another extreme.

Tamping down of sensory stimulus, typical of a Zen practice environment, may help precipitate more-purposeful thought processes, deeper thinking. But cognition has its limitations. It cannot penetrate to the origin of thought itself. Which, we imagine, comprises the essence of Buddha's insight. What order of thought is it that is not dependent on conventional thinking, language, or concept?

Sensing Thought

Thinking is the most persistent, and potentially pernicious, of the senses, in its power to corrupt our worldview. But in Zen we respect and appreciate the thinking mind:[62]

> If you wish to move in the One Way, do not dislike even the world of senses and ideas. Indeed, to accept them fully is identical with true Enlightenment.

The world of senses and ideas is part and parcel of the Way. The monkey means us no harm, usually, and provides mechanisms for coping with everyday life. It is dedicated to our survival, with notable exceptions. Where mind turns against body, it manifests as what is considered neurotic or psychotic behavior: self-cutters, ascetics, flagellants, and most suicides.

The self-centered bent of conventional thinking can intrude greatly in the way of going beyond thought. Thought is, after all, the monkey's forte. We are very good at thinking. But it can also become an addiction. We know that thought takes time, always retrospective in nature. If we pay close attention, we can catch it in the act of trying to keep up.

Thoughts can be powerful, as in a "Eureka!" moment. And may seem tangible, even painful. But in Zen, thoughts are regarded with some skepticism, as the automatic, if unpredictable, output of the brain. This is in accord with Buddhism's three-part sense-realm (S. *dhatu*) model: the organ, the object, and the field of operation, frequency on the spectrum. All six senses operate with, or without, intentional thought, including thinking.

Wavelength of Thought

Placing thinking on the electromagnetic spectrum may seem a reach, because we do not know its specific range limit, as science claims we do with seeing and hearing. Just as ultraviolet and infrared frequencies are said to be outside the range of visual perception yet are still a form of light, and just as very high- and low-frequency sounds cannot be detected by human ears but still exist as sound waves; just so, thought may extend beyond that slice of the spectrum to which we are normally attuned, transcending physiological limitations of the sensing brain. Thinking outside the brain.

If you can embrace thinking as yet another sense, categorically, you can appreciate that it is functionally connected to the other dhatus. And they, in turn, provide food for thought in the form of sense data to the brain. They appear to overlap, like a Venn diagram.

Even when we sleep, the mind conjures up objects: kaleidoscopic images, sounds, and events, triggering vivid, sometimes lucid dreams. This is striking evidence of mind's power of imagination. The presence, frequency, and vividness of dreams suggest that it is not wholly dependent on the senses and their objects. In the absence of concrete objects, it simply makes things up. But this is not the only credible interpretation of dreaming, of course.

Linguistic Relativity

The area of study called linguistic relativity delves deeply into which comes first in this chicken-egg scenario—the concept? Or the percept? Summarizing the theory:[63]

> The principle of linguistic relativity holds that the structure of a language affects its speakers' worldview or cognition. Popularly known as the Sapir-Whorf hypothesis, or Whorfianism, the principle is often defined to include two versions. The strong version says that language determines thought, and that linguistic categories limit and determine cognitive categories, whereas the weak version says that linguistic categories and usage only influence thought and decisions.

It seems certain that our native language influences our thought processes. But when we consider the thinking mind, it is clearly capable of going beyond language altogether. In visualizations that engender art and design solutions, auditory processes that inform musical composition, and kinetic movements of dance and choreography, new forms of language (e.g., musical or choreographic notation) are developed to codify and communicate them. Visceral learning often proceeds through a process of sensory immersion, observation, and imitation of one's mentors (e.g., in the arts and sciences). This direct learning surely transcends limitations of language, as it does in Zen practice as well.

Conceiving Perception

Conceptualization engenders fixed concepts about the senses themselves. Conception interacts with perception as a kind of closed loop. Interpretation of sensation is influenced by conscious, as well as unconscious, causes and conditions (e.g., inherited biological traits, DNA, social memes, and stereotypes).

These influences modify perception, often on an unconscious level. Sensation is biased by immediate preferences: pursuing pleasure, avoiding pain. Conscious memories, along with subliminal resonances on past experience that may have nothing to do with our present reality, trigger subtle emotions, such as paranoia, ennui, or dread.

With repetition, like exercising a muscle, concepts about reality and our place in it develop into mental habits, becoming personality traits hardwired into our nervous system. They become our persona, or self-identity. This makes for a stubborn monkey.

Being blindly unthinking can become a major problem in daily commerce. Coping with the vicissitudes of life is dependent on feeling, thinking, and speaking with sensitivity, which is further complicated by the dualistic nature of language and cultural idioms.

In zazen, our mindset ultimately becomes what Dogen refers to as non-thinking: not relying on conceptual thought, but not suppressing it either. Whether or not thinking occurs at any moment on the cushion basically makes no difference to our progress in zazen.

Sleeping Off Thought

It is worth examining the boundary between sleeping and waking states, with particular attention to the quality of awareness and its effect on thinking. On the cushion, the body-mind switch may be thrown to the off position, as when drifting off to sleep. But without concomitant loss of consciousness. Everything else falls asleep, but we stay awake and alert. A semisleep state infuses the thinking mind, as well as the other senses. We may feel physically tired, but also tired of thinking.

Sitting upright in stillness, you may experience a disconnect, a sense of floating. As your body comes into complete alignment with gravity, physical effort becomes evenly distributed. All tactile sensation evens out. It can feel like entering a trance. But try to sustain a keen awareness in the present. Vacillating from drowsiness to alertness, we emerge refreshed. Like taking a nap, recharging your batteries.

Data from electrophysiological studies link sleepiness and deep meditation by virtue of their similar theta-level brain waves. In the beginning, we may regard sleepiness in meditation with a certain disdain. We are supposed to be waking up, after all. But, knowing as we do how closely connected sleeping is to awakening, drowsiness itself may be seen as a sign of progress.

Zen ancestors are reputed to have taken vows never to lie down. They slept sitting upright, all night, a practice followed to this day in extended retreats (J. *sesshin*). In Japan, Zen meditators utilize a chin board to keep them from falling over during all-night sessions.

Sleepiness is a known issue, in other words. It is the second barrier, after pain. Sitting through sleep is a testament to unrelenting aspiration to awaken Zen mind. This is indicated in the first classic Ch'an poem:[64]

If the eye never sleeps, all dreams will naturally cease. If the mind makes no discriminations, the ten thousand things are as they are, of single essence.

All dreams will naturally cease if we wake up to real form, underlying appearance. The Zen meditator is not lost in thought, or in dreams about reality. "Dreams" characterizes the ordinary, awake state of mind, definitively described by Buddha:[65]

Subhuti, how is it possible to explain this Scripture to others without holding in mind any arbitrary conception of things and phenomena and Dharmas? It can only be done . . . by keeping the mind in prefect tranquility and in self-less oneness. . . . And why? Because all the mind's arbitrary conceptions of matter, phenomena, and of all conditioning factors and all conceptions and ideas relating thereto are like a dream, a phantasm, a bubble, a shadow, the evanescent dew, the lightning flash.

Eventually, on the cushion or off, thought beyond thought occurs. The thought of emptiness. The empty thought of Buddha, the "blessed one." Blessed, but not because his is a "holy" thought. Zen's truth is "Vast emptiness; nothing sacred," attributed to Bodhidharma.[66] Blessed because it is a great relief to finally put down the burden of judgmental thinking, as declared in the same poem:[67]

The burdensome practice of judging brings annoyance and weariness. What benefit can be derived from distinctions and separations?

So, thinking itself is not the problem, but rather how we use our faculty of thought, and to what purpose we apply it. But our precious power of thinking becomes distorted in service to our annoying, and ultimately weary, judgmental mind.

First-, Second-, and Third-Level Nen

The very exclusivity of dependence on thinking comes at the expense of the mind's other powers, the intuitive, trusting mind (S. *bodhicitta*). Thinking itself inhibits deeper insight beyond ordinary thinking. The Japanese language offers up a tripartite model of cognition, based on a concept called "nen":[68]

> These two kinds of actions of consciousness are both called nen, a term . . . we may approximately translate as "thought impulse." The nen alternate with each other, from moment to moment, and we may feel as if they were arising almost simultaneously. But nen-actions that occupy the stage of consciousness come forth one at a time. Let us call the outward-looking action the first nen, and the reflecting action of consciousness the second nen. The second nen, which illuminates and reflects upon the immediately preceding nen, also does not know anything about itself. What will become aware of it is another reflecting action of consciousness that immediately follows in turn. This action is a further step in self-consciousness. It consolidates the earlier levels. We shall call it the third nen. In our example . . . we have first the observation, second the awareness of that observation, and third the acknowledgment of ourselves becoming aware of the observation.

This formulation's first, second, and third levels of nen are analogous to high concept on the third level, less complex on the second level, and basic on the foundational first level. This model recalls the empirical method: contrasting external, sense-derived information with internal reflection, as two parallel tracks. It forms a rough correlation to physiological levels of outer cortex, inner cortex, and brain stem. All higher conception, such as Einstein's thought experiments, would correspond to third-level nen. The less complex cognition of a child, and those of higher-intelligence animals, to second-level nen. Primitive instincts of the brain stem—the so-called lizard brain—and lower-intelligence organisms would correlate to first-level nen.

Zazen may be thought of as a process of regression in nen, from complex processes of third nen in the beginning, simplifying over time to second nen, and ultimately reducing to first nen. Another model for profiling Zen's process of unlearning.

We turn away from intentional thought and return to natural thought. Then nonthought. Nothing lost, nothing gained in the process. Zazen plummets to zero-level nen, the very ground of awareness, supplanting thoughts of a trivial nature with the nonthought of enlightenment. Which necessarily transcends ordinary thinking, encompassing all levels of nen simultaneously.

Becoming Supersaturated

Zen's meditation is experimental as well as empirical (i.e., based on observation). Zazen does not presuppose an objective or goal but is open ended, exploratory. Because of this, concentration in zazen is not forced mental attention to any single object—such as Nature or a mantra. Or an image: a candle flame, Buddha, or a bodhisattva. Traditional meditations, but not characteristic of Zen. We do not ruminate on a teaching or simply engage with whatever train of thought happens to arise.

Again, concentration in Zen is cumulative, analogous to a supersaturated solution, say of salt. In your high-school chemistry class, the teacher may have demonstrated this phenomenon by stirring salt crystals into a large jar of water. Soon, the solution becomes saturated. No more crystals will dissolve. Heating the water with a Bunsen burner dissolves the remaining crystals; it becomes supersaturated. Finally, the teacher turns the burner off, passing around a petri dish exhibiting a single, tiny crystal. Then, dropping it into the cooled solution—shazam!—the liquid instantly changes state, to a single, solid crystal.

Made from Concentrate

Concentration in Zen is like this. Over time, by virtue of repeated zazen, our attention—our entire being—becomes highly concentrated. This is sometimes referred to as ripeness, like an orange ripening on the tree. How long this takes for you to come to peak ripeness depends on many factors. But when ripe and ready, any stimulus—no matter how slight or mundane—may trigger a change of state. In awareness, that is. Insight into the Great Matter.

This illuminates the "most important thing in Buddhism," from Dogen:[69]

Now that you know what is the most important thing in Buddhism, how can you be satisfied with the transient world? Our bodies are like dew on the grass, and our lives like a flash of lightning, vanishing in a moment.

The Great Matter is nothing more than awakening to Truth, first recorded in the story of Shakyamuni Buddha. It is the reason for being of Buddhism itself. The final turning point, in the practice path of Zen's ancestors. For them, and for us today, it opens the gate to the original frontier.

Waking up is hard to do, and not something that we can do intentionally. We can foster ripening on the cushion. But we cannot force the gate open. Faith, in Zen, means having this kind of confidence, not a belief, that such an auspicious event can come about with a perfect storm of causes and conditions. Some are naturally riper and readier than others, even when first beginning practice. Life experiences contribute to spiritual maturity. In traditional Buddhism, this includes carryovers from past lives, a so-called karmic remainder.

Some of us are slow horses, others fast horses, to use an analogy attributed to Buddha. But anyone can eventually come to complete state of concentration, the deepest of Samadhis. This is the role, and goal, of thinking—and its flip side, nonthinking—on the original frontier.

Perception Is Not Reality

The next two sections, on seeing and hearing, move into the arenas that we associate with perception proper. Most conscious information conveyed by sense data—to which we attribute importance, and through which we construct our worldview—is gathered through these two realms. We do not consider thinking as a sense, in the vernacular. Nor does tactile sensation compete with visual and audial for first or second place in perception. Once we overcome physical resistance, and mental frustration has abated, our zazen turns to fully embrace the influx of sight and sound. This begins the process of deep sensory adaptation.

Sensory adaptation flows both ways, in opposite directions. That is, our baked-in, normal process of adaptation—numbing and dumbing down—can be countered by reverse adaptation, induced through meditation. Learned ignorance can be unlearned if we are willing to relinquish our preconceptions, deeply embedded in perception. All dimensions of mind are subject to adjustment in zazen. Like Alice, we never know what is around the next bend on the winding Wonderland path to the original frontier.

Everyday perception adjusts, and adapts, to anomalies in the environment, such as loud sounds or unusual sights, in order to maintain survival mode: feeling safe and maintaining status quo. In zazen, however, this view of normalcy is broken down through reverse adaptation, as it were. We push the envelope of perception by sitting still enough, for long enough. Everything goes up for grabs. We are nowhere safe in this world, at least not for long.

Eventually, looking at things from the other side of the original frontier leads to a more complete view, Buddhism's "right view." Normal, everyday perception may already be topsy-turvy, but zazen can help turn it around. Powers of reasoning can also lend a hand.

The Real World in Bucky Words

As an example of real-world reasoning, Buckminster Fuller reminds us that our concept of up and down is, stated more precisely, in and out. Speaking to a group of Russian scientists in Leningrad, he makes an acerbic point: [70]

> Many of you think of yourselves as scientists, and yet you go off on a picnic with your family, and you see a beautiful sunset, and you actually see the sun setting, going down. You've had four hundred years to adjust your senses since you learned from Copernicus and Galileo that the earth wasn't standing still with the sun going around it. . . . But you scientists still see the sun setting. And you talk about things being "up" or "down" in space, when what you really mean is out and in in respect to the earth's surface.

This was one of Bucky's pet peeves: imprecision of language, especially as indulged by experts who should know better. He felt that it contributed to the overall dumbing-down of society. The same may be said of those experienced in Zen. We should be careful about expression, so as not to lend to the rampant confusion regarding reality.

The idea of what is up, and what is down, derives mainly from a perspective of about 5 to 6 feet off the ground—that is, hunting on the savannah (e.g., in early Africa). From which vantage point the world also appears to be flat, since we can see only about 3 miles in any direction unassisted, and on a flat plain. The earth curves out of sight at that distance. The first invention to expand this horizon was climbing the tallest tree, hill, or bluff in the vicinity. Binoculars came later. As did flight and, eventually, orbiting the earth.

We have slowly come to adopt Fuller's corrective—prodded by spectacular images from space missions of the past few decades—that what we call "up" is really "out." We go out from spaceship Earth—and into outer space. What we call "down" is really "in." We come back in from outer space—into the atmosphere, and onto the surface of Earth. Or that of the moon, or any other solid celestial body. But we still have flat-earthers among us.

As Bucky also pointed out, seafarers like him have long referred to "sailing in" to land, where the terrain is relatively static, and "sailing out" to sea, where it is in constant, fluid motion. For sailors, the technically correct navigational terminology of space exploration is nothing new. If we landlubbers would take this reorientation to heart, it might alter our perception enough to induce disorientation, seasickness, as if we were floating in outer space.

After all, all objects in the universe are floating in space. Actually, most are falling through a trajectory, what Fuller called the "geodesic"—the arc of least resistance, to oversimplify—determined by the ever-changing matrix of gravitational attraction of massive objects in the neighborhood. In our case, Earth is the proximate gravity sink, in thrall to the greater one of old Sol. We do not feel the geodesic directly. But everything we do feel, see, and hear is affected by it. Perception is inseparable from the matrix but has adapted to it.

On the byways and backwaters of the original frontier, we gradually get used to the lay of the land, testified to by an ancient Ch'an poem:[71]

Penetrate the source and travel the pathways, embrace the territory and treasure the roads.

C. SEEING: Eyes & Sights

I place seeing third, in diminution of relative resistance, after touching and thinking. Once you are relatively comfortable in the posture, and the internal chatter has diminished to a dull roar, your attention can turn to other things. Vision. What's up with that?

Owing to its primary position in most people's perception and its double-edged meaning in Zen, contrasting ordinary sight with extraordinary insight, this subsection runs a bit long. I hope you will see your way to the end of it.

Seeing is the most focused of the senses, in the literal sense of keenly homing in on form, color, contrast, and such like. At the same time, peripheral vision encompasses the vast, surrounding environs, even reaching far into outer space, to the moon, the sun, and the stars beyond. We are impressively farsighted. Technology has amplified sight more than any other sense, penetrating into the micro and macro dimensions of the universe.

Sight is given first place in traditional order, probably owing to its primary position in perception, at least for sighted human beings. The preponderance of information registered by the mind comes through vision.

For me, personally, vision has always been number one in the sensory mix, stemming in part from my preoccupation, and professional occupation, in visual arts and design. That training in photography or drawing is primarily training the eye to see. In zazen, we are also training ourselves to see, but beyond seeing. Seeing naturally comes to the forefront, after feeling and thinking finally take a back seat.

The common expression "Seeing is believing" indicates the primacy of sight for all, in the normal hierarchy of the senses. We speak of "seeing through deception" and imagine extraordinary powers of sight: seeing in the dark, clairvoyance, or Superman's x-ray vision.

Do You See What I See?

In Zen, however, we learn that seeing is not believing. Our vision is not to be blindly believed, not in an unquestioning way. We find that we actually do see in the dark: if nothing else, we see the darkness. Looking more fixedly, we see light in the darkness, and vice versa. We "see through" the wall in the zendo, as the gaze becomes fixed on a point in space, beyond the wall. The wall is seen to be floating in the foreground of the sphere of vision, the total realm (S. *dhatu*) of sight.

These claims are not merely semantics, or only a manner of speaking. They become more credible in zazen. Deeply examining your field of vision, freed of preconceptions regarding its nature, you will come to see what I mean. But this does not mean that you see what I see, or that I see what you see. Even when we are looking at the same scene. Master Bodhidharma weighs in on seeing in the physical sense, and in the sense of understanding:[72]

To find a buddha, all you have to do is see your nature. . . . You should realize then that everything you see is like a dream or illusion.

Critically scrutinizing sense data has been a tradition in Zen from the beginning. The great sage peers further into the inner abyss of sight:[73]

If you don't see your own miraculously aware nature, you'll never find a buddha even if you break your body into atoms. . . . The buddha is your real body, your original mind . . . but this mind isn't somewhere outside the material body of four elements.

Zen seeing means seeing into the nature of mind, finding buddha there. Waking up to the reality that is in front of, and behind, our own face. A startling footnote, on the meaning of atoms at that time, signifies seeing through reality as we usually perceive it: [74]

The early Buddhist Sarvastivadins recognized subatomic particles . . . which can only be known through meditation . . . perceptible only by the eyes of a bodhisattva.

This remarkable assertion from ancient India propels us headlong through the Zen mirror, challenging our seemingly fixed, relative scale of perception, like *Alice Through the Looking Glass*. Sitting fixedly, with fixed gaze, has a liberating effect on ordinary perception.

Seeing Meaning

Sight is so dominant in modern culture that higher achievements of mind, and admirable attributes, are expressed in terms related to vision. These include veneration for "vision" itself, imagination, visualization, envision, and the revered "seer," a sage who sees into the very meaning of life. Visionary is another exalted term, usually reserved for only the most accomplished of leaders, philosophers, creatives, and inventors. Sight is also the root term of the most vital, central concern of Zen: insight.

The centrality of seeing to any and all knowing is unwittingly enshrined in the vernacular, as in the curt "See?" or "I see what you mean." World "view" is the most comprehensive term for philosophical outlook. Buddhism's right and wrong views provide further examples, embracing both personal and social realms. The media adage "A picture is worth a thousand words" denotes the primacy of visual over verbal, the illustrative over the descriptive.

You Can't Unsee That

But seeing has its downsides. For example, we are daily witness to horrific examples of suffering and violence—on the news, through television and other visual media—all registered mainly through the eyes. Warnings that a report includes "graphic" images have become pervasive. Increasingly vivid, video documentation of acts of mayhem, savagery, and violence has become the norm. Competitive media have dropped all pretense of propriety or sensitivity, especially with regard to victims and their families.

In an age of supersaturated imagery—from social media selfies to the now-traditional television and movies—the trope "You can't unsee that" has come into vogue. We suffer from persistent, internal retention of unwanted visuals, burned into memory. Information overload contributes to the general sense of uncertainty, amping up stress levels across the globe. Traveling to the original frontier looks more and more inviting.

On a technological level, the glut of computer-generated special effects and visual illusions, approaching 4-D virtual reality, is trending to becoming indistinguishable from real images. A recent online video shows a full-scale, moving hologram of whales frolicking in the ocean, watched in real time by a rapt audience of students smack in the middle of a gymnasium.

Traumatic experience is recalled as vivid images, often with full-blown soundtrack. Victims cannot erase them from their minds. Dreams are primarily visual, with muted sound and limited sensation. But they can trigger real reactions, causing us to wake up in panic or experience "night sweats."

Evidence of the onset of physical aging and decline becomes apparent visually, witnessed in the bathroom mirror on a daily basis. This may be one downside of being sighted. And you are most likely reading this text with your eyes, to belabor the obvious.

Closing Your Eyes

Seeing absorbs so much bandwidth that in order to savor a flavor, a fragrance, or a kiss; to fully experience a massage; or to listen deeply to a piece of music, our first instinct is often to close our eyes. This selectivity applies to all the senses.

In order to watch something intently, such as a movie or sports, we get comfortable, so as not to be distracted. If you want to lose yourself in music more demanding than background sound, such as jazz or classical, you do not want to be running on a treadmill. You may prefer to dim the lights, and hope that no one is grilling fish in the next room.

The six senses are distinctly different and, in a very real sense, compete for our attention. We may think we are multitasking, simultaneously assimilating a multisensory experience, like Cirque du Soleil. But we only appear to be able to do so, owing to the rapidity of attention-switching. We may be able to walk and chew gum at the same time. But in walking alone, we can focus on only the front or the back foot, not both at a time.

In zazen, all sense realms gradually merge into one undifferentiated sense of being. Seeing seems most resistant to merging, owing to its specificity, its snapshot-like exclusivity. Like a camera, the field of vision necessarily leaves out more than it includes.

Seeing Your Blind Spots

This expression can be taken on several levels. Physical manifestations are encountered in zazen first. In time, we confront our social and psychological blind spots as well.

The fact that we do not ordinarily perceive our blind spots—the optic nerve, or "punctum caecum," in the retina—is another example of conceptual mind editing perception. It fills in the blank area, like a built-in Photoshop application. In zazen, the fixed gaze makes us distinctly aware of these spots, one in each eye, floating in the air in front of us. Blinking exaggerates them.

Of course, we all see things differently. The apple I see is not the same apple you see, if only by dint of different perspectives on it. Conceptually, we see apples even more distinctly, owing to ingrained, personal traits. I may like Granny Smiths; you may not. More to the point, I cannot get into your head, and you cannot get into mine.

Zen's focus on experiential reality means that in physical terms, it is impossible for any two people to see the same apple, or even its red or green color for that matter. Differences lie between the noumenon, the thing in itself, and the phenomenon, a thing as it is perceived (see Immanuel Kant). Not to mention the apple, or orange, that I, or you, alone, can eat.

Practicing zazen diligently, our self-assured assumptions about our world begin to break down, including their distorting effect on the senses. Vision, being the most sensitive of the senses, may be affected more dramatically than hearing or feeling. But all six eventually take a compellingly curious turn.

Fixing Your Gaze

In Soto Zen, we typically sit facing the wall to minimize distraction. The gaze comes to rest on a fixed point in space, downward at 30–45 degrees, the eyes' natural position at rest, some 3–9 feet in front of where we sit. We are not really looking at the wall. It is just another object in the field of vision.

Buddha is said to have remarked that if we take away the walls and the objects outside the building, the surrounding trees and mountains, we would see as far away as the moon, the sun, and the stars beyond:[75]

> Ananda, if you exhaust the field of your vision, from the sun and moon to the seven mountain ranges with all kinds of light, all that you see are phenomena which are not YOU. As you [shorten your range] you see passing clouds and flying birds, the wind rising, and dust, trees, mountains, rivers, grass, men, and animals; they are all external and are not YOU. Ananda, the great variety of things, far and near, when beheld by the essence of your seeing, appeared different whereas the nature of your seeing is uniform. This wondrous bright essence is really the nature of your perception.

Vision is not limited to, or by, its objects. They float in the foreground, against a background as dark and vast as outer space. Perceived reality is like a kind of marvelous projection. This is not my original idea but is attributed to Buddha himself. Seeing normal vision for what it really is: projection of an image onto a three-dimensional screen. In those days, there was no cinema, no television, only shadow puppet shows. So he could not have meant projection in the modern, technological sense. Nor in the psychological sense, layering personal interpretation over reality. But seeing our field of vision as some kind of projection, we can't help but wonder: What must be behind the screen?

Next time you are in a movie theater, vicariously absorbed in the narrative, fully engaged in suspension of disbelief, pull back a bit. Notice the crowd around you, the soft light of the sconces on the walls, the murmur of your fellow moviegoers, the scents and sounds of their popcorn-munching. Next time you are meditating, same thing. Draw back to include the peripheral theater surrounding your personal meditation movie, and for a moment at least, disrupt your suspension of disbelief. You may see for yourself what Buddha meant.

Seeing in Motion

If your gaze remains fixed long enough, a subtle change in perception will set in. You will likely begin sensing subtle, animated patterns. The retina is comprises innumerable cone- and cylinder-shaped cells, catching light and secreting chemical effluents. Visions are the predictable result of maintaining a fixed gaze. Reducing outer stimuli heightens inner stimulation, in inverse proportion. Sensory deprivation tanks are the most familiar case. But an intense outer stimulus can also trigger inner reactions. You may recall such an experience at your last eye exam. Staring wide-eyed into the seamless white hemisphere of an instrument designed to find weak spots in your retina, subtle patterns of movement emerge in your overstimulated field of vision.

An old Zen saying captures the interactivity of the sensory interface: "When you speak, IT is quiet; when you are quiet, IT speaks." By extension: When you move, IT is still; when you are still, IT moves. If you sit still enough, for long enough, everything else begins to move.

Artworks of schizophrenics, and those inspired by psychotropic drugs, often reflect intricate, atomistic patterning, deriving from fluid vision. Complex, organic geometry appears in temple carvings from separate primitive cultures, such as the Maya, Aztec, and Inca in the Americas and others from around the world. Horrific countenances of demons and gods, dragons, and temple guardian dogs are iconic in the religious art of many cultures.

They also show up, not coincidentally, in the design of automobiles. Headlights and grills resemble faces, eyes, and fangs of fierce animals. Or the masks of comic superheroes. Bilateral symmetry is the unifying thread.

Facial imagineering (thank you, Walt Disney) probably comes with the territory of being born as a human being. We are preprogrammed to recognize Mom, in our mind's eye. It is not surprising that faces would be reflected in the mirror of Zen.

Light in Dark, Dark in Light

We become acutely aware of the deep blackness surrounding our field of vision. Even though, technically, we cannot see it, since it lies outside the periphery of our vision. Both areas, peripheral and central, begin oscillating from light to dark, and dark to light, seeming to transcend the visual field's boundary. A stanza from an ancient Chinese Zen poem hints at this phenomenon:[76]

In the light there is darkness, but don't take it as darkness. In the dark there is light, but don't see it as light. Light and dark oppose one another like the front and back foot in walking.

Light and dark carry a symbolic meaning in common parlance today, connoting good and evil, respectively. But in Zen, spiritual is not separate from physical. Front and back feet are continually changing place, like black and white sides of the yin-yang symbol. We approach the deeper meaning of Zen's teachings from physiological rather than philosophical or psychological parameters. Primarily through sensory immersion, or absorption.

Inner versus Outer Light

Another Ch'an poem points to the relativity of internal, versus external, vision:[77]

In darkest night it is perfectly clear; in the light of dawn it is hidden.

Normally, inner vision is overpowered by the blinding light of the sun, or intense lighting. In subdued light, inner radiance is more readily apparent. Ambient light in the zendo is kept at a moderate level. In ancient times, oil lamps provided artificial lighting. So the prescribed level is closer to candlelight than to fluorescent.

Ultimately, seeing adapts completely, neutralizing perceived differences between peripheral and central vision. Vision unites in an all-encompassing field. The dark half, behind our head, becomes unified with the bright half, in front of our face. Internally luminous, bathed in light, it appears as soft moonlight, illuminating the original frontier.

Seeing Beyond

Whereas normal vision is one sided—we can see what is in front of us, but not what is behind—in zazen, the realm of vision expands, including what is not seen. No longer looking out, or looking in, we grasp the concrete meaning of there being no inside, no outside.

Master Hakuin testifies to this internal/external illumination in closing his paean to meditation, Song of Zazen:[78]

How vast is the heaven of zazen Samadhi! How bright and transparent the moonlight of wisdom! What is there outside us, what is there we lack? Nirvana is openly shown to our eyes. This earth where we stand is the Pure Lotus Land, and this very body, the body of buddha.

The only real heaven, Hakuin suggests, is found in the transformation of Samsara—everyday life—into Nirvana, the Pure Lotus Land. The path to that transformation is Samadhi, found in zazen. Permeating the entire universe, the moonlight of wisdom radiates from the internal heart-mind (J. *shin*) in this present, eternal moment. This is not a vision of a faraway, imagined paradise. Heaven and hell are potentials both here, immediately at hand.

Topsy-Turvy Views

One line of the Heart Sutra mentions that "Far beyond all inverted views, one realizes nirvana."[79] The more charming "topsy-turvy views" are found in the early translation chanted at ZBTC. Inverted views are our conventional worldviews, which skew dualistic, biased toward the self. Disclosures of my adventures in seeing may not be convincing that you are not seeing straight. But not all may be as it appears in your field of vision.

Experiments conducted by the psychologist George M. Stratton in the 1890s lend a literal dimension to the phrase. Investigating the strange physiological phenomenon of inverted vision,[80] Stratton developed special spectacles that inverted his field of vision, wearing them daily for a week or more. At first, the effect caused disorientation and nausea, but after a week or so, his vision reverted to normal, as long as the spectacles were in place. But when they were removed, the world was upside down again for a while. The mind, in the interim, had adapted to the anomaly. Which, for Stratton, demonstrated the intricate interconnection between vision and tactility, or proprioception, the sense of our body's location in space.

Seeing Delusion as Normal

For followers of Zen, Stratton's findings illustrate the amazing power of discriminating mind to establish—and reinstate—normalcy, in spite of distorted input from the sense organs. The monkey mind maintains normal seeing, hearing, feeling, and thinking in interpreting sense data, so long as the particular sense in question is not too closely examined. Ordinarily, the accuracy of our perception is taken for granted. We ignore the anomalies popping up in an ever-changing, distracting environment. This amounts to an ingrained ignorance. But in zazen, we turn our attention to examining this misperception.

A finding from more-recent research would seem to support Stratton's thesis. It indicates that newborns' vision is, literally, upside down. For the infant, what we regard as "up" (overhead) is experienced as "down" (below our feet). As the child matures, this perception flips, replacing it with our conventional shared vertical axis. This would seem a natural transition, as the baby learns to stand, and walk, in gravity. Up and down makes little difference in the crib. Or in outer space, for that matter.

An adult, transient state of inverted vision is a well-known, if rare, syndrome, known as the disorder "metamorphopsia." Its causes and conditions are not fully known.

Such findings lend credence to Zen's premise that so-called normal perception is suspect. And, therefore, so must be our normal conception of reality, based as it is on defective, or at best incomplete, information.

Seeing Stillness in Motion

Another example: The eyes are constantly in motion. In rapid, subtle movements called saccades, they jump between points of relative fixation several times per second. But like our inverted orientation to gravity, we are normally unaware of them. Usually, focus shifts from object to object in our field of vision, or feature to feature within a single object.

Our mind adapts to subliminal motion, and as with any constant, unrelenting stimulus, we become numb to it. We adapt. The monkey mind maintains the fiction of stillness, stability, and balance in the midst of constant movement. Otherwise, we would be falling down at every moment, overwhelmed by the rush of sensory data.

The discriminating mind imposes a false stillness on reality, a remark attributed to Buddha. Ordinarily, we need to see our world as fundamentally constant, the better to register any change—feeling, sight, sound, or odor—that may indicate a threat. Which is necessary for survival, but insufficient to grasp Zen's reality. Which is dynamic, not at all still. To see this for ourselves, ironically, we have to sit still. Ergo, zazen.

Intently fixing the gaze tamps natural movement of the eyes down to a minimum. This is not the false stillness identified by Buddha—imposed by the monkey on an internal, mental level. But instead, relative stillness—self-imposed on an external, physical level.

Intentional stillness in zazen affects all of our senses simultaneously, if sequentially, and to different degrees. It may appear in feeling as a sense of floating. Or in hearing as a deafening silence. In seeing, as moving patterns of light and color, graying out, or radiant inner light, light in the darkness.

In interpreting sense data, monkey mind imposes false stillness as our daily normal. Contrary data flowing from senses are simply ignored, the root of Zen's principle of Ignorance, the first link in the "Twelvefold Chain of Interdependent Co-arising." We ignore certain stimuli in favor of others deemed more important. But we do so at our own peril. The main barrier to insight is this automatic filtering of the mind, its daunting ability to ignore reality.

Seeing What You're Seeing With

Sitting still enough for long enough gradually removes the filters on awareness. Movement that would ordinarily remain subliminal rises to the level of consciousness. Facing a blank wall—in moderate light—internal vision comes to the fore, precisely because external stimulus is restrained. The same is true of the other senses, but vision, being the most acute, is the most acutely affected.

The static wall is relatively unchanging, but vision itself is not at all static. Neither is the wall, of course, but it changes at a much-lower frequency than vision, on the molecular scale. On a subatomic scale, the wall is radiant with the invisible frequency of particle decay. Fixing the gaze causes the radiance of vision to fluctuate noticeably, particularly where bright areas contrast with dark surfaces or shadows. Subtle differences in hue, texture, and pattern stand out in stark relief. Boundaries between light and dark manifest the afterimage effect, shimmering at the edges, exaggerating the slightest wavering of the gaze.

Your True Colors

After some time, if you suddenly shift your gaze to the side, a powerful afterimage moves with it. Where a strong color area exists, the opposite hue on the color wheel appears as a floating, glowing afterimage. Reddish begets greenish, and vice versa.

When not shifting your gaze, the objects within it are continually overlaid with their afterimages, moment by moment. The surface, reflected light, chemical responses of the retina, interpreted by the brain, determine the outcome. The afterimage calls into question the "true color" of any object in our field of vision. Your true colors do not necessarily come shining though. Is it the bright color we see when we shift our gaze? Or the duller color when we hold them still? This subtle but startling shift in awareness is a tangible example of sinking into the Samadhi of seeing. We are closing in on the movement of time itself.

Movement of Time

Another implication of the afterimage effect is that it reveals the emergent movement of time on a momentary basis, which may be belaboring the obvious. The immediate past, with its lingering afterimage overlaid on the present, slowly fades away in the electrochemical membrane of the retina. Time is literally passing before your eyes.

An arcane Buddhist hypothesis, "The Theory of Instantaneousness,"[81] posits that the smallest unit of time (S. *ksana*) is so brief that hundreds of them pass in a single snap of the fingers. In one ksana, the entire universe arises, abides, changes, and decays, according to this ancient idea, which may be pre-Buddhist. The passage of this primordial instant, dubbed the "chronon" by a modern physicist,[82] is so brief that it does not register in consciousness. Changes that are accessible to perception, such as that illustrated by shifting afterimages, may be regarded as resonances on this fundamental frequency. Movement where there shouldn't be movement suggests that we are literally seeing into the momentary flux of arising, abiding, and decaying, tracking the immediate passage of time.

Adapting to Seeing

As the gaze settles into ever-greater fixity, afterimage effects fade into background. Our eyes fidget less. The binocular structure of vision—differentiating left and right orbs—emerges. Each field registers separately as a two-dimensional oval, one on the right side of the nose, one on the left. The overlap of the two—between the noses, so to speak—forms a central arena of three-dimensional focus. This distinct separation into three is usually blended into a unified field by the mind. This may be the "third eye" of legend—looking back at the other two.

As we become more still, we begin to sense still more movement. Rotating moonlight-like blue-white waves rhythmically sweep the field, something like a radar screen. Radial pulsations of brightly colored light seem to come from a distant center point, alternating outward and inward. A bit like an animated nimbus, the flaming halo familiar from Buddhist iconography. Others originate in the extreme periphery, flowing into the middle field.

When we sit very still, our awareness attunes to ever-finer levels of motion, including in our field of vision. The stiller, the subtler the motion perceived. Motion manifests in reverse proportion to stillness. This may be an example of what Dogen referred to as the subtle, fine, or mystic mind of Nirvana (J. *nehan myoshin*).

Closing the eyelids—not recommended in zazen—we see internal fireworks, amplified by rubbing the eyes. Fluctuations in the visual field are always present, lost in a kaleidoscope of images constantly impinging upon the retina. This internal light obviously comes from an internal source, not from the sun or artificial light.

Fluid micromotions of the eyes, and soft chemical excretions of the retina, are exaggerated by facing a blank, unchanging wall. Images appear to be emanating from the wall, or emerging in the space between the wall and eyes. Motion, light, colors, forms and shapes, and frequently faces, sometimes monstrous, even seductive and sexual. But they are merely the surface of the mind's ocean. But that does not mean they do not have a real, physical source. Gazing steadily, we can even see our heartbeat's pulse, softly flickering.

The power and effects of the fixed gaze go with us when we leave the cushion. But we have to be careful as to when and where we practice it. It is not recommended while driving on the expressway, for example, for obvious reasons. Though it may come in handy at the office, fostering greater equanimity at your desk, or in a board meeting.

Earth Shaking

Watching over the Sangha, attendant priests often face inward during meditation sessions. The major portion of their downcast, fixed gaze is filled with the floor. We once had tight-woven, wall-to-wall carpet, tan in color, with parallel linear ridges a quarter inch wide. It resembled the raked sand of a Zen rock garden. I could see another layer overlying that pattern, a subtle, distinctly organic texture—perhaps partly a result of foot traffic—creating numberless, overlapping, slight impressions in the surface.

The upper layer conjured images of faces staring back at me—humans, dragons, and other phantasms—the familiar shifting, organic shapes. The underlying linear grid provided a visual counterpoint. Both transposed, separating and recombining, in a kind of soft, rhythmic dance, the dance of yin-yang, fostering a quite pleasant feeling.

This same phenomenon must pertain to all the senses but is most pronounced in vision, for me at least. Insight is sometimes referred to in Indian texts as the earth trembling in six ways (i.e., in each of the six senses). We commonly speak of the earth moving when describing overwhelming experiences. Such as falling in, or out of, love.

Seeing in Four Dimensions

Another incident, as compelling as the animated zendo carpet, occurred on retreat one crisp, overcast, fall afternoon. Facing the shoreline of a lake in zazen, my downcast gaze was filled with the watery surface. Bluish tints of reflected sky on the water, lapping at the shore, rendered the tiny wave patterns in stark relief. One-quarter slope was the darkest, shadow side of the peaks, penetrating to the depths. Opposite, a highlight reflected bright sky. Two shades of gray, on adjacent slopes of each wavelet, completed the rendering.

Suddenly they separated into four distinct layers, differentiating each hue as a flat grid of single-colored patterns. All four floated simultaneously in my field of vision as separate, layered planes, brightest on top, darkest on bottom, rather than individual wave forms on the surface of the water. A bit like photographic separations for four-color offset printing: yellow, red, blue, and black combined in overprinted layers to render the full-color image.

I could return to the surface of the lake as a unified image as I wished, and as easily allow its separation back into planes. Bemused, I vacillated back and forth. The wash from passing motorboats would disrupt the vision temporarily, then it would settle back into place.

A similar phenomenon happens when facing a field of grass. The brighter tips of the plants unite to form a top plain; middle and darker hues form the background levels. In design and art circles, these are known as figure-ground relationships and reversals, made famous in optical illusions such as those by M. C. Escher.

These simple shifts in awareness may represent a rather pedestrian example of what Dogen described, in the tract on "the most important thing" in Zen, as the "backward step":[83]

Therefore, put aside the intellectual practice of investigating words and chasing phrases, and learn to take the backward step that turns the light and shines it inward.

This phrase, adopted from a Chinese ancestor from the prior century whom Dogen much admired (Hongzhi Zhengjue, 1091–1157), indicates a 180-degree turnaround from perceived normality, beginning with taking in the unified field of vision instead of individual objects. Then seeing inwardly, as well as outwardly. We find no absolute separation of inside and outside in all the senses. Zen seeing is unfiltered by intellectual duality.

Have You Seen the Dragon?

These recollections of lively visual phenomena remind me of an old Zen story my teacher recounts in one of his published talks:[84]

> When the ceiling in the Myoshinji Temple became dull, the Zen Master, Gudo, sent for Kano Tanyu to paint a dragon on his ceiling. But Gudo told the artist, "For this special occasion I particularly want to have the painting of the dragon done from life." Naturally the painter was taken aback and said, "This is most unexpected. As a matter of fact, I am ashamed to say that I have never seen a living dragon." The painter asked wonderingly: "Where can one see a living dragon? Where do they dwell?" The Zen master answered: "Oh, that's nothing. At my place there are any number. Come and see them and paint one." Tanyu went joyfully with the teacher, and when he arrived, at once he asked: "Well, here I am to see the dragons. Where are they? The teacher, letting his gaze go around the room, replied: "Plenty of them here: Can't you see them? What a pity!"

The story relates that Tanyu studies Zen with Gudo, until one day he sees the dragon. But the master asks him only how the dragon's roar sounds, which sends Kano back to the cushion for another year. Finally one day he hears the roar and paints the famous dragon. True story. The chapter is illustrated with a photo of the actual painting.

It may be helpful, here, to take a moment to discuss the importance and meaning of the dragon as a symbol in Zen. With the monkey and the ox, we are accumulating quite a Zen menagerie. Multiple references in the literature include one compelling mention by Dogen:[85]

> Earnest Zen trainees, do not be surprised by a real dragon or spend a long time rubbing only one part of an elephant. Exert yourself in the Way that points directly to your original [Buddha] nature.

This references the story of a legendary artist who specialized in dragon statues and paintings. One day he was frightened, nearly to death, by the sudden, unexpected appearance of a real dragon. One scholar interprets the meaning of this dragon as zazen itself. I suggest it refers to the change in awareness—visual and acoustical, as well as tactile—that eventually comes about in zazen. Actually seeing the dragon.

Dragons are dynamic, fiery beings, electric in intensity. Always seeking to quench their terrible thirst, longing for the refreshing element of water, symbolized by a ball in its teeth or under its chin. The dragon symbolizes both the thirst that is driving us and the power to overcome that thirst. The elephant is an analogy attributed to Buddha for investigating only one part of the truth, mistaking it for the whole. The point is to go directly to the whole truth, avoiding obsessive distractions and unnecessary distinctions and separations.

Have You Heard Its Roar?

This part of the story may seem to belong in the next section. But we are honoring the nonseparation of the senses. They all impinge upon each other. In the martial arts, the vital-force energy (J. *ki*; C. *chi*) is the power of the dragon—as in the popular Bruce Lee movies—unleashed through training. It is also a central image—the coiled serpent—of the force unleashed through Kundalini Yoga. The serpents (S. *naga*) protecting Shakyamuni and Nagarjuna in Buddhist iconography are further examples.

Images that arise in zazen often resemble the faces and bodies of dragons or other beasts. Do not be surprised. But not only the sense of vision is involved in taming the dragon. All six are. It is the direct manifestation of the Original Mind, the real dragon. Paraphrasing Pogo the Possum: We have met the dragon, and it is us.

Childhood Visions

My personal history of insights about sight predated my involvement in Zen. A curious vision from my early boyhood—one that you may find reflected in your own sitting space—had to do with motion in stillness, as applied to seeing. Walls are not really blank, smooth, or featureless. Surfaces exhibit textural details, however subtle: the unevenness of plaster under the paint, weaves of carpets, textures of curtain fabrics.

My bedroom was a low-ceilinged, rustically finished, gabled attic room above the kitchen of the farmhouse where we lived. When I lay on my back in bed, the ceiling of faded wallpaper filled my entire vision, like a tent. It had been papered over many times. The layers beneath had not been thoroughly stripped, leaving an organic pattern of shallow bumps under the surface. As dusk settled in, I would stare at these complex shapes, half asleep, half awake. They would begin moving, subtly coalescing together and separating, in multiple layers, in an enchanting dance. Without knowing it, I was having a fixed-gaze phenomenon, seeing into the motion that is in stillness. Something similar occurs in zazen.

Playing with Vision

As a child growing up on a small farm, with both parents working, I spent a lot of time alone. I learned to entertain myself, which partly explains my abiding interest in creativity, and whatever capacity I may have for it. Perhaps you also spent formative years in relative solitude.

I taught myself to draw at an early age, nine or ten, inspired by the cartoons of Walt Disney, among other influences. My focus on seeing may be the more intense, since drawing trains the eye to see more clearly, or at least differently, from an untrained eye.

An example of self-entertainment, one that seems to apply to all children, is crossing your eyes, just for the heck of it. We were told it would stick if someone slapped us on the back. Children of all cultures invent similar childhood games in isolation from others, a well-documented phenomenon. Creativity, like buddha-nature, is innate from birth.

I would close my eyes while navigating my room, just to see what it would be like to be blind. I could "see" the surrounding room in my mind's eye, with its few furnishings. More like spatial feeling, sensing the room's shadowy form. I began to grasp what Buddha said about blindness in the *Surangama Sutra*. The mind has the faculty of sight, even if the organ of the eye is dysfunctional:[86]

[Buddha said:] "When you meet a blind man and ask him what he sees, he will tell you there is nothing but darkness in front of him. Therefore, though things may be screened from view the [faculty of] seeing continues." Ananda said: "If a blind man sees nothing but darkness before him, how can this be called seeing?" The Buddha asked: "Is there any difference between the darkness seen by a blind man in front of him and that seen by a man who is not blind when he is in a dark room?" [Ananda replied]: "World Honoured One, there is no difference." The Buddha said: "Ananda, when a blind man who used to see only darkness suddenly recovers his sight and sees every thing clearly, if you say that it is his eyes which see, then when a man who saw darkness in a dark room suddenly lights a lamp which enables him to see what is there, you should say that it is the lamp that sees. . . . Therefore, you should know that while the lamp can reveal form, seeing comes from the eyes but not from the lamp. Likewise, while your eyes can reveal form, the nature of seeing comes from the mind but not from the eyes."

In this sutra, Buddha examines the nature and function of each of the six senses, in an effort to persuade Ananda, with sheer logic, that it is the mind, penetrating throughout the sense organs, that is the true source of all perception. Plasticity of the mind/brain has been convincingly confirmed by modern science, in devising ways to bypass the eye, for example, by feeding live video images directly to the brain electronically.

Evidently, the lack of any one, fully functioning sense triggers enhanced sensitivity in the other senses as a natural compensation. Blind people often have extraordinary powers of hearing and a keen sense of the spatial surround, engendered by the necessity of navigating complex and dangerous environments. Similarly, deaf people have heightened visual acuity, exemplified by receptivity to the quick and subtle gestures of sign language and facial expression, exemplified by lipreading.

Eyes Wide Shut

Some years after simulating blindness in the confines of my bedroom, I conducted a related experiment, with disastrous results. An uncle and aunt invited me to spend the summer with them in the hilly town on the Mississippi River where they lived. They bought a 24-inch bicycle for me to ride around the neighborhood while they were at work.

One evening at dusk, riding around the block on the sidewalk, I noticed a bright streetlight at the corner at the bottom of a long but not very steep hill. I reasoned that I could approach the corner with my eyes closed, and when the light was at its brightest, turn left. I learned that you can't judge the peak of brightness until you are past it. Rolling right into the space between the lamppost and a concrete pylon, not wide enough for the handlebars to go through, I opened my eyes just in time to see my bike hitting the pole. And myself flying in a beautiful arc over the handlebars, landing headfirst in the street.

I combed my hair to cover the bruise the next morning, so that I would not have to explain myself to my hosts, who would have felt responsible for my safety. End of experiment.

Showering in the Shadows

Something safe enough to try at home involves taking a shower and closing your eyes to avoid the sting of shampoo or soap. See if you can still see the outline of your limbs in motion, glowing in the darkness, like a three-dimensional shadow. Motions of legs and arms, in a kind of phosphorescent blue-black image—appear behind, or through, the eyelids. This may be my imagination but is very distinct. It may represent the visual corollary to proprioception, feeling the disposition of the body in space. Optometrists or ophthalmologists may understand and be capable of explaining these phenomena. But that would take the mystery out of it. Another example of beginner's mind, not merely blissful ignorance.

Seeing in the Dark

Try another experiment next time you are lying in bed, drifting off to sleep. Instead of ignoring what you are seeing—which you may think must be nothing, since your eyelids are closed—look closely, and deeply, into the darkness. Focusing, instead of softening, your vision. You will find that there is something there to be seen: fluctuations in the darkness, phosphorescent areas, movements of boundaries between light and dark domains. They become more distinct and sharply rendered in contrast as you stare into the depths. This may keep you awake a bit longer. But whatever happens, and whatever it may mean to you, these phenomena are always there, whether we are aware or them or not. They probably reflect currents moving on the neural networks. But they do not require explanation in Zen.

Internal Light Show

In bright daylight, on the other hand, looking directly at the sun—eyelids closed, of course—we see bright lights and brilliant colors. These are not reflected from any objects yet have recognizable patterns. Rubbing or fluttering your fingers against your eyelids—another adolescent experiment—triggers quite a show. Think internal fireworks. Available at your fingertips, and not only on the Fourth of July.

This child's play may not be as childish as it sounds. Researcher Andrijah Puharich, investigating extrasensory perception and other paranormal powers (S. *siddhis*) in the 1950s, conducted experiments with known psychics, including Yuri Geller, using hi-tech gadgetry such as Faraday cages to screen out random interference. In one experiment, he flashed high-intensity strobe lights on their eyelids. When the frequency was tuned to about sixteen flashes per second—the minimum for registering fluid motion in cinematic projection—distinct visions were triggered. The experiments included setting up long-distance communication tests to determine whether the visions were provably clairvoyant.[87]

From this, it seems that seeing is not limited to external light and objects. Internal energy may suffice. And external stimuli may trigger internal visions.

Insight Is Not Perception

In Zen, insight is the doppelganger of sight. Zen insight means, literally, seeing into the truth of Zen's teachings. Zen's insight is not an intellectual "Aha!" or an object of perception, but a fundamental reboot of the ground of perception itself. Ordinary vision apparently has a refresh rate, much like that of your computer monitor or a television screen. Each of our senses is fine-tuned to its own frequency range on the electromagnetic spectrum. But we can be hopelessly out of tune, in terms of our awareness.

Certain teachings attributed to Buddha, much as Hakuin's, offer detailed descriptions of deep meditation, including startling comments regarding the senses:[88]

Ananda, in this profound and clear state of your penetrating mind, you will be able to discern everything clearly in your body and will suddenly see lively tape-worms. This is your clear mind spreading in your body and shows its effective functioning, the temporary achievement of which does not mean that you are a saint. If you do not regard it as such, it is an excellent progressive stage, but if you do, you will succumb to demons.

Ananda was one of Buddha's ten main disciples, a younger, close relative. Buddha warns against the tendency to misinterpret a select fifty of the various mystical or visionary experiences that may occur during meditation. His main cautionary tale is that no matter what happens, we should avoid assuming that any such epiphany is tantamount to awakening, since this will inhibit further progress on the path to final, thoroughgoing realization (S. *anuttara samyak sambodhi*).

Buddha's comment about tapeworms challenges our credulity. We are left to wonder if this describes some sort of hallucination, though he presents it as real. Tapeworms may have provided a familiar reference in those days, an apt analogy to explain what would otherwise be an indescribable vision.

Not Your Everyday Hallucination

The onset of dramatic visions in zazen is sometimes referred to as *makyo*, a Japanese term that literally means "ghost cave" or "devil's cave":[89]

> It is a figurative reference to the kind of self-delusion that results from clinging to an experience and making a conceptual "nest" out of it for oneself. Makyo is essentially synonymous with illusion, but especially in reference to experiences that can occur within meditation practice.

For us in the West, the term may connote hallucinations, delusion, fever, or mental illness. Or, more benignly, simple sensory confusion. Categorizing such strange experiences may be an attempt to normalize them, rather than explore them with an open mind. It may be better to simply sit back and enjoy the show. Such interesting phenomena may even encourage us to keep going in Zen, when energy and interest begin to flag. We do not know how insight begins, after all. This could be the start of something big.

Encountering such startling changes, whether visual, aural, or tactile, your first reaction may be that they come from an overexcited imagination. But you should suspend judgment. In the rarefied stillness of zazen, we may be seeing traces of the organs with which we are seeing, the so-called retinal circus popularized in literature of the 1960s LSD movement.[90] If so, it may be an instance of your "clear mind spreading in your body."

Enlightening with the Universe

I can personally testify to seeing grayish, rapid, twitching movements gradually coming into sharp focus while in zazen, as well as while lying in bed. More closely resembling images of branching synapses than tapeworms. Such visions may represent an optical resonance on some microlevel of the nervous system, registering in the visual cortex.

That such visions, however disturbing, represent your clear mind spreading in your body implies that the mind is not limited to one level of perception: the so-called classical scale, on which we perceive the outer world through the senses. It is as if, like Alice, our mind can move freely between scales, simply by taking a bite of a different cookie.

In this same sutra, Buddha indicates that this clear mind also spreads to its external objects, another startling idea. It seems reasonable to assume that our consciousness may be capable of spreading throughout our own body. After all, the two are inseparable. But it is a greater leap to accept that the same penetrating awareness can include objects of perception external to our being.

But this assertion simply restates, on an intimate, personal level, Buddha's description of his original awakening experience, in which he declares—in delight and surprise, one assumes—that he and the whole universe were enlightened together. It is reflected in Dogen's claim, quoted above, that "all things realize correct awakening; myriad objects partake of the buddha body." These expressions describe phenomena under the influence of zazen. In Zen, separation into inner and outer is largely irrelevant.

Light Comes from You

Another saying that may strike you as odd comes from my own teacher, who once remarked, "The light by which you see things comes from you!" Generally, we regard light, by which objects in the field of vision are illuminated, to be that of the sun, direct daylight, or reflected off the moon at night. More rarely, from starlight. Or from artificial light sources. Light may come from different sources, but certainly not from inside us.

It is tempting to interpret Matsuoka Roshi's usage of light as generalized—as in the phrase "Seeing it in a different light"—an interpretation, aspect, angle, or point of view. Or as indicating insight, as in "The light finally dawned on me" or "I see the light."

But I was there at the time, and I know for sure that he meant, concretely, the light by which we see things. Light that actually illuminates our field of vision. That light comes from us may not strike you as particularly rational, but as some sort of mystical claim.

In light of modern research on the brain, however, this idea may not be so irrational. From my limited understanding, it is impossible for us to directly see the objects in our field of vision. Instead, we are able to register only a reconstruction, constructed by our own brain. This is illustrated by the common experience of mistaking something we see for something else. Doing a double-take, we realize our mistake and see it for what it is.

But according to Zen's model of sight, even when we see a thing for what it really is, it is still only in the mind's eye. The monkey mind is constantly editing reality to follow its script. Traditional examples of this point are used to illustrate Buddhism's "emptiness," including horns on a rabbit or hair on a tortoise (emptiness of that which never is), or a coiled rope misperceived as a snake in a dark room (emptiness of that which is not what we think it is).

Zen Vision

Anomalies within the normal functioning of eyesight are, for me, endlessly fascinating. I assume them to be a natural product of the interplay among exterior objects, the frequency of light itself, and the living pulse of inner vision. Resonances within the sense realm of vision, or dhatu, in its holistic, nondual, and dynamic aspect. My interest does not, however, derive from mere speculation. A Ch'an poem points to the interactive aspect of the senses:[91]

> All the objects of the senses transpose and do not transpose. Transposing, they are linked together; not transposing, each keeps its place.

The ancient sage is not speculating, either, but reporting personal insight into the overlapping yet independent nature of the senses. Another Venn diagram. My personal record likewise evidences the relative falseness of normal vision, its built-in limitations that tend to inhibit insight.

Demystifying Insight

This lengthy dissertation does not begin to exhaust the implications of vision in Zen, with its opposite poles of sight versus insight. My teacher said that his father, his first Zen teacher, "lit a light in my heart, which is still burning today." In Japan, it was not unusual for your father to be your first Zen teacher. It was customary to have more than one teacher, usually three: your initiation teacher, your training teacher, and your transmission teacher, eventually performing your final ceremony as a Zen priest.

Matsuoka Roshi told several stories about his unusual relationship with his father. This touching example implies that there is an inner source—a faculty of vision, or of light—that illuminates all things, independent of outer light.

You might reasonably ask, How did his father do this? By teaching? By living together? By doing zazen together? What activities, words, or experiences lit this light? One answer might be "All of the above." This goes to the Zen tradition of dharma transmission, chronicled in such classics as *Transmission of Light* by Keizan Zenji, which documents exchanges between masters and students in the history of Zen. But we do not attribute any direct, causal relationship to the actions of a Zen master directly triggering the student's insight. Transmission is 100-plus percent dependent on the sincerity of the student.

Dogen declares that this light embraces all things:[92]

> Grass, trees, and lands that are embraced by this teaching together radiate a great light and endlessly expound the inconceivable profound dharma.

A radiance that transcends daylight, and at the same time includes it. But even the full light of day—coming mainly from a single-point source, the sun—is set against an underlying darkness, as deep as outer space and as close as your peripheral vision. Dark and light become inseparable, as one complementary unity that is not-two. They define each other, and not only on the physical plane. Sensory and conceptual seeing merge in one true vision: right view or right understanding. As in "I see what you mean."

Seeing beyond Duality

When we no longer see any separation of inner and outer, light and dark, seeing itself has to change. Normal seeing of distinct, exterior things eventually becomes simply seeing, absent any particular objects. All objects merge into the unified field of vision.

We may postulate seeing, then, as

1. seeing (subject—the organ)   2. seeing (predicate—as insight)
3. seeing (object—the reality)

Zen seeing, then, is seeing seeing itself. The tedious redundancy of this construction illustrates the difficulty of expressing nondual truth in language, which is inherently dualistic. Just as thinking goes beyond thinking in Zen, seeing goes beyond seeing. Other expressions might be "Seeing that is non-seeing" or "Seeing that is beyond seeing."

Zazen transforms ordinary sight into insight, if only we sit still enough for long enough. The same principle holds true for all six sense realms, within the realm of nondual sensation. It is the enchanted scenery of Wonderland, the landscape of the original frontier.

D. HEARING: Ears & Sounds

I place hearing fourth, in sequence of confrontation, in zazen. It occupies last place of the four major senses, on the sliding scale of diminishing resistance. Hearing emerges after the barriers of tactile discomfort, mental confusion, and visual distraction are overcome. Sound precedes smell and taste at the end of the spectrum, in amenability to sensory adaptation.

Hearing may take longer to come to the foreground, partly because, like smell and taste, it is closer to feeling than it is to seeing. Hearing has an ambient quality, whereas seeing tends to be more sharply focused, at least under normal daylight conditions. At night, or in a dark room, seeing takes on a more ambient aspect as central vision takes a back seat to the peripheral. Hearing manifests a analogous separation into inner and outer sound sources.

Once it has come front and center, hearing adapts more quickly, and more completely, than seeing. We register the slightest visual changes, such as passing shadows from clouds. But changes in ambient sound, both from internal and external sources, register strongly. We are highly attuned to sound, especially sensitive to unexpected noises.

Listen to the Music

If you happen to be trained in music or pursue professional activities related to sound, hearing may loom larger, much earlier, in your personal experience on the cushion. Owing to the influence both of visual arts and music during my formative years, for me the two are mixed. Again, your results may vary; I am merely reporting mine.

Growing up in a musical family—my father leading a jazz quintet in the 1940s, my brother being a professional jazz pianist—a soft spot for the aural complements my predilection for the visual. My sisters both took dance lessons, one turning professional. So I also gained an early appreciation for the performance arts. Perhaps you can place your own personal penchants somewhere on the sensory spectrum.

Such personality traits, born of both nurture and nature, may seem to compete against each other, as it were, vying for our attention. You cannot do everything. But in the process of refining your Zen life, they come to complement each other. Our conditioned preoccupations tend to level out in zazen through a kind of sensory balancing act.

If you are oriented to hearing, through a love of music, for instance, you may in zazen become more acutely aware of visual stimuli. Or develop a more kinetic sensitivity to your body. If you are athletic, or preoccupied with fitness and working out, you may become more attuned to your sense of hearing or seeing. Thus, a more well-rounded person may emerge from your time on the cushion. We find ourselves paying attention to what we usually ignore.

Mary Had a Little Lamb

That all vibration is sound is an ancient teaching, expressed in the mystical syllable "OM." The sun is said to emit a tone at an extremely low, B-flat pitch, the music of the spheres. We may regard our sound-surround as a form of music, however chaotic and cacophonous. Some contemporary classical, jazz, and electronic composers appreciate this. In the famous piano composition of John Cage titled "4'33"" ("Four minutes, thirty-three seconds"), the pianist, after opening the piano, sits silently for that exact period of time, then closes the piano, rises and bows, and exits the stage. The audience is treated to the various ambient sounds in the concert hall: shuffling of feet, coughing, and so on. Which composes the music of the piece.

In zazen, you may begin hearing a familiar song, a melody that you cannot get out of your head, such as the old childhood ditty *Mary Had a Little Lamb*. It repeatedly runs through your mind, driving you to distraction.

While irritating, this phenomenon serves to illustrate one of the critical functions of the thinking mind: its talent for bringing order out of chaos. Recognizing that this is a predictable occurrence when sitting in meditation, there is still something you can do about it.

Focusing on each individual note of the melody, one pitch at a time, you will find that you are actually hearing, not imagining, each tone. Each resonates from a real, but ordinarily subliminal, source. As if the brain is chock-full of sound-emitting, electronic diodes.

As you embrace each of these pitches as real, if fluctuating, you will find that, taken together, they form a grand, dissonant, pulsating chord. This may or may not be related to tinnitus, ringing in the ears, considered a disorder or decay of the hearing organs.

My point here is that the mind naturally attempts to bring order out of this chaotic, subliminal wall of sound. It picks and chooses various pitches, stringing them together into a familiar sequence of intervals, such as the tune about Mary and her lamb. This phenomenon is highly contagious, like yawning. Now that I mention it, you may be hearing that song.

Getting Beyond Noise to Just Sound

You may also find external sounds to be distracting at first, especially the sound of the human voice. If you can hear someone speaking, even softly, it can be difficult to ignore and will test your patience during zazen. If what they are saying can be understood, it is even more distracting, as the monkey grasps at the words and their meaning. An indistinct murmur, or an unfamiliar foreign language, is easier to ignore. Like the buzz of chatter in a restaurant. This is why Zen centers tend to stress—and sometimes enforce—observing silence, especially during zazen sessions. But white noise, such as that of a fan, is not usually an issue.

Eventually, in zazen, even human voices will come to be experienced as "just sound." A line from a poem of Dogen—one of his *108 Gates of Dharma-Illumination*—points to this reductive truth:[93]

> Right speech is a gate of Dharma-illumination, for [with it] concepts, voice, and speech all are known as sound.

It takes a moment of time, and some effort, for our brain to interpret any sound, including the sound of a human voice, even in our native tongue. If we hear people speaking in a foreign language, the automatic, unconscious translation into meaning that usually happens does not, indeed cannot, occur. We recognize the voices as human and may identify the language. But the further removed from our own speech, the closer it comes to registering as sound in the abstract.

The Moment Before

In zazen, we do not settle into the present moment, in the ordinary sense, but into that micromoment just before interpretation can take place. All sensations received by the ears, and registered by the brain as sound, are discriminated by the mind into such categories as speech and voice; then conceptualized as music, noise, or static; and further judged as soothing or irritating, and so on.

When we begin to register our own speech and that of others in Zen's neutral, concrete way, we see—or, more literally, hear—that even speech can be reduced to mere sound. Our specific, meaning-laden language breaks down into individual words and syllables. Then on to discernment of its abstract dimensions: pitch, intensity, and resonance. And, finally, we arrive at just sound. Here we find the complementary nature of sound and silence.

Ordinarily, we might adjudge right speech to be "right," only by virtue of the practice of kind or loving speech as being a gate to dharma-illumination. But elsewhere, Dogen, as always, stresses the experiential:[94]

> We vow with all beings from this life on throughout countless lives to hear the true dharma.

Dogen's "hearing the dharma" is not the mere understanding of the meaning of the written or spoken record, but as manifested in all sound. He quotes a famous Chinese poet:[95]

> The voices of the river valley are the [Buddha's] wide and long tongue.

The True Dharma (in Written Form)

Of course, Dogen also embraced hearing the dharma in the conventional sense, as in studying the Sutras and following the Precepts. But the "true dharma" is less accessible to the thinking mind than is the written record.

In order to know what the great master is getting at, we must come to the point of hearing all conceptual levels of sound as, at base, pure sound: the True Dharma. Dharma is the content of all sound, not exclusively conceptual, as expressed in words. In order to hear in this way, we have to settle into the present moment, just before automatic interpretation into language and concepts can occur.

"Dharma-illumination" may call to mind the visual sense, rather than speech. But Dogen's poem indicates insight into all of the senses, through unraveling, untying the six knots. The other five senses are also mentioned, along with all major Mahayana teachings, adding up to 108 Dharma gates. Speech derives from thought concepts, the human voice, and language. Insight into hearing is tied directly to the speaking tongue. Your experience of illuminating insight in zazen will reduce these complex phenomena to pure sound, resonating throughout the eternal moment. Dogen touches on this repeatedly:[96]

> This being so, the zazen of even one person at one moment imperceptibly accords with all things and fully resonates through all time.

Your own experience of pure sound, if and when it occurs, may seem meaningless and somewhat unnerving. It renders the familiar nature of sound surpassingly strange. I first experienced it in my pre-Zen days, under the influence of a psychedelic. Sitting at a table with my mother and my brother's mother-in-law, their chatting suddenly morphed into incomprehensible baffle-gabble, an abstract gabfest. I could willfully return to understanding what they were saying, but it was a relief, and entertaining, just to hear it as sound. It was quite musical, in its own way, like listening to foreigners speaking animatedly.

The same phenomenon has recurred in the intervening decades, providing an option for tuning out of distracting chatter intentionally, not an uncontrollable "flashback," the dreaded symptom of permanent brain damage prevalent in that period of drug-induced insight. The eeriness of this change illuminates the difference between real sound and our preconception of it, contrasting autopilot engagement against listening critically. Typically, we hear what we expect to hear, if not always what we want to.

The familiar example of repeating a word, such as "elephant," illustrates this disjunction. The term deconstructs itself, given sufficient repetition. It is rendered into the sound of mere syllables, losing their association with the giant pachyderm, and with each other, finally parting company with meaning altogether.

Experience versus Interpretation

Just as we give experience first priority over expression, similarly, interpretation must take a back seat to experience. We stop short of interpreting or overanalyzing our experience of sensory input in zazen. A caveat may be in order, to distinguish between raw sensation and our interpretation of it. Both are real, but in different ways. Buddhism posits a distinction between "real and existent dharmas" and "real but nonexistent dharmas." Dharma has the connotation of a being, or object, as well as teaching. The actual, concrete sound of the voice is real and existent. Our interpretation of it, as meaningful words and concepts, qualifies as real, yes, but nonexistent.

In Zen, the debate is not whether sound and language are real or not, in some absolute sense, but how they exist in reality. All forms exist by virtue of emptiness, the dynamic process of unceasing change, in which forms arise and are embedded temporarily. Likewise, all five aggregates of sentience—form, sensation, perception/conception, impulse, and consciousness itself—exist within a network of codependent and mutually causal conditions.

It is not that sound, as language, is unreal. It is that the construct of language does not exist in the same physical sense that the sound itself does. When anyone speaks, their voice is manifesting the Dharma, no matter what they actually say in words.

This seeming dichotomy is akin to a visual analogy by Master Dogen on a painting of rice cakes:[97]

An eternal buddha says, "A picture of a rice cake does not satisfy hunger."

One interpretation holds that everything we perceive is like a painting of a rice cake, not the real thing. It does not satisfy our hunger. Likewise, nothing can satisfy our spiritual hunger, since everything is empty, including emptiness itself. In this respect, a dream—or a painting of a rice cake—is no less real than the waking world, or an actual rice cake. Since all things are but passing dreams, they are just paintings of rice cakes.

Words and concepts, then, can be no more of a barrier to awakening than anything else. They are, in and of themselves, demonstrably empty. Concepts of reality are problematic only when mistaken not to be empty: not subject to change, cast in concrete, unlike reality itself.

We reify concepts, believing that the words actually capture reality. In some cases, such as $E = mc^2$, the evidence is very convincing. But existent versus nonexistent realities clash when words fail. Both are real, but in different ways. The first can be found in its dharma location; the second resides only in our minds. The first is the thing in itself; the second, our interpretation.

Ambient sources of sound—wind in the trees, rain on the roof, birdcalls, dogs barking, passing trains and traffic—all become part of the Zen soundscape. If you find them distracting, not to worry; they will become less so in time, even soothing.

Listening to Life

Our own internal sources of sound also become amplified, though no one else can hear them, unless your digestive system gurgles loudly or your breathing is raspy. The gentle flow of the breath, the beating of the heart, electrical activity within the brain and neural pathways, the pulsing circulation of blood—all may become palpable, magnified in zazen. It is perfectly natural that such subtle sounds—to which the mind is normally deaf—enter fully into your consciousness, given the hypersensitivity of zazen. They provide the soundtrack for our movie, chronicling our journey into the profound stillness of the original frontier.

You may find this more disturbing than external sounds. Hearing your own heart, or breath, is usually associated with crisis, a threatening situation, or other forms of distress. It may set off alarms, the knee-jerk reaction of the monkey mind. You may feel panicky, nauseated, or dizzy.

The latter two reactions are noted in another pamphlet from the Chicago Temple. It suggests focusing on the forehead, if nauseated, or on the knees, when dizzy. This is a spoiler alert that we will, indeed, become nauseated, dizzy, or both at some point in zazen. The precarious position of being perched at the top of a "100-foot pole"—one of Zen's more alarming analogies for the rarefied heights to which zazen will take us—feels this way.

Eventually, however, our newly normal, higher threshold of sensitivity to what are ordinarily subliminal sounds becomes familiar, even reassuring. It is soothing to hear your own heart, beating at a calm pace. Or listening to the breath as a deep sigh of relief. We can even synchronize our breath and heartbeat, the former slowing the latter down.

One ancient tradition from India points out that even the familiar inhaling-exhaling cycle has two distinct sounds. Inhaling sounds something like *hangh*; exhaling, *sa*. The full cycle sounds like *hangh-sa*. I know that sound. You might want to get to know it too.

Unraveling Sound

Buddha likened the senses to six knots tied in a scarf. He exhorted his disciples to untie them, one knot at a time, during meditation.[98] The scarf represents undifferentiated consciousness, running through all six. This is Mind, in the most general sense of the term. The unraveling is necessary to counter the normal entanglement of mind with each sense organ, and in turn each organ with inner and outer objects, as well as each sense "transposing" with the others. You might think of this process as "unraveling enlightenment," as Sensei titled one of his public talks. Hearing is considered most amenable to unraveling, as attested by several of Buddha's own disciples.[99]

Buddhism's Bodhisattva of Compassion (S. *Avalokiteshvara*; J. *Kannon*; C. *Quan Yin*) is associated with hearing. Her spiritual transformation is said to have followed solely from hearing, attuned to the sounds of suffering in the world. Zen emphasizes deep listening as a central focus of zazen. Immersion, in one sense at a time, is recommended as an expedient exercise, but not to the point of disregarding the other senses.

From Zen's premise—that particular sounds reduce to just sound—it follows that all sound is, essentially, the sound of change. Change is the impersonal, universal meaning of Buddhism's Dukkha. Anything and everything that we all hear, at any and all times, is, by definition, the sound of dukkha: the soundtrack of inexorable change.

Cutting through the Senses

In the *Surangama Sutra*, hearing is the sense most cited by Buddha's disciples as their personal gate to insight. Others were awakened via taste, smell, vision, or tactile sensation. Again, your results may vary on the basis of a whole host of factors. But even being perceptually disabled, disadvantaged, or challenged—by blindness or deafness, for example—does not disqualify a person from realizing this potential.

We may take this hypothesis on faith, as a theory yet to be proven in our own personal experience. To test it in zazen, we direct our attention to our senses, one at a time. Once any one of our senses begins to unravel, the others are bound to follow, like so many tangles in the scarf. Or, for that matter, an electrical cord, rope, or garden hose. One has to begin somewhere, teasing out whichever thread is loosest, the most accessible to untying.

Hearing Space

Hearing may owe its relative ease of unraveling to its nature as the most spatial of all the senses. In it, we find no distinct boundary between inside and outside, and no outer limit. Much as binocular vision enables three-dimensional seeing in the field of vision, two ears provide the function of bilocation—the ability to pinpoint the source of a sound—in the surrounding environs. The inner ear also plays a central role in the vestibular system, sustaining our physical sense of balance. Hearing involves much more than simply registering sound.

Hearing also seems less tangible than the other senses. But loud sounds—an explosion, a passing siren, or loudspeakers at a rock concert—cross the boundary into feeling and can cause physical pain. Even a loss of hearing, if intense enough and repeated enough.

Our overall sensitivity spikes early on during zazen, including especially hearing. Initially, and more deeply over the long term, hearing adapts to the relative quiet of our sitting place at home, or in the zendo. Internal sounds become more pronounced; external sounds more vivid. Even distant sounds seem more immediate, expanding our sense of space.

Our acoustical range expands perceptually, if not actually, with heightened receptivity to higher and lower frequencies. This hypersensitivity is an instance of reverse adaptation, as we adjust to deeper stillness. The monkey's habitual muting of the chaotic sound-surround gradually falls away. The meditation space becomes something like an echo chamber, on a highly nuanced level. We become acutely aware of the subtlety of sound.

Sensing Silence

People conventionally associate meditation with sitting in silence. And to the degree practicable, most Zen centers and monasteries maintain a significant level of quiet. But silence, in Zen, is not the absence of sound. The sound is in the silence; the silence is in the sound. Silence is inseparable from sound, and sound is inseparable from silence. Even the deaf hear the silence. Our entire surrounding field, or sphere, of sound eventually becomes unified, set against a deeper background of relative silence. Sound and silence are interdependently co-arisen. In Zen, we see no dichotomy, no opposition of sound and silence. This is implied in *mokurai*: "silence is thunder."

Sound, or hearing, has always occupied a special place in the history of Zen. Anecdotes record different Zen masters' experience of awakening, triggered by sound. A stone striking bamboo while sweeping the walk; a frog jumping into a pond. A dying Zen master, asked by his students as to where they might enter the original frontier, said, "Do you hear the sound of the squirrel on the roof? Enter there." Another master directed them to the babbling of a nearby brook.

Sound is always and everywhere such an entry point, itself a gate of dharma-illumination. Hearing becomes deep listening, attending to the universal "sound of silence" (Paul Simon). Master Dogen captures this ringing sound even more poetically:[100]

This is not only practice while sitting, it is like a hammer striking emptiness: before and after, its exquisite peal permeates everywhere.

The deep silence of Zen is in the sound, the motion is in the stillness, and vice versa: sound is in the silence; stillness is at the heart of the motion. Like the sprocket of my 24-inch bicycle, at the exact center of the earth, the moon, or the sun, there is a still point. A center that is still, relative to itself, while everything around it is in motion. That still point is inside you, and me, as well.

Entering into deep stillness is the greatest action we can take. Action and stillness are also not-two. In Zen's stillness, mind and object, being and environment, merge. This is the fundamental dynamic in zazen on the conceptual level, a progressive merging of all apparent opposites into "Not one, but not-two."

In zazen we listen deeply to the true dharma, the sutras expounded everywhere, and at all times. Can't you hear it? The sound of sounds permeates the original frontier.

E. SMELLING: Nose & Scents

I place the sense of smell next, fifth in order of resistance or diminishing level of difficulty in zazen, followed closely by taste. Not because either puts up much resistance, but precisely because they do not. For you, depending on the sensitivity of the two organs, taste may come before smell. Unlike the four major contenders, the olfactory and gustatory senses do not usually cause much trouble in meditation.

Smell comes into play before taste, in my estimation, because it is directly connected with breathing, the most immediate and continuous of life-sustaining resources. Breathing is the focus of the second set of instructions in zazen, between dispositions of posture and attention. Taste is a step lower on the material hierarchy, since its object is not airborne but solid organic matter, and fluid chemistry.

Smell adapts quickly in the ambience of the zendo, which often features incense. After all, we are not eating or drinking anything while sitting in zazen. Both senses quickly become nonissues, being far less resistant than bodily sensation, and less demanding of our attention than thinking, seeing, or hearing.

The zendo is not normally subject to changing aromas but maintains a relatively neutral redolence, often with a subtle residue of incense (J. *kunju*). Registering and differentiating scents is largely dependent on chemical reactions. Tiny volatile molecules, suspended in the airstream, fit into specific receptors in our nasal membranes, like miniature Chinese puzzles, or a microscopic space module docking in a port. Taste functions similarly, via chemical nutrients interacting with taste buds on the tongue.

Fragrant Memories

Smell is arguably the most primal of the senses, the most closely associated with memory. It is thought to be an ancient sense, of early evolution, by which primitive human beings took samples of their environment, as we observe other animals doing. Odors signaling danger can be critical to survival, along with alarming sounds or unusual sights.

Instant, negative reaction to acrid smells, and revulsion at certain odors—such as sulfur or sewage—are olfactory red flags we all share in common. We instinctively detect presence of any bacteria, or chemistry, that might cause disease or injury. "Stench" and "stink" identify the negative end of the smell spectrum, while "fragrance" and "aroma" label the positive extremes. Terms such as "scent," "smell," and "odor" occupy the neutral, middle ground.

Intimations from Childhood

As a young boy growing up on a small farm, I had personal experience with a broad spectrum of smells, from attractive to repellent. Among my chores were feeding the horses and cleaning up after them, which provided a rich palette of odors: the oats, alfalfa, and straw at the front end of the process, and the manure at the back end.

It also fell to me to keep the home fires burning in the coal furnace during winter, and to keep the drainage ditch from the septic tank clear in summer. Each offered a panoply of tactile and visual impressions, accompanied by unusually strong odors, from the sour stench of sewage to the sulfurous vapors from the coal.

Not knowing any better at that age—as to whether these smells were a good thing or a bad thing—I quickly adapted to them, overcoming any built-in revulsion. I assume that sewer workers in major cities likewise get used to the stench, which I later found very familiar, rising from the street grates in Chicago, New York, Atlanta, London, and Tokyo, among others.

I was fascinated by the shiny surfaces of the "clinkers," as we called the fused coals, and the bright sounds they made when bumped together—thus the name—carrying them out to line our long driveway to the farmhouse. We now know that coal ash contains many dangerous chemicals and, in large quantities, is hazardous to the environment. But to me, they appeared as organic sculptures, with beautiful, iridescent surface colors.

Grandma's Cooking

Another example of the marriage of smell and memory comes from the lifestyle of my grandparents' generation. The wood heating stoves, and the cook stove in my grandmother's kitchen in our hometown and, later, their place in the Missouri Ozarks, were compellingly redolent. During summer vacations there, the aromatic nature of the wood itself, usually hickory, ash, or oak—as in the old folk song on making moonshine in a still—filled the air and formed an early association with food in my sensibilities. But a more curious and intense residual memory of smell came from her dishpan, sitting on one end of the stove top.

Since they depended on well water, fresh, clean water was very precious. So Grandma Nelly would leave the same pan of wash water on the stove for several days. At the end of that time, it began to smell more like soup than soap. Of course, she rinsed the dishes, pots, and pans before and after, so there was no danger of contamination. But the yeasty aroma lingers in memory. The smell of the woody incense used in Zen meditation halls harks back to the aromatic air of the Ozarks, taking me back home where I belong, on the original frontier.

Montezuma's Revenge

Decades later, while teaching classes in meditation and creativity at the Centro International de Documentación (CIDOC), in Cuernavaca, Mexico (founded and led by Ivan Illich), we took up residence in a communal compound hosted by a retired Catholic priest, Padre Francois. The kitchen had running water, but conservation was valued. I set up what I dubbed the "Zen-Ozarks" system for dishwashing. It entailed a three-tub approach, designed for efficiency and sanitation, in lieu of a professional steamer. On the basis of Grandma's method, and similar to what I have seen at Zen centers, I feel sure that it protected my family, along with the other residents, from Montezuma's Revenge.

A visual memory from the trip to Mexico stays with me. Stopping along the highway some distance south of the border, I wandered into the desert to relieve myself. There was no traffic to be seen for miles in those days. I suddenly noticed the sand, stones, and cacti in the brilliant sun, and every minute particle seemed intentionally placed, arranged in beautiful patterns. It had to be either that no human or animal presence had disrupted the surface, or infrequent rains had erased any such intrusion. It reminded me of the Civil War soldier's impression of the banks of the creek in "An Occurrence at Owl Creek Bridge," by Ambrose Bierce. He imagined that he escaped being hanged, the rope breaking. Clambering out of the water near his home, he was struck by the unbelievable beauty of the forest floor, just before the rope snapped his neck. One of the lingering olfactory memories I cherish is that of the air in Mexico. It literally smelled like exotic, peppery spices.

Survival instincts and fantasizing aside, an old saying claims that to the enlightened, all odors are perfumes. The social import of smell is indicated by the quaint old English phrase that a certain persona non grata is "not in good odor." Or the gangster's "I smell a rat!" And the muckraker's "This stinks to high heaven!" Smell still has social as well as survival value.

Sniffing Out the Science

Sense data from the nose go directly to the brain's olfactory cortex, embedded in the same region where emotions and memories are thought to reside. This zone can trigger the release of endorphins and regularly acts on the limbic system, defined as such:[101]

A complex system of nerves and networks in the brain, involving several areas near the edge of the cortex concerned with instinct and mood. It controls the basic emotions (fear, pleasure, anger) and drives (hunger, sex, dominance, care of offspring).

Note that our basic emotions are conjoined with our baser drives, instincts, and moods. A scientific take on the monkey-mind-body connection. The choice of the term "control" to define the role of the brain reflects a predominant cultural meme: "mind over matter." From the perspective of Zen, a more neutral term—such as "harbors" or "coordinates"—is more appropriate. We have to treat as a hypothesis—or a theory, at best—the idea that the brain is actually in control of anything. Monkey mind, of course, likes to feel that it is in total control.

Smelling a Conflict

A brief caveat: appeals to science from time to time in these comments may appear to be an attempt to bolster certain claims, providing a respectable veneer of authenticity. But it is meant, instead, to add an appropriate layer of objective circumspection. That is, the underlying mechanisms, as we understand them, do not really explain the phenomenological experience of the senses, or the adaptive transformation that they undergo in zazen.

Buddhism finds no basic conflict with the findings of science, as my teacher, as well as HH the Dalai Lama, has mentioned. And the way that Zen works is not independent of the way the physical body works. Zen meditation, as a method, works precisely because of the natural functions of the body, not in spite of them. And we might add that zazen works mainly because it focuses our attention directly on our physical and physiological reality, rather than denying it or engaging in speculation about it.

Surviving by Smell

In any case, smell is well connected to our primal drives and emotions. This makes sense because the sense of smell finds its home in the nasal passages and the mouth, our body's main interface with vital sources of sustenance: air, water, and food.

Breath is our source of life-giving oxygen, which we need in constant supply, moment by moment, in order to avoid suffocating. The outer limit is usually something like five minutes before loss of consciousness, with resultant brain damage and death, may set in. Unless you are an oyster diver. Lack of water or food takes a bit longer.

The smell of the air we breathe is the canary in the mine shaft. This is driven home by evermore frequent warnings of smog alerts, and bad air days, in our congested inner cities. Beijing, Shanghai, and New Delhi currently compete for the honor of being the poster boy.

Smelling for Profit

The pleasurable side of smell is dramatized by the overwhelming deluge of scented items on offer, demand for which supports a robust product re-search-and-development industry. The ostensible benefits and pleasing effects of scents from nature's cornucopia of spices and flowers, historically including ambergris from whales (shout-out to Moby Dick), are marketed as aroma-therapy. Artificial fragrances are concocted in the lab and sold with claims that they positively alter our mood and have beneficial effects on our health. This represents a predictable outgrowth of the cosmetic and perfume industry, with its emphasis on celebrity and beauty, conflated with hip and holistic New Age health memes.

The connection of smell to memory is more evident—more scientific, if somewhat nostalgic—than profit-driven claims of the benefits of scent-based products. Familiar aromas trigger vivid memories, such as grandma's cooking, grandpa's pipe tobacco, or a favorite incense. In an age of wretchedly excessive marketing, a little incense can go a long way.

Stop and Smell the Incense

If you are familiar with protocols at Buddhist centers or monasteries, you know that incense is often burned before, and during, meditation sessions. The upside of this custom is that consistent use of incense reinforces a conti-nuity of atmospheric ambience from session to session. Which can be helpful in settling the mind more quickly. The downside is that smoke particles pollute the air and invade the lungs. And strong perfumes can be noxious.

This constitutes a notable exception to the relative irrelevancy of smell as a source of resistance: increasing sensitivity to air pollution, including such afflictions as asthma, and allergies to mold. In which case, smell, or allergic reaction, raises a red flag immediately.

For these reasons, incense use is decreasing in American Zen centers, even falling entirely into disuse. More attendees declare that they are allergic to incense. Consequently, many Zen leaders are eschewing the use of incense altogether. This reflects the pragmatic conformity of Zen, adapting to necessity.

I have always had a positive reaction, personally, to incense of the woody variety. Highly perfumed incense, more characteristic of India, is more distracting, if not irritating. Temples and monasteries of old were drafty, nothing like the airtight buildings we occupy today. So it is beyond reasonable to treat incense with moderation, erring on the side of health and wellness.

Adapting to Smell

So long as no strong odors intrude, such as from cooking, your meditation should proceed undisturbed by the olfactory sense realm. For this reason, the kitchen is some distance from the zendo, mitigating the impact of odors as well as distracting sounds while preparing meals.

Some animals, notably dogs, are known to be much more sensitive to smell than humans. But recent research has shown that even human beings can distinguish literally thousands of odors, even if each sample is only slightly different from another.

In the hypersensitivity of deep zazen, each breath can be discerned as subtly different from the one before. This heightened sensitivity is transitory, of course, eventually succumbing to progressive adaptation, as with all the senses. Because smelling adapts more quickly than seeing, hearing, or feeling, it soon becomes inoperative.

Sensitivity is mitigated, or masked, by nasal congestion and apparently diminishes with age, as does taste. We often experience the movement of breath as tactile sensation, rather than as odor. The sharp shock of freezing air temperatures in winter, for example.

Smelling Feeling, Breathing, and Hearing

In zazen, the smooth flow of air moving through nasal passages, whether scented or not, becomes extraordinarily soothing, especially as the breath slows down. Breathing should also, naturally, become quiet. If you can hear your own breathing, it is likely that others can. If you are breathing noisily, it might indicate an unconscious constriction in your nasal passages. If you focus on the exact center of the breath stream, you will find silence there, where the airflow is unrestricted. As the breath becomes natural, there is less and less resistance to the flow. This will relax any constriction in the air passages, in lieu of congestion. We become aware of such subtleties, observing the breath closely in the stillness of zazen.

We also become acutely aware of the rapidity of the breathing cycle, slowing down naturally, gradually becoming deeper and more quiet. Breathing should be more like sighing than labored palpitation, just as posture should feel more like stretching.

Quiet breathing goes hand in hand with deep listening, leading naturally to the Zen protocol of observing verbal silence. This holds true whether in solo or group meditation. The natural breath, once we have rediscovered it, goes with us everywhere. Even at home, at work, or at play, not to mention at rest.

We also train ourselves to move as quietly as possible when movement is necessary, especially in the zendo. Heightened sensitivity to sound is part and parcel of finding stillness in the Three Actions of body, speech, and mind.

As our body becomes still, our breath does as well. With the stilling of the breath, our sense of smell becomes refined, then neutralizes. Finally entering into olfactory stillness, so to speak. As your sense of smell adapts, the subtle incense of emptiness, like refreshing water, nourishes your mind. Speaking out of this stillness, our words calm and comfort others. We catch a sniff of the Dharma, inhaling the bracing aroma of Samadhi. We never forget the spicy fragrance of the original frontier.

F. TASTING: Tongue & Flavors

Taste comes sixth, dead last in sequence, in terms of confronting resistance in zazen, for similar reasons as smell. Tasting adapts quickly, putting up little resistance to sitting still unless we are hungry, or nauseated. But because the tongue is also engaged in speech, off the cushion there is a level of social difficulty associated with it, beyond its physiological function. More on this later.

Given ordinary circumstances—being in good health, and having no particular problem with the gustatory system—taste should not be a major hindrance in zazen. Because it is not as directly connected with breathing, taste is less of a player than is smell. Taste does not usually occupy our attention unless we are eating. Even when one is eating, flavors are transient. They last only the length of your tongue. Again, remember that we are discussing the senses as they come under scrutiny in zazen, not as they might be ordered on another set of criteria.

Chemical Intelligence

Taste, like smell, may be regarded as primarily chemical in essence. Based on solids and liquids rather than gases, the gustatory realm is a bit grosser, technically as well as socially. However, distasteful flavors—such as sour, bitter, or rotten—trigger reactions similar to repulsive smells. Our health, even survival, may be at risk, from threat of sickness or poisoning from tainted food, for example.

Bad breath can be a symptom of disease and is usually accompanied by a bad taste in the mouth, to which, of course, we adapt. Owing to the ready adaptation of both smell and taste, a person is usually unable to detect when they, themselves, may have bad breath. They cannot smell their own breath, having adapted to it.

Perhaps owing to their chemical connection, smell and taste are highly dependent on physical variations in their organs, which produce broadly different sensibilities. Professional wine tasters and smell testers are endowed with sensitive tongues and noses. They make their livelihood detecting the subtlest notes of flavor and sniffing out the finest differences in aroma, in the development of wines as well as perfumes. Individuals display widely differing sensitivity to taste, depending on the array of taste buds on the tongue. The same is true of smell, where sensitivity depends on the number of nasal receptors.

Taste and Smell Inseparable

We all know that smell and taste usually work together. Smell and taste are tightly interwoven, as you may have noticed when suffering from a head cold. Food loses most of its flavor when it cannot be smelled. Without smell, taste becomes mostly texture, the tactile side of the tongue.

A common complaint in extended-care facilities for the aged—one my own mother mentioned often in her declining years—is a perceived lack of taste in the daily fare. When I joined her for a meal, the food seemed fine to me. This perception may be related to diminished sensitivity to smell, and taste, that comes with aging, rather than blandness of the menu. Hospital food is universally panned as bland and tasteless, partly owing to a lack of spices. But other factors of aging may play a part, such as loss of appetite accompanying depression, illness, and mobility restrictions. These understandably affect the enjoyment of life in general, and diet in particular. I can testify from personal experience of relying on cafeteria food in my undergraduate days that this complaint is not necessarily age-related, but only exacerbated.

Taste adapts immediately in zazen, owing to the lack of stimulation. Unlike smell, which resides in the constant cycle of breathing, flavors come from intermittent cycles of eating and drinking. Both adapt much like a chemical solution, neutralized through balancing acid and base components. Indigestion is usually a symptom of chemical imbalance, skewing to the acidic, given the typical American diet. We should avoid meditating immediately after eating, according to Hakuin Zenji. He advised sitting with the stomach only two-thirds full.

Good for What Ails You

Zazen can be good for what ails you physically. Enhanced calmness affects the digestive system positively. Direct confrontation with craving itself—as the driving force of monkey mind—can have a tempering effect on compulsive consumption. Indulgence of any sensory pleasure brings satiation. Overindulgence can bring pain. Ecstasy becomes agony.

This is certainly true of the seductions of taste. The finest gourmet entrée loses its luster when served at every meal, day in and day out. Excess consumption of comfort foods, such as sugars and starches, leads to obesity and worse. In Zen, all such compulsions are seen as a form of greed, one of the Three Poisons. Consequences of greed can become karmic.

With the lack of outer stimulation and constancy of sensation in zazen, taste becomes no-taste, as a consistent aroma becomes no-aroma. Adaptation applies to all sensory stimuli, but taste and smell have a much narrower range. Which is why they are more quick to adapt than touch and hearing, and especially seeing and thinking.

In Zen, the suggestion that we can have too much of a good thing begs this question: How much is enough? This is also a question in art and design philosophy, a fundamental premise of minimalism. Finding the middle way in all things, especially in balancing sensory appetites, is a central part of Zen practice, both on the cushion and in daily life.

This is illustrated by the formal way of taking meals in the monastic setting. Called *oryoki*, a Japanese term that carries the connotation of "just enough," a meal typically consists of two or three simple items; for example, grain (rice), soup, and salad. They are served in separate, small nesting bowls, like papa, mama, and baby bear bowls in the Goldilocks story. Ordinarily, seconds are available. But on long retreats, appetite typically diminishes day by day.

Feeding Buddha

In India and China, in Dogen's Japan, and even today, Zen practitioners, especially monastics, are admonished to set aside preferences for certain foods. Mendicants from Buddha's time were told to eat whatever is put in their begging bowl, without complaint. Beggars can't be choosers.

One outcome of this tradition (J. *takuhatsu*) is that monastics cannot insist on vegetarian fare. In Buddha's India, of course, most of the common diet was vegetarian. Meat was scarce. But Buddhists in Tibet, for example, grow up eating yak and yak products. One mythical story of Buddha's life is that he died from tainted pork. But this should not be taken as contradicting Buddhism's compassion for sentient beings.

Buddhism and vegetarianism are not necessarily linked, though many of the early teachings seem to indicate as much. From the perspective of a meat-saturated society, it is difficult to imagine a more natural diet in a time when meat was rare. Nowadays we expect a chicken not only in every pot, but at every meal.

Whatever your diet, the sense of taste adapts immediately, even just after eating. If we think about it carefully, the taste of even the most exotic, savory, or other delightfully flavored morsel lasts for only an ephemeral moment in the mouth before we swallow it. Time and treasure expended on pursuing fleeting, gourmet pleasures are hardly worth the effort.

Tasting Reality

Not eating or drinking during zazen means little stimulus to the taste buds. But taste becomes hypersensitive as part of the adaptive process. We become aware of a subtle, ambient taste, not stemming from food or drink. Saliva and leftover chemistry from meals, toothpaste, or mouthwash, combined with effluent from hundreds of microorganisms inhabiting the mouth, contribute to the presence of a subtle, constant flavor.

Mentioning the microbiology of taste may seem gratuitous, and even disgusting—which term, ironically, derives from the same root as gusto! And

I certainly do not mean to suggest this as an intentional focus of attention in zazen. But the unromantic dimensions of what it is to be alive, incarnated in a physical body, can come to the fore in deep meditation. We begin to appreciate the meaning of the dismissive Ch'an portrayal of the human body as a "stinking skin sack." And yet, according to Zen, this human birth is the essential prerequisite for spiritual awakening.

Sensitivity to sensory stimuli in general becomes much subtler than normal, increasing dramatically in zazen. The most minute of changes in body chemistry, such as digestion, or reaction to stimuli (as to an especially strong perfume) can trigger reactions of revulsion, or even nausea. But a different order of nausea may occur as a result of the emotional intensity of zazen, with no direct connection to biology, ambience, or atmosphere. Akin to the subtle nausea reported by creatives when facing a blank canvas or beginning their next novel.

Tasting Tastelessness

Taste, like smell, usually adapts so quickly that for our purposes, both may be reasonably subsumed under bodily sensation rather than regarded as distinctly separate senses. They become minor factors in comparison to the flood of stimulus from eyes, ears, and the body, and the overwrought activity of the thinking mind.

With taste and smell thus subsumed, we are left with four main attentional domains: seeing, hearing, and feeling as direct sensation, and thinking as the overriding, mental sense. Though not truly separate, the tetrapartite model simplifies paying attention, providing fewer limbs of the sensory tree for the monkey. Focusing on immediate physical sensations one at a time, or altogether, provides relief from obsessive focus on thinking.

Zazen helps cultivate the ultimate refinement of all levels of taste, in its most general sense. Highly developed tastes for consumption, variety, and entertainment are supplanted by a taste for—well, nothing special.

Zen is like water, relatively tasteless. Physical taste associated with the tongue, when fully neutralized, reveals the fine flavor of emptiness. Like the taste of pure water, neutral but refreshing, taste is, always and ever, tasting taste, itself.

Talking about Speech

Before we leave the sense of taste, let's take a brief look at speech, the other salient function of the tongue. The Three Actions, natural functions of body, mouth, and mind, go to intent when interpreted as forms of desire. They include greed for food, gluttony, in the sense realm of taste. Each of the senses has a corollary impulse or desire, which at an extreme becomes a specific form of greed, associated with that dhatu.

Social dimensions of the action of the mouth include a predilection for speaking out of turn and engaging in unkind, or dishonest, speech. This is one of the first five Precepts. Lying necessarily includes lying to yourself. In order to lie to someone else, we have to lie to ourselves first. We tell ourselves that it is okay to lie. In some cases, it may be. Or we may even believe the lie. But we should know the difference.

The same can be said for the body in pursuit of sensual pleasure, through sexual relations or a sybaritic lifestyle. In terms of eyes and ears, the parallel would be in pursuing pleasure through visual beauty, musical extravaganzas, and so on. Early versions of the Precepts warned against such indulgence, for monks and nuns. Less for lay people.

Public aspects of indulging the senses have to do with time off the cushion, in social interactions. They become apparent in zazen, however, and represent the call to action of moderation in all things, a tenet of Buddhism shared by most rationalist philosophies and theistic morality systems.

The original frontier is not exempt from these all-too-human frailties. They do not magically evaporate when we cross the boundary. But we do get a taste of what it would be like to live free of them in our personal lives. This is the original flavor of freedom found in the original frontier.

Sensing a Summary

Summarizing our survey of Buddhism's six senses, as reexperienced in zazen:

1. We aggressively confront feeling on the gross, physical level of tactile, bodily sensations. Finally transcending the first barrier of resistance, pain.

2. As the body adjusts to its new posture, we next engage thinking as monkey mind, the second barrier. It resurfaces from time to time throughout the remainder of the process.

3. We move on to look fixedly into the third and most acute sense, seeing.

4. Then we listen deeply to the fourth, hearing, commanding our undivided attention.

5. Finally, we note the neutralization of smelling and tasting, in fifth and sixth places.

All six undergo considerable adjustment, adapting to our new normal Zen awareness. We loop back through the cycle again and again, on ever-deeper levels. Like drilling for water. In zazen, we revisit these various way stations in a dynamic process. But with each visit, we penetrate deeper into the stillness that is at the heart of form and emptiness.

By now we should begin to see what the Heart Sutra is getting at when it modifies each of the senses, in turn, with the prefix "no": no seeing, no hearing, no smelling, no tasting, no touching, no thinking. Given emptiness, that is.

The true state of sensory awareness, as dynamic in nature—and not as static as we ordinarily conceive it—is central to intuiting this so-called emptiness (S. *Shunyatta*). This does not suggest that the senses totally disappear. We do not deny their reality. We simply see through an incomplete, one-sided idea of them to get the rest of the story.

Following detailed examination of the nature of each of the senses, and how our appreciation of them changes during zazen, we return to a holistic, transsensory awareness. The Six Senses and the Five Skandhas may be discussed separately but cannot actually be separated. They are complementary and interactive in operation, tracing the natural process of our adaptive progress in zazen. Again, these modes and models of presenting Zen teachings should not be taken too literally, and certainly not linearly.

Sitting upright and still, breathing deeply with fixed gaze, and immersed in a quiet, moderate environment, the stimuli flooding our sense organs become relatively constant. The normally distracting level of change in our daily lives is attenuated. Sameness rules, inducing sensory change of an order far beyond the depths we normally experience.

Seeing, hearing, smelling, tasting, and touching merge into a unity that is at once strange and yet familiar. Resonances on the nervous system, transsensory in origin and usually subliminal, register in consciousness. Owing to relatively unchanging input, a cache of energy accumulates in the neural, electrochemical networks of our body, pushing the envelope of awareness to another level of the micro-macro universe of sentience.

Energy builds in all six sensory realms simultaneously, a cumulative effect analogous to an electrical charge building on a capacitor. Like a slow-moving, low-voltage, gentle electrocution. When storage capacity is reached, the spark jumps the gap. Framed metaphorically here, you will nonetheless recognize it when you observe this process empirically in zazen. Then you can choose your own analogy. For what is the original frontier but a metaphor?

EMBRACING NONDUALITY
WITHOUT LOSING YOUR GRIP
ON REALITY

Moving beyond the senses, the larger implications of exploring the original frontier are equally challenging. Having established, one hopes, the radical departure from commonsense sensibility that nondualistic awareness of zazen brings about, we will attempt to expand our horizons. Indulging in speculation can be titillating, a kind of guilty pleasure. Just as music enchants the ears, images tickle the retina, and massage delights the muscles, thought can bedazzle the brain.

However, thinking is not diametrically opposed to nonthinking. Like all dual dyads, they are two sides of a complementary dynamic. We can engage in thinking without indulging in thinking. Wisdom is to know the difference. If our thought is informed by direct experience, we cannot go too far astray.

One of the strangest dimensions of the Zen frontier is that duality, native to our home country, does not obtain. The normal division of the environment into such sensory mundanities as dark and light, hot and cold, wet and dry, is flipped 180 degrees. One startling Zen declaration is that "water is not wet." This mental mode of intuitive ambiguity requires an attitude adjustment of a different order. It goes beyond simply seeing through the senses.

On a conceptual or philosophical level, Zen challenges received wisdom by pointing out that where we see dichotomies and contradictions, they do not really exist. In the same way that the senses do not exist, at least not as one-sidedly as we think they do. We learn the rest of the story through unlearning these memes in zazen.

Let us consider some of the salient dual pairs, putative opposites, that under the bright light of Zen are not so clearly distinct and separate. That is, they depend on each other for their very existence as concepts (i.e., as real, but nonexistent, dharmas).

Subheads in this section pair selected conceptual "opposites" with the conjunction "and," as in the first instance, "Form and Emptiness." But you are free to substitute "Form versus Emptiness" or "Form/Emptiness" if it more clearly captures the relationship of the dyad. Needless to say, this selection is not exhaustive. That exercise would amount to an entire dictionary of dyads.

Form and Emptiness

An all-embracing pair of complements is found in Buddha's fundamental formulation, Form is Emptiness, or Emptiness is Form. But this is not the same as saying form = emptiness. The equation format implies that the two elements on opposite sides of the equal sign are indeed independent and exist separately but are in some sense equivalent. A dozen apples equal a dozen oranges, in the sense that both contain the same number of edible fruits. But they are in no other way equal. I am told there is a mathematical sign indicating that the two components under consideration are not equal, but inseparable. Suffice it to say that form has no meaning outside emptiness; emptiness has no reality separate from form. All other such dyads are also like this.

The fact that the nonduality of dual pairs has to be explained illustrates the limiting nature of the discriminating mind, and the limitations of language, rather than being a logical fallacy of Zen. That we can speak of these pairs as "opposites" does not indicate a bifurcation of physical reality. That "non-duality" requires hyphenation reveals that the unified term is not even proper English. Even Einstein's famous formulation, quantifying the relationship between matter and energy, implies the inseparability of the two, rather than suggesting that matter exists separately from energy, and vice versa. Radiant forms of energy are not matter, but they still behave as particles, given the right circumstances. Matter is simply "impounded energy," a phrase used by R. Buckminster Fuller. From the perspective of these great geniuses, the original frontier is surpassingly strange but also hauntingly familiar.

Stillness and Motion

Meditation is associated with being or becoming quiet, and is sometimes referred to as entering into silence. Soto Zen has been criticized, notably by adherents of the Rinzai sect, as a form of feckless quietism. Turnabout being fair play, Soto advocates have as often denigrated Rinzai as intellectual or word-oriented (J. *kanna*) Zen. But in advanced zazen, we find that all is not at all quiet, on any front of the original frontier. We enter into progressively deeper stillness, against which the dynamic nature and noisiness of body, mind, and environment—particularly ambient acoustics—stand out in stark relief.

Stillness is more fundamental than silence. Stillness is not limited to only one sense—as silence is limited to hearing—but permeates and affects all six senses. Zen meditation is reentering into the profound stillness that is at the heart of all existence. All things are in Samadhi—balanced, centered, and still—at all times. But ordinarily, we don't know, or feel, it.

In the very center of this stillness, we encounter the thundering silence that is mokurai. This is the direct experience of Dogen's "hammer striking emptiness." But it does not strike only once and never again. He goes on to claim that "its exquisite peal permeates everywhere," and to ask "How could it be limited to this moment?" In other words, this stunning silence pervades all of spacetime. In it, once is forever.

Always and Only Coexisting

According to Zen, stillness, as experienced in meditation, is not separate from motion. This apparent contradiction is captured in this term, mokurai, which also connotes stillness in motion, and motion in stillness. The two are not-two. And, like matter and antimatter, they obliterate each other in realization, as we hear from a Ch'an poem:[102]

> Consider motion in stillness and stillness in motion; both movement and stillness disappear. When such dualities cease to exist, Oneness itself cannot exist.

Motion and stillness, silence and sound, and all other conceptual binaries always and only coexist. This accords with a more modern expression of this ancient Zen tenet. The term "tensegrity," coined by R. Buckminster Fuller, combines one such dyad—tension and compression—in one word. The famous engineer, inventor, and philosopher pointed out that both physical realities and structural systems exhibit similar interior interrelationships:[103]

> [S]cientists now know that the proton and neutron always and only coexist in the most exquisite interorderliness.

Vintage Bucky, making up that last word, where there is none in English adequate to convey his meaning. After explaining that tensing a rope in our hands is an immediate, sensory experience of tensegrity, the first level of the process of extracting general principles from particular case experiences (his definition of intelligence), he elaborates:[104]

> This [recalling the experience] is a first-degree generalization. The discovery of always and only coexisting tension and compression is a second-degree generalization. Finding a whole family of always and only coexisting phenomena is a third-degree generalization, and conceiving therefrom "relativity" is a fourth-degree generalization.

Tension and compression, a fundamental dyad of engineering, dependably operate on axes at 90 degrees to each other. If you pull on a rope, for example, you are exerting tension along the length while the cross section compresses. If you squeeze a basketball, you compress the vertical axis between your two hands, while the horizontal circumference expands. Much like the ovoid shape of the earth, with gravity and rotation compressing the poles, while simultaneously stretching the equator. Such "opposites" are not truly opposed but instead mutually define each other.

On the cushion, and in daily life, we directly witness our own special-case experiences. Dualities extracted from them by our intelligence are general principles, compounded of first-, second-, third-, and fourth-degree generalizations. Much like the aforementioned first-, second-, and third-level nen. This is our conceptual experience of personal relativity.

Zen and Relativity

Pairs of dual concepts amount to different ways of saying essentially the same thing: distinctions with a difference. When we say "hot," we are implying "cold." "Subject and object" may be read personally as "mind and body" and socially as "self and other." But any one of these pairs cannot be completely sundered. They come bundled in one package, like the positive and negative poles of a magnet. Quoting more fully, the same Ch'an master clarifies the relativity of duality on a very personal level of consciousness itself:[105]

> When no discriminating thoughts arise, the old mind ceases to exist. When thought objects vanish, the thinking-subject vanishes, and when mind vanishes, objects vanish. Things are objects because there is a subject or mind, and the mind is a subject because there are objects. Understand the relativity of these two and the basic reality: the unity of Emptiness. In this Emptiness the two are indistinguishable, and each contains within itself the whole world.

The mind can be a subject, with the body being its object, at least in our imagination. Mind and body can conflate as self, as distinct from all other minds and bodies. "Self" can be opposed to "other" in the generic sense, all things that are not specifically our mind and body. But Dogen assures us that this, too, is a kind of delusion. Real enough, but not telling the whole story:
[106]

> To study the buddha way is to study the self. To study the self is to forget the self. To forget the self is to be actualized by the myriad things. When actualized by the myriad things, your body and mind as well as the bodies and minds of others drop away. No trace of realization remains, and this no-trace continues endlessly.

This dropping away of body and mind (J. *shinjin datsuraku*) is one of Zen's most memorable phrases, marking Dogen's profound initial awakening in China. According to the story, it was triggered by hearing his Ch'an teacher, Master Nyojo, admonishing a dozing monk, saying:[107]

> To do zazen under this Zen master is to drop off body and mind. What are you doing, dozing the whole time! How could you accomplish the true awareness of self like this?

This human body is necessary, but not sufficient, to bring about Zen insight. It requires working the body to the ends of Zen, including overcoming sleep as a barrier in zazen. But as this is so, what we really need has always been with us. It doesn't require carrying around any excess baggage. We can travel light while mapping the original frontier.

One implication of the nondual wholeness found in Zen is that when we say "body," we are already implying "mind," and vice versa. Body and mind cannot exist separately, nor can the body and the spirit, or so-called soul. To take the conventional reasoning to heart—to believe that mind and body actually are separate—is a kind of category error in Zen.

In Buddhism, it is considered unusually fortuitous to be born as a human being, in that it represents a rare opportunity to awaken, spiritually. The human body is the necessary vehicle or pivot point (J. *yoki*) for this transformation. Dogen makes this point with a sense of urgency in his first written guidelines for Zen practice:[108]

> You have already had the good fortune to be born with a precious [human] body, so do not waste your time meaninglessly. Now that you know what is the most important thing in Buddhism, how can you be satisfied with the transient world? Our bodies are like dew on the grass, and our lives like a flash of lightning, vanishing in a moment.

This is the urgent reality underlying the physicality of Zen's emphasis on upright-sitting meditation. There is no time to waste. Other sentient beings do not enjoy this advantage. They are not, however, absolutely excluded from the Path, according to Buddhism. They too share buddha-nature. But the causes and conditions of their existence make self-awakening highly unlikely for them. For humans, the prospect of awakening is also not very likely, at least not in one lifetime. Our situation does not constitute a kind of cosmic, karmic lottery, however, but requires only intense effort and sincere repentance on our part to overcome the barriers to insight. Along with a sense of urgency.

Inner and Outer

It may be useful to consider connections between the direct effects of zazen and some of Buddhism's classic teachings. Perception, also known as Receptivity, is one of the Five Aggregates of Clinging (S. *skandha*). Likely adopted from Hinduism or earlier teachings, the five Skandhas—meaning heaps, or piles, or in modern parlance, aggregates—represent a comprehensive quintet, dividing the complex world of sentient beings into five relatively distinct, interrelated clusters integrating the inner and outer, material and immaterial worlds:

Form, Sensation, Perception, Impulse, and Consciousness.

Traditionally positioned third in sequence, Perception is the middle aggregate, bridging between the external and the internal, the material world of Form and Sensation (matter and energy), and the mental-emotional world of Impulse and Consciousness. The senses form the primary interface between inner and outer domains of sentient beings.

This apparent separation into inner and outer is yet another bifurcation intentionally imposed by the discriminating mind. True as far as it goes, but only half true. The sense organs may separate us from the environment, but by the same token, they join us to it.

Perhaps the most obvious example is the skin, considered our largest sense organ owing to its extensive surface. Who you are seems to end at your fingertips, but they also connect you to your environment through touch. Under the microscope, the skin is revealed to be a vital zone of high traffic, with fluids and microorganisms crossing in and out through the porous membrane. The same may be said for the six portals of Buddhism: two eyes, two ears, the nose, and the mouth.

Not to mention the unmentionables: the end of the digestive tract and the genitals, as well as the vestigial umbilical cord. We are intricately and intimately interconnected with our world, with no absolute separation of inner and outer.

Perception and Conception

In Zen we face the double bind of accepting that our experience of sensation, perception, and conception is in some wise delusional and yet reflects reality, partly owing to built-in biases in favor of survival, which conforms to biological science. We like to believe that not all impulses and desires are based on simple selfish motives, but even apparently altruistic behaviors can be reduced to indirect strategies evolved to preserve the species. All that aside, we are individually confronted with the everyday koan of seeing through the delusional aspect of our awareness to the reality at its core.

Part of the reason that Zen practice takes so long for any significant shift to occur in our awareness is the power of the monkey mind to resist this counterintuitive effort. Our faculties of conceptualization, reacting to events—past and present, pleasant or unpleasant—trigger a subtle, but powerful, interference phenomenon. Conceptual feedback interferes with primary perception, rendering the data we receive from our senses even more distorted. Again, PTSD is an extreme example. Where there is no real and present danger, we still feel threatened.

In Zen, we come to regard these seemingly inseparable arenas of awareness as worrywart partners in monkey business. Conceptions are initially born of raw perceptions, but they come to exert a retroactive, reverse-conditioning effect on our immediate perception. We perceive reality as we conceive it, not as it actually is.

Which is why we must transcend the Skandhas, as well as the senses, if we are to see through the hardwired distortions stemming from the stew of conditioning, selective memory, and survival instinct. We may be forgiven for feeling like giving up in the face of such seemingly intractable intransigence. We seem to have no free will in the transaction.

Free Will and Karma

In the liturgical service associated with Soto Zen, we chant the stanza of Repentance:

All my past and harmful karma
Born from beginningless greed, hate, and delusion
Through body speech and mind
I now fully avow

Consider the phrase "through body speech and mind." Zen recognizes that most of our desires, and resultant actions, come from being incarnated in this physical body. I am using the term "incarnation" here in its most general sense—that we are corporeal beings, not in the sense of Hinduism's reincarnation. This ancient doctrine posits a self-existent self, or soul (S. *atman*), transmigrating from one life to the next, discarding old bodies and donning new ones, much as we change our clothing. This is not Zen's principle of rebirth.

Buddha did not find evidence for this belief in his direct insight, any more than we find the mind-body distinction of Cartesian philosophy in our Zen practice. Body and mind, matter and essence, and physical and spiritual are all co-arisen and interdependent in Zen. The Three Actions taken through body, mouth, and mind do have consequences—and not only in the limited sense used by politicians—through their inevitable, karmic effect. Buying into the reality of karma is one of the keys to the original frontier.

But the important point here is that the body is, itself, the root source of thirst, hunger, sexual cravings, and desire for creature comforts, as well as most of our mental and emotional needs, such as for safety and security. We don't just make this stuff up. Conceived of as independent of the body, the machinations of the mind, upon closer examination, are seen to be almost entirely in its service. Our mind clings to our body, and our body clings to our mind. Even this expression implies their separation. This, again, is the fault of language and not of the reality.

The concept of free will seems necessarily in opposition to karma, as popularly understood: what goes around comes around, in the dismissive vernacular. Free will is usually opposed to fate, necessity, predestination, or God's will. But Zen does not deny the exercise of free will or consider it merely notional. Karma operates over Zen's Three Times—past, future, and present— the last being the concrete dimension in which we actually live, the only time in which we can take action. Karma's Sanskrit root means "action."

Karma and Action

Taking action—in particular, intentional or willful, self-centered, motive-driven action—leads naturally to consequences of karmic dimensions, for individuals as well as groups. Actions—and elections—have consequences, as we are frequently reminded and as we witness on a daily basis. Karmic consequences can be considered a special class, however: those that have lasting effects rather than the somewhat trivial results of everyday activities. Breathing, for example, is something we do not do intentionally. But the consequence of not breathing means that we die in about five minutes. Whether that is good or bad is up to you to decide. Free will consists in the choice of actions that we elect to take in the present.

Actions of omission, as well as of commission, can result in significant, if unintended, consequences. If you can accept karma as an operating principle of existence and not merely a belief, the most you can do about it is zazen. If we find what we lack in meditation, we will not be creating undue karmic consequences, looking for satisfaction in all the wrong places.

Doing and Nondoing

Karmic consequences flow from actions, which are always some form of doing. We like to feel that we are acting freely, choosing between two or more options. Doing zazen, we are definitely doing something we intentionally choose to do. But it is markedly different from most anything else we do, both in its unnatural stillness and in our intentions for doing it.

Initial reasons, goals, and objectives for doing Zen—which we all have, at least in the beginning—are much like rationales for other activities, such as any regimen of self-improvement. But beginning goals fall away in time, revealing a deeper, underlying purpose. Eventually, zazen progresses to a level of nondoing, obviating any remaining notions we may have about why, exactly, we are doing it.

Each time we experience nonthinking, it is less strange, and more familiar, than when we first encounter it. It gradually becomes our new, normal state of awareness. We have been liberated from thinking, in the sense of obsessively interacting with our thoughts. We are thinking of nothing in particular.

It begins to dawn on us that for considerable periods of time, we are also doing nothing in zazen. It has become second nature, far beyond habit. And beyond any guilt feelings about wasting time doing nothing. Conventional doing—intentionally acting to achieve an outcome—is over for us. The body is doing the sitting as well as the breathing. The brain is doing the thinking, for what it is worth. Meanwhile, we are merely observing. As long as we are observing, there is still doing. But it persists on a liminal level of intention.

Observer and Observed

Science attempts to describe reality separate from the observer. Einstein's $E = mc^2$ is a standout example. It matters not who makes the claim; the formula holds true, independent of the observer. But Buddhism includes the observer in the equation, from the very beginning. The whole point of Buddha's insight is that it included his own place in the grand scheme of things. However, finding this place required surrendering his prior, assumed place: the constructed self. The self, as an independent observer, does not survive this experiment.

When your meditation becomes truly intimate, there is no longer even an observer observing anything. The notion of the self, itself, becomes truly notional. As my teacher would often say, "Sit until you forget that there is someone sitting." The Zen mind emerges, bridging inside and outside, noninteracting, intrinsically intimate, and not subject to conventional understanding. Dogen was fully intimate with this experience:[109]

The actualization, that is by nature intimate, never has defilement.

When you realize such intimate actualization of the truth, it cannot be "defiled." That is, your experience cannot be reduced to an object of your subjective mind or subjected to logical analysis or common understanding. Thus, it cannot be captured by the ordinary use of language either. All fingers are pointing at the moon, at this point. Dogen goes on:[110]

The manifestation, that is by nature verification, never has distinction between Absolute and Relative.

Verification of your practice is self-manifested in your practice. Being so, it is beyond all consideration of conceptual thinking, let alone the judgment of another person. It is even beyond any application of absolute and relative, parallel classes of truth traditionally posited in Zen. The relative is the many: eye, ear, nose, tongue, body, and mind. The absolute is not asserted to be one, but not-two: no eye, no ear, no nose, no tongue, no body, no mind, in the sense of independently existing entities. The relative is thinking, doing, and interacting. Or not thinking, not doing, not interacting. The absolute is nonthinking, nondoing, noninteracting. This kind of doing cannot be done, or not done. It is beyond doing. It may be bare "being." Dogen then moves on to make it personal:[111]

The intimacy without defilement is dropping off without relying on anything.

Dropping off body and mind cannot actually be done, either, at least not intentionally. Zen promises it can happen, however. Experiencing intimacy without defilement requires dropping off your body-mind, as well as those of others: seeing through the delusion of both. But this can happen only by sitting without relying on anything: neither intellect; nor breeding, to be quaint; nor DNA, to be more modern. None of the circumstances of birth, of Nature and nurture, have any dispositive or determinative effect on your original nature.

Even our grasp of the teachings of Buddhism, however elevated, is of no avail. Far less any personal ideas or opinions we may harbor regarding all the above. None of the mental tricks, trinkets, and trash we have used to get by, up until now, are of any use at this remove. Ironically, we grasp the meaning of "not a single toehold," a salient expression of ancient Zen, by ceasing to grasp at anything. Anything at all conceptual brought into Zen meditation is simply excess baggage. We leave it at the zendo door.

Continuing along Dogen's line of thinking beyond thought:[112]

The verification beyond distinction between Absolute and Relative is making
effort without aiming at it

In doing zazen we are definitely making an effort, in a particular and unusual way. But as long as that effort is connected to a preconceived outcome, however vaguely envisioned, it is skewed to that degree. If there is a target, it is one we have made up. In the very act of aiming at it, we are sure to miss the mark.

Relative and Absolute

Goals and objectives are tangled up in the opposition of relative and absolute, reducing them to philosophical constructs. As such, they have little chance of providing verification.

Opposing relative to absolute is used to characterize truth, Zen's philosophy. The relative truth of Form is set up against the absolute truth of Emptiness. But the whole truth transcends relative and absolute aspects, unifying form and emptiness, both being true.

Verification of truth beyond absolute and relative considerations cannot be accomplished by ordinary, goal-oriented effort. The requisite action—or better, nonaction—takes place in the midst of our not aiming at anything. This is a difficult double bind, a real koan, requiring aimless effort. We must take a deep breath at this juncture and surrender to Zen's fundamental ambiguity. Finally, Dogen returns to the concrete, exemplified by Nature:[113]

The water is clear to the earth; a fish is swimming like a fish.
The sky is vast, extending to the heavens; a bird is flying like a bird.

The truth discovered in zazen is fully evident in observing a fish swimming through clear water, or a bird flying through the vast sky. Or your sitting in zazen, like a human being.

Whether the great master intended it or not, a swimming fish often symbolizes a person practicing Zen. Like yourself, swimming in Zen waters without knowing their limit. The bird flying through the air may likewise be taken as a symbol of realization.

To the fish, swimming is flying; to the bird, flying is swimming. For us, swimming is our everyday action; flying is liberation from the constrictions of our limitations. Liberation in the midst of life—swimming in the ocean of Samsara—is offered up as a transcendently natural benefit of Zen, the direct route to Nirvana. Samsara becomes Nirvana, and vice versa.

I hope this brief analysis gives you a peek in the tent of Dogen's poetic intent, on the basis of his practical experience. Others may differ with my interpretation. But you will be hard-pressed to find a more concise use of language than this lovely little poem, to point at that which is ultimately beyond language. It is written to us as a postcard from the original frontier.

Mind and Environment

Not only are mind and body not-two, according to Zen. Your mind and your surrounding environment are also conjoined. Matsuoka Roshi would often comment that "Cleaning is cleaning the mind" while we were doing cleaning practice (J. *soji*) at the Zen center. He would also say, "I like to keep it empty around here."

Providing an environment that is clean and conducive to Zen practice is one form of perfecting generosity (S. *dana paramita*). Achok Rimpoche, a venerable Tibetan teacher, made this point during a talk at our center. He expressed admiration for our zendo, with its plain white walls and natural wood trim. But he went on to remind us that in Tibet, everything is white, everywhere you look. Then he added, chuckling, "So, we like a little more color." Tibetan temples are known for their bright red and gold interiors.

Sitting with fixed gaze, and for some time, however, even the brightest colors neutralize. So the particulars of the meditation environment are not determinative. Dogen reminds us of the importance of providing the walls:

Grass, trees, and lands that are embraced by this teaching together radiate a great light and endlessly expound the inconceivable, profound dharma. Grass trees and walls bring forth the teaching for all beings, common people as well as sages. And they in accord extend this dharma for the sake of grass, trees, and walls.

Vintage Dogen, in which lush, visionary images are interwoven with down-to-earth, practical teaching. The very walls of the zendo extend the dharma, as does all of Nature. All beings are engaged in a vast, collaborative project, evolving and propagating higher awareness.

Thus, another aspect of nonduality on the original frontier is that the practice of Zen, and the environment in which it is practiced, cannot be separated either. Taking care to set up a supportive environment is conducive to Zen, at home or in your community.

But as my teacher said, eventually it will be possible for you to meditate virtually anywhere, and under virtually any conditions. He related the true story of a Japanese man during the San Francisco earthquake of 1906 who sat out the disaster on a couch in zazen, on an upper floor of a hotel shaking to its foundations, while everyone else ran for the exits.

You should have confidence that Zen's promised merging of subject and object, body and mind, self and other—and, by extension, being and environment—will eventually come about, regardless of the state of your practice space. Genuine insight cannot be dependent on the specific character of your environment, however humble.

The deeper effects of Zen may emerge in your basement, or in your own backyard. And when you least expect it. It is not necessary to seek out exotic locales to practice Zen. However, especially for beginners, distractions at home can be difficult to ignore.

Urban and Rural

The attraction of getting out of the rat-race commute, decamping to a remote redoubt to refresh and reboot, has existed as long as there have been cities, including the original city-states of Greece, Rome, Egypt, and other early civilizations. As Sensei would often say, "Civilization conquers us." For related reasons, Zen communities establish rural retreat centers in remote places, as well as more-accessible urban locations. Pastoral settings can be conducive to intensive retreat. Zazen Samadhi can be strengthened by immersion in Nature, deep in its own, natural Samadhi.

In the busy city, a Zen center offers convenience, the opportunity for frequent group practice. In the country, a retreat center offers solace and sanctuary, far from the madding crowd. Both environments support a balanced approach to meditation, complemented by practice at home.

Matsuoka Roshi would often describe zazen as being as stable as a mountain. The Hindu saint Sri Ramakrishna likened meditation to a tree. As a sapling, it needs a fence surrounding it, so the elephants do not trample it. When fully mature, however, the great tree cannot be toppled, even by the biggest elephant.[114]

Like the fence surrounding the sapling tree, every aspect of your Zen environment—from a small sitting space in the corner of your room at home, to a large public meeting hall—should be optimized to support your effort in sitting. Ambient conditions should be kept largely the same from session to session, to the degree practicable. Sound, light, and temperature are best maintained at moderate levels. Avoid spaces where clutter and other distractions abound, and times of day when interruptions are likely.

On long retreats, you are encouraged to sit in the same spot, facing the same wall, to increase the sameness of sensory stimulus. This spatial fixity magnifies the temporal flux—subtle differences occurring from moment to moment—augmented by the power of repetition, and enhances the natural process of sensory adaptation.

Sameness and Difference

Sameness brings out differences. By intentionally acclimating our consciousness to a constancy of stimulus, we frustrate the natural predilection of the mind to seek out novelty. The monkeyish side of the mind prefers difference, any slight variation, to the nagging tedium of sameness, preferred by the monkish side of the mind.

Minimizing disruptions by managing the practice place amounts to a kind of intentional suppression, countering the monkey's insatiable lust for variety and entertainment. Proof of the latter is found in the sheer size, reach, and power of the entertainment industry. Half or more of what is presented as "news" amounts to entertainment these days, promotion of such newsworthy items as a celebrity's next movie or an author's next novel.

The intellectually valid counterargument—that no experience is ever exactly the same twice—is all the more reason to err on the side of sameness in your meditation space. Controlling for sameness provides the necessary contrast, elevating subtle and subliminal differences to new levels of conscious awareness.

Sitting still enough, for long enough, will naturally still the mind, like calming a spooked horse or taming a wild stallion. Blinders have a similar effect, but in effect, we are removing our blinders. Stillness in the body is magnified through sameness in surroundings. Each time we return to the same sitting space, immersion in stillness is more immediate and more pronounced compared to sitting in different environments. Burning the same incense connects this conditioning directly to the sense of smell and, in turn, to memory. Consistency and repetition foster the accumulation of concentrated effort, like any form of distillation.

Difference and Sameness

However, practicing in a variety of locations from time to time is also an effective strategy to mature your training. Difference brings out the sameness. Becoming inured to distracting conditions in the midst of zazen is strengthening, like tempering iron with fire. Outstanding athletes are noted for their ability to focus under pressure, including drastically changing circumstances such as large, noisy crowds; variations of terrain; and inclement weather. Similarly, Zen training develops the "iron mind" (J. *tesshin*) necessary to meditate in any environment or situation. Dogen connects the environment to seeking dharma:[115]

> When you first seek dharma, you imagine you are far away from its environs. But dharma is already correctly transmitted; you are immediately your original self.

It does not really matter where, specifically, you find yourself in spacetime. The original frontier is not limited by geographical boundaries. Wherever you are, there it is. Later in this same teaching, Dogen confirms this point:[116]

> When you find your place where you are, practice occurs, actualizing the fundamental point. When you find your way at this moment, practice occurs, actualizing the fundamental point.

Where you are, and at this moment, is the intersection of spacetime, the nexus of personal relativity. Note that practice occurs when conditions are ripe; we do not make it happen. Toward the end, he sums it all up:[117]

> Here is the place, here the way unfolds.

"Here," of course, is in zazen. But also, immediately and intimately, here in time and space. But again, simply being in the present moment is not the endpoint of Zen. We need to cross the boundary into the original frontier.

Beginning and Ending

People often ask, out of curiosity, When did you begin your Zen practice? Usually we can remember particulars, such as the year, if not the exact season or date. What initially drove us to seek out Zen tends to be memorable as well. Ordinarily, some kind of crisis. If and when further crises occur in our Zen life—including a crisis of confidence, or trust, in our teacher—it can lead to a wholesale rejection of Zen. Intense personal conflicts in training are sometimes too strong to overcome residual trauma. It is not the fault of Zen, however. Fortunately, not a single negative incident ever occurred with my teacher, which I attribute to his character, not mine.

In Zen practice, we go through a process of testing the waters, much as with any other project, such as writing a book. Jumping in at some point and just sitting, or writing, then reworking our approach, consulting with others, and editing out what we find to be more than necessary. But our judgment is not always correct, owing to the vagaries of the monkey mind. In the process of maturing Zen practice, it is natural that we may feel disappointed, giving up before we get to the final draft.

If you feel this way, I suggest that you go ahead and stop practicing zazen. For a while. When you do so, you will discover what many have before you: the unacknowledged and unappreciated effect that Zen has been having on your life all along, unbeknown to you. After a couple of days, or a week or two, you may find yourself falling back into the same-old-same-old habit patterns from which you had begun to free yourself. Or so you had thought.

This is a common experience reported by many people: they didn't know what Zen was until they stopped. This does not mean that we develop a dependency on zazen, however. It is too simple, and too difficult, to become addictive.

While we may not see the effects of Zen on our persona, others may. Members often say their spouses push them to get back to the Zen center more often. Implying, not too subtly, that their behavior displays a diminishing return on their capacity for patience. In one memorable case, a person was promoted at work, partially for being so good at working with others. But he still saw himself as the inveterate troublemaker.

You will notice different levels of Zen's effect, from the mundane—not crying over spilt milk, to the practical—knowing the right thing to do in a situation that otherwise might leave you stumped, to the sublime—having a solid practice to guide you through the bumpy roads of the original frontier.

Like most worthwhile endeavors, Zen requires repetition, and longevity, to have long-lasting effect. More important than consistency, regularity, frequency, or duration—the measurables of meditation—is just to doggedly return to zazen, in spite of whether you think it is working or not.

It requires a degree of humility to continue practicing in the face of diminishing returns, just as it does to continue exercising to stay physically fit as we age. As some wag said, getting old is not for sissies. Zen is not for the faint of heart either. But we must continue to renew our commitment, inspired by the example of our ancestors as well as that of our community. "We teach each other Buddhism," as Sensei often said.

If you continue practicing through thick and thin, you may come to the same conclusion that I have. That we never really began Zen, so we can never really end it either. For Zen is not just another activity that we take up in life. It is about the very essence of life. So we have been working on Zen all along, without knowing it. And even if we try to quit, we will simply continue practicing Zen in a less obvious, and perhaps less effective, way. We really cannot stop practicing Zen.

Zazen and Meditation

You may still feel that zazen and all other forms of meditation are more alike than different. And on a superficial level, you would be correct. Any two given approaches may emphasize sitting still for long periods of time. Both may focus on breathing. Both may suggest that thinking has to be set aside. But the very sameness brings out the difference, in stark relief. The devil, as well as the buddha-nature, is in the details.

Whether you are a sincere seeker of the Buddha Way or interested in only the secular benefits of meditation, you are invited to compare and contrast Zen's stripped-down approach with whatever alternative methods you may encounter. I think that zazen will prevail, in the long run. Any meditation that works has something of Zen in it.

This means, above all, not giving up too soon on your own meditation. But this also lobbies against the usual approach: surveying the many meditations on offer, trying a bit of this and a bit of that. Deciding this one doesn't work, or this other one looks better. This is the natural way of sampling until we find the way that works best for us, and settle down with it.

But this kind of modus operandi, if continued at length, has been likened to drilling many shallow holes, rather than one deep hole, hoping to find potable water. Zen drills down deep in one high-potential location for a well. It is about doing one thing well, as Dogen reminds us: "Doing one practice is practicing completely."[118] This is the focus on zazen in Soto Zen. It bears repeating that zazen is in a totally separate class from traditional meditations. Zazen is objectless. Or it becomes so, with time and effort.

How well zazen works turns out to be largely a matter of how well we work it. Just as any form of government will work—as long as the people are happy and willing to make it work—most any method of meditation (or for that matter, any skill you are trying to develop) will work to achieve its aims, as long as we are willing to make it work. And we don't give up.

Zen works on so many levels that it is difficult to treat comprehensively, even in a text this exhaustive. In my less-than-linear approach to discussing Zen and zazen, I hope that some of the ways that you can make Zen work for you have begun to become clear.

APPLYING ZEN
TO YOUR LIFE BY APPLYING
YOUR LIFE TO ZEN

Once we have managed to sit through deconstruction of the senses, undergone intentional personality disintegration, and embraced the dichotomies of life as built into nondual existence, we still have to return to everyday life, face the madding crowd, and get on with it, as the somewhat sardonic title of a popular book on Zen has it, *After the Ecstasy, the Laundry.*[119] But the common confusion that we have to apply Zen to life—or even that we can—calls for yet another attitude adjustment. It is not easy living on the original frontier. And at a certain point of departure, there is no turning back either.

Many people come to meditation for its well-known effect of calming the mind, hoping to benefit their hectic daily lives. Setting aside whether this is a worthy initial aspiration, and recognizing that it plays into our cultural weakness of wanting to exert control, the main problem with it is that it is backward. Rather than fretting about how to apply Zen to your life, simply apply yourself wholeheartedly to Zen. If you do so diligently, Zen will naturally apply itself to your life. If we try too hard, artificially, to apply Zen to daily-life situations, the very attempt will likely get in the way of any hoped-for effect.

Rather than focusing on any one goal, such as applying Zen, or being in the moment or worrying about what stage of meditation we may be in at present, we simply observe the transient nature of our own perceptions and conceptions amid the passing pageantry of life. Experience is not so compartmentalized, no matter how hard the monkey tries to make it so.

We examine awareness itself—in the moment, yes, but critically, with a willingness to recognize past influences, embracing present and future consequences. We may think of this as an exercise in intentional discrimination, squared. Using the power of discrimination to discriminate against discrimination itself. Foiling the preferential biases built into the monkey mind. This reinforces the importance of simply paying attention:[120]

There's an old Zen story: A student said to Master Ichu, "Please write for me something of great wisdom." Master Ichu picked up his brush and wrote one word: "Attention." The student said, "Is that all?" The master wrote, "Attention. Attention." The student became irritable. "That doesn't seem profound or subtle to me." In response, Master Ichu wrote simply, "Attention. Attention. Attention." In frustration, the student demanded, "What does this word 'attention' mean?" Master Ichu replied, "Attention means attention."

Pay attention, period! The question—especially in light of the current popular obsession with mindfulness—is this: Pay attention to what, exactly?

Paying Attention

Paying attention—direct mindfulness of the present moment—is practiced as a disciplinary attitude in Zen. It is done so as to counter our native, discursive bent of mind, not as an end in itself. This is similar to the place and function of directed attention in other forms of meditation, as mentioned by Goleman, such as Satipatthana: settling or quieting the mind, as practiced in Vippassana: insight meditation. A loose parallel to this exists in Zen: stopping and seeing (J. *shi-kan*). If we cannot stop the usual nonsense in our mind, we have no chance of seeing beyond it. But the nonsense has to come to a natural end, not forced.

In Zen, we regard the beginning, middle, and end game as equally important, essentially indistinguishable. This is indicated by the appreciation for beginner's mind, Zen's emphasis on sustaining an open-minded attitude, throughout the activities of our daily lives.

The busy, hungry mind is inclined to look for something new and different, exciting and entertaining—or at least interesting—all the time, like a high-strung monkey. It is more entertaining to sit and think about something— anything at all—than to sit and not think, or to think about nothing in particular. In Zen, we turn this natural, insatiable curiosity away from conceptual speculation, in favor of simple observation of the passing, sensory scene.

Thinking is as natural as breathing, and, ordinarily, just as continuous. But at risk of repeating myself, thinking is not our inevitable, or sole, mode of consciousness. In Zen, we regard thought as a secondary function. Consciousness itself does not depend on thinking but requires only attention. This is sometimes referred to as bare awareness.

Bare Awareness

We train ourselves to pay strict attention, without resorting to conceptual analysis. However, bare awareness also includes paying attention to the random musings of the monkey, and even to the maddening noise of the media, the nattering nabobs. If we pay full attention to propaganda, for example, we can recognize it as such. And turn it off.

When we first experience Dogen's "backward step," opening up the mind to any and all input without prejudice, we find a welcome and palliative alternative to compulsively worrying about breaking news, daydreaming, reliving the past, ruminating over old grudges, scheming, or anxiously planning for the future.

But bare awareness is not, by itself, a final objective of Zen. Living in an end state of just noticing what is happening, moment by moment, amounts to a kind of mindlessness. Nor is Zen's approach a kind of cognitive therapy, replacing unpleasant thoughts and feelings with pleasant ones, which reduces to a kind of positivistic, structured daydreaming. Zen is, instead, liberation from the tyranny of dependency on distractions altogether, including thought.

Stimulating your mind to think is not the focus of Zen. Admittedly, this is what I am trying to do at the moment, though to the contrarian end of nonthinking. Finding more things to think about is to be assiduously avoided, especially during meditation. This is one reason why Zen centers and monasteries, especially zendos, are so simple and spare by design. We already suffer from overstimulation, especially mental stimulation. Intentional thinking is not necessary to realize Zen mind and can be counterproductive to that aspiration.

This is another reason why Zen teachers often discourage reading about Zen. Books can simply fill the mind with ideas, specifically about Zen itself. These ideas, in turn, predictably intrude during zazen, distracting us from the immediacy of the meditation experience. During daily life off the cushion, they detract from reality itself. This is the problem with "bedside Zen": treating

Zen as an interesting subject to study, rather than a method to practice.

My use of "reality" is not meant to convey a conceptual or perceptual distinction in which my reality is the real one, and markedly different from yours. This is a form of hubris often implicit in claims of the guru class. Instead, Zen's reality points at unfiltered experience beyond concepts, beyond even perception, in which yours, while not the same as mine, is equally real. The concrete reality that we all share, if from different perspectives.

It may seem irrational to point to a reality beyond perception, since the two appear to be synonymous and simultaneous. But it takes time for raw sensation to be translated into perception, so the two cannot be simultaneous. There is a slight, internal lag time. Further, there is an external gap as well. To belabor the obvious, it takes time for the light by which we see others to reach the retina, for sound waves to reach the eardrums, for the itch to reach the brain. We never see each other in real time, but only in the immediate past.

We always see, hear, and feel what just happened in the prior moment. Or we recollect the past minute, hour, day, week, month, or year(s), depending on how faraway in time the source of the stimulus is. Things do come back to haunt us. Memory does seem real.

But the reality is the present, eternal moment, which each of us experiences separately. It is forever beyond, or before, perception. This moment is right at the center of our personal spacetime continuum, which finds its vertical axis in the spinal column, its living pulse, in the spinal cord. The present cannot be synonymous with perception because the apparent simultaneity of an event, and our perception of it, is an illusion. The cockroach running across the floor, the breeze through the curtain, the clouds passing before the moon, the flickering of the morning star—perceived simultaneously—all happened in the past and at different times.

Meditating on Mindfulness

Mindfulness is a term we hear a lot these days. In some circles, it is synonymous with meditation itself. It is often used, as is Samadhi, to describe both the method as well as a hoped-for effect of meditation. People practice mindfulness meditation in order to become more mindful, a rather circular aspiration. Defining mindfulness as being in the moment, however, or as *The Power of Now*,[121] as one popular self-help book profiles it, is to miss the main point of Buddhism's Right Meditation—the alpha and omega of Soto Zen.

Zazen is distinctly different from the popular approach called mindfulness meditation in more than one way, but one in particular stands out. In a current bestseller, the author repeatedly refers to sitting with his eyes closed during meditation, which raises the question of how mindful this approach can be if it ignores vision. The main vehicle through which sighted people absorb most of their information and understanding of the world is that of seeing. How does closing your eyes contribute to being in the moment? True mindfulness cannot be of only the other senses. Or only thoughts and emotions. Or of thoughts about emotion, emotions about thought, thoughts about thought, or emotions about emotion.

Of course, meditating with eyes closed will have some effect. For someone who has just experienced their first intensive meditation retreat, as this author had, its effects may appear as a real, and distinct, change of mind. But they may merely reflect the temporary novelty of first reactions to relative stillness. Surprised by immediate enhancement of the senses—greater appreciation for the taste of food, stronger visual and acoustical impressions, etc.—mindfulness seems to trigger immediate, permanent changes.

But, like Dr. Suzuki's cautions against reading too much into any early experience or Buddha's warnings in the *Surangama Sutra*, getting stuck in a preliminary fixation can inhibit any further development.

Being mindful is not part of our normal experience, which is likely why the fad has gained traction in the media. Most of us find just the opposite. Suffering anxiety, planning for the future, daydreaming, or revisiting the past are more the norm: terminal distractedness. If you are like most people, you have a difficult time just being in the moment—or consistently remaining so—for any sustained period of time. Pulled this way and that by changing demands of our daily routine, mental and emotional nudges and tugs of our busy mind. So mindfulness sounds promising, whether on the cushion or on the commute. The promise of improved mindfulness is a big part of the attraction of meditation, precisely because it carries over into our daily-life situations.

For first-time meditators, immediate impressions of mindfulness may seem fresh and new, rather than something we have simply forgotten, in the pursuit of busyness. Take the time to smell the roses and sip and savor your tea slowly. Notice this, notice that. And above all, enjoy! These are the hallmarks of meditation, as popularly conceived. It is treated as a kind of do-it-yourself therapy, which may be a necessary palliative for our crazy-making culture. Zazen is surely therapeutic, but it is not a form of therapy.

The opposite of mindfulness is, simply put, forgetfulness. Or at an extreme, mindlessness. As children, we were constantly surprised by everything. We were also relatively thoughtless, but in a good way. When we take the time to slow down for a moment, or for a week or more, we begin to remember this in a visceral way.

Mindfulness, Yes. But of What?

Mindfulness meditation questions how we direct our attention to solve problems, but begs a fundamental question: Mindful of what? Just being in the moment may be necessary but is not sufficient to get to the bottom of existence. Examining thoughts in a more mindful way may only lead to more dependence on thought. To get out of this closed loop, we have to penetrate to a deeper mindfulness, such as becoming mindful of the Four Noble Truths of Buddhism. We don't have to, of course, but who wouldn't want to?

Zen mindfulness is more than simple awareness of what is transpiring at any given moment in time. If this were all there is to Zen, it wouldn't have lasted 2,500 years! It begins with the senses but soon penetrates to profound stillness, underlying the sensory surface.

But Zen is a hard sell. Even some who have been trained in Zen prefer to represent mindfulness meditation to the public, owing partly to the current wave of interest in mindfulness. It has become a buzzword and thus is an easier sell. "Everybody's doing it" goes the mantra. Zen is more demanding, both to practice and to teach.

And then there are the presumed limitations of Zen. It is so serious, demanding, ancient, and monastic. And Asian. Not American, like mindfulness. Zen is old, and out of date, by comparison. But nothing could be further from the truth. Zen is always modern. And zazen is the ultimate, stripped-down method of meditation methods. The ultimate in do-it-yourself. Which is very American.

Another component missing in mindfulness meditation, as well as other star acts on today's meditation marquee, is Zen's emphasis on brute, physical-body practice—staying in contact with all of your senses, including the visual field. Most other styles seem to regard meditation as primarily a mental exercise.

Zen's assertion that body and mind cannot separate is not very controversial today. Many scientists and philosophers would agree. But that the mind and the environment also cannot separate would raise some eyebrows. If you keep your eyes open, you will see for yourself. This is the only way you will know the difference for yourself, and for sure.

Zen Sickness of Falling into the Moment

Merely dwelling in the present, avoiding or ignoring any consideration of past and future—and worse, equating this to enlightenment—is equivalent to practicing mindfulness with your eyes closed. In the first case, you are dismissing the bulk of the iceberg of time. In the second, you are slamming the door on your primary source of information. You are practicing meditation with the greater part of your mind closed. Of course, it is more healthful to train our attention on the present rather than obsessively rehashing the past, daydreaming ourselves into alternative realities, or fantasizing about the future. But a focus on the now does not change, and cannot sidestep, karmic causality.

Staying in the moment does not provide an escape hatch from reality. We may wish to discount Buddhism's admonition that we ignore, at our peril, the interconnectedness of the Three Times: past, future, and present. But consequences inevitably intrude upon our fantasy.

Zen embraces the transcendent Buddhist teaching that causes and conditions affecting our world are not composed solely of present, proximate circumstances. In order to liberate ourselves from analysis paralysis, overweening self-criticism, or heedless disregard of the results of our behavior, in Zen we simply fess up and face the consequences.

Carrying rose-colored mindfulness to its absurd extreme, we may find ourselves sitting in the moment in meditation, assuming all is well. Blissfully, blithely unaware that meanwhile, our world is crumbling from neglect all around us. Zen is not about finding your bliss.

Meditation and Medication

Zazen is the mother of all meditations. But most meditations share characteristics in common. One challenge confronting meditation's claim to be therapeutic is dealing with major illness and minor ailments, whether physical, mental, or emotional. If you have a nagging discomfort, a recurring itch, or even chronic pain, Zen teachers may suggest that you simply sit with it. That is, rather than trying to ignore it or considering it a cause to stop meditating, make it the focus of your zazen. It may be mostly your imagination. But for deeper psychological neuroses, it is not a good idea to be cavalier. Meditation is not a panacea. But it can help, in concert with other treatments, as prescribed by your doctor.

Mindfulness mentors apparently concur. Zen practitioners develop a similar attitude and report similar changes in headset, as do mindfulness mavens, in confronting minor maladies. Nagging symptoms are depersonalized through dispassionate observation, losing most of their power. Emotional reactions to illness are less agitated, and pain associated with the malady is less severe. The tendency to self-medicate is tempered by self-meditating. The latter is safer than the former, even under medical supervision. Google "opioid" to assess the consequences for yourself.

Our typical go-to method for dealing with any discomfort or pain is to mask it with our drug of choice, of which there are so many on offer these days that it makes you wonder if they are just renaming remixes of the same old chemicals. Coming up with creative brand names for them has become its own, robust industry. Just watch the evening news on television, which apparently only older folks do anymore. Every imaginable ailment has its perfect pill, with an interminable list of side effects, up to and including death. It is no wonder that the USA has been called the "Prozac nation,"[122] or faulted for our worship of youth. The inevitable decline of aging is often denied, glossed over, or ignored in the public arena. We are encouraged to block the slightest physical discomfort, even at the risk of our health, but also prefer to engage in happy talk, avoiding any hint of negativity.

In Sickness and Health

But how does this abnormal attitude toward health and happiness in modern times comport with Buddhism's teachings of the acceptance and understanding of suffering? We usually associate human suffering with pain, manifesting on multiple levels: physical, mental, emotional, and societal. Or even more broadly, existential suffering, angst. Indignities suffered through inexorable aging and potentially catastrophic illness—witness recent outbreaks of Ebola and measles—are largely consequences of living in modern society, often as a result of willful carelessness and peccadillos of our fellow human beings. We all suffer fools from time to time, if not gladly.

In this foreboding context, the attraction of such a simplistic brand of mindfulness—being in the moment, drug-induced or not—is understandable. And why it is much in vogue. But the popular take on mindfulness is not that of Zen. Zen openly embraces suffering, in all its iterations. Zen does not duck, or pull, punches. We lump all imperfections under the rubric of dukkha, inadequately translated as "suffering." Change, the impersonal, universal driving force of dukkha, comes with the territory of the original frontier.

Zen urges us to recognize that our discomforts, on any and all levels, are the result of natural change, greatly exacerbated by our own resistance to it. Our discomfort is reduced in inverse proportion to our willingness to drop our resistance. Personal suffering is mostly the product of our own imagination. Buddha is even said to have taught that we only imagine that our legs are in pain, in zazen. To which we say: Pretty strong imagination; imagination on steroids! But if we stop resisting mentally, our legs can stop resisting physically as well. The body will adjust to the posture, in time. Zazen is, after all, the most natural way to sit. The chair, while undeniably a great invention, has had unintended, deleterious consequences.

In zazen, we make the body sit, rather than trying to make the mind behave. Rather than attempting to ignore pain by sheer force of will, or popping a pill, we embrace it. No pain, no gain. Of course, it may take a triumph of the will to overcome the pain in your legs. Largely caused by stretching of the tendons—made much worse by the monkey mind—it cannot go on forever. But if we must cut off sensation to do meditation, we may as well invest in a sensory deprivation tank. Where the body goes, the mind has to follow, eventually.

Zen is not about getting away from our present reality, including, most especially, the sense realms. It is all about fully engaging with them, in order to see through their deceptive, delusional aspects. This same attitude carries over to all aspects of life.

Suffering and Salvation

Please return for a moment to this question: What, precisely, are we to be mindful of in Zen? Beginning with cultivating our ability to pay unrelenting attention in the moment, and resisting the natural tendency of the ox to wander off mindlessly in search of greener pastures. But Zen mindfulness includes awareness of the truth of Buddhism's compassionate teachings, notably the first on record, the Four Noble Truths. Being mindful means that we become aware of their significance to our lives, not merely as food for thought. We become painfully aware of the truth of suffering, in all its manifestations. But Zen offers the antidote.

It bears repeating that "suffering" is a poor substitute for the original meaning of dukkha. Other choices include unsatisfactoriness, that vague sense that not all is right with the world. Today we are saturated with awareness of suffering all around the globe, to the point of fatigue. So it seems counterintuitive, and countercultural, to intentionally make suffering a focus of attention. Very un-American.

But if we are to fully understand the first Noble Truth—the Existence of suffering, first we must fully experience the reality of suffering. If we are to fully abandon its origin—craving, thirst, or another choice, greed—we must pay enough attention to at least recognize our own greed. Greed is not good, whatever the Gordon Gekkos of the world would have you believe. If we are to fully realize the Cessation of suffering, we must make genuine effort to relinquish craving as it arises in real time. If we are to fully follow the Path, we must begin with right meditation, which cultivates right mindfulness, and on down through the eight dimensions of the Path, culminating in right view. The Four Noble Truths—articulating the existence, origin, and potential cessation of suffering, actualized through the Eightfold Path—compose the content of Zen's mindfulness. This is the indelible connection between Zen and Buddhism, which some may wish to debate or even deny. Zen without Buddhism is a nonstarter.

Salvation comes in the midst of life, in living out these truths on a daily basis. It does not come after death as a reward for living according to the rules. It is bad enough that we have to go through aging, sickness, and death in the first place, the whole enchilada of suffering. We do not have to make things worse by beating ourselves up over it, being too harsh on ourselves, or blaming others. The blame game does not improve the taste of the enchilada. The most shameful blaming of all is the threat of eternal damnation after suffering this veil of tears. Navigating the original frontier is difficult enough without recriminations.

Practice and Enlightenment

We regard zazen practice to be the original source, and ultimate manifestation, of true mindfulness. We appreciate its halo effect on daily life but return to the cushion to recharge our mindfulness batteries. Zen mindfulness is not simply staying in the present moment, but deepening our awareness of the reality-based nature of Buddhism's teachings as they are manifested in the present moment. This entails delving into Zen on a deeply personal level, diving into the deep end of the pool.

Zen's mirror of mindfulness is all inclusive, reflecting the good, the bad, and the ugly with equal dispassion. It is not merely the exercise of maintaining a positive mental attitude. Or thinking only good thoughts. The practice and experience of heightened mindfulness in zazen is very different from our usually distracted, dreamy state of awareness.

Zen mindfulness, sometimes called "every-minute Zen," is not a final goal, but more an attitudinal training technique. It helps us establish right discipline, wherein right mindfulness interacts with right effort and right meditation. Right discipline colors right conduct, in which we become mindful of our speech, action, and livelihood. And sometimes painfully mindful of inappropriate conduct on our part.

The exercise of right mindfulness, in concert with the rest of the Path, can eventually lead to Zen insight. But simply being present is not, in itself, equivalent to right view and thought. It does not guarantee right speech, action, and livelihood, or right effort and meditation, the other way stations on the Eightfold Path.

Emptiness and Mindfulness

Zen's mindfulness does not simply entail a willful refocusing of attention. First-person evidence, observed within our experience, is the only way to confirm the concreteness of the teachings of Buddhism. One becomes mindful of a primordial emptiness (S. *shunyatta*).

How does emptiness look? How does it sound? How does it feel? We say that emptiness is beyond seeing, hearing, and feeling. So, thinking certainly cannot be an issue; it cannot ultimately hinder enlightenment. But as long as we are thinking about it, the very activity can distract us from the ubiquity of Zen's emptiness as the dynamic activity of mind.

Zen's mindfulness—beginning with mindfulness of form and emptiness as inseparable—is a prerequisite of a profoundly transformative process. It entails reexperiencing, not just reconceiving, the very basis of our being. Which, according to Buddhism, is marked by emptiness, with its three intrinsic aspects: impermanence, insubstantiality, and imperfection. This blunt expression of truth may trigger a certain amount of anxiety. But accepting and embracing it should actually provide a certain amount of relief, as expressed in an ancient Ch'an poem:[123]

To live in this realization is to be without anxiety about nonperfection. To live in this faith is the road to nonduality, because the nondual is one with the trusting mind.

Zen practice may lead to relative perfection, or refinement, of our life. But we do not imagine that we have anything to do with achieving that perfection. It already is perfect, just as it is. It is just that natural perfection does not conform to our human standards. This is why we have to engender a basic trust in the original mind. It is, by definition, perfect.

Another Ch'an poem reminds us:[124]

Hearing the words, understand the meaning; don't establish standards of your own.

Relinquishing our compulsion to prejudge everything on the basis of our own standards— especially clinging to our own opinions regarding the Noble Truths of Buddhism—is the most difficult prejudice of all to abandon.

Being okay—if not comfortable with our own imperfection, at least accepting of it—is only a matter of realistic humility in the context of Buddhism's teachings. But actually, you will likely benefit from enhanced self-confidence with extensive Zen practice. This can help improve your performance in many areas of life, as it does in the martial arts, as well as in such anxiety-provoking activities as public speaking. We become more at peace with change and more comfortable in our own skin; as the saying goes, more comfortable with discomfort.

Continuity and Change

Through change, we consume change, someone once said. As we age, we encounter a higher frequency of change, in all aspects of life. One theory is that the speed of electrical impulses on the channels of our nervous system slows down, creating the impression that the outside world is accelerating. My father once said that life is like a merry-go-round that goes faster and faster the older we get. This provokes a sense of urgency, affecting our attitude. Our attitude affects our intensity in Zen, and conversely, our intensity affects our attitude.

We develop a circular pattern of mutual cause and effect: first, the direct effects of our practice on awareness, then changing awareness directly affecting our practice. The overall effect on our attitudes toward Zen practice and daily life recycles in a positive-feedback loop. These attitudes constantly adapt, just as the nature of our Zen experience changes, evolving in subtle and not-so-subtle ways over time.

Importantly, our assessment of whether or not, and to what degree, Zen is "working" for us also evolves. The novelty of meditation wears off quickly, as you may already have noticed. You may also have noticed that you are surprised, from time to time, that everything old, including Zen, suddenly seems new again. But our new, noticeable calmness and collectedness also diminish from time to time. And then returns, with changes in the stages of our life, not just in meditation. The two are mutually modifying, not-two.

The same may be said of periodic disruptions to calmness. Anxiety, once seemingly overcome, may reemerge with a vengeance. Interpersonal crises beget personal crisis, at which times we need Zen even more.

Over the course of our lifetime—from childhood through adolescence, schooling, dating, marriage, parenthood, career changes, midlife, empty-nest syndrome, divorce, retirement, assisted living, and on into our dotage, aging, and death—our Zen practice adapts to changing circumstance yet forms an underlying constant.

Like the keel of a ship, Zen keeps us upright through the stormy sea of life, the ocean of Samsara. This is mindfulness in Zen: taking the long view, rather than just being in the moment.

Matsuoka Roshi, who held a black belt in judo, often spoke of the relationship of Zen to the martial arts. Describing verification in zazen, after being asked how do you know when it is working, he said it comes as a "sitting-mountain feeling," the signature of Samadhi. He claimed that by having Zen, you could defeat an opponent having superior technique (J. *waza*).

Mountains are potent symbols of continuity and stability, attested to by frequent use of the term "mountain" (J. *zan*) in dharma names given at Zen initiation (J. *jukai*). This may stem from the tradition of referring to outstanding Zen masters by the name of the mountain where their monasteries, or hermitages, were located.

Our ability to confront, head on, the many situations that create conflict for us—whether in the fighting ring or elsewhere in life—is enhanced by the spiritual confidence we derive from Zen. Like an island mountain, high above the shifting tides, this feeling of great stability carries over into our daily activities. Anyone should be able to live a Zen life, not only martial artists, monastics, or Zen masters. While we do not master Zen, but it masters us,

Zen certainly can help us master life. Becoming more measured in our reactivity to anticipated events, as well as emergencies, fosters a positive frame of mind, energizes our daily activities, and reduces wasted energy in overreacting and second-guessing. Change defines continuity, and vice versa, on the original frontier.

Power and Surrender

In the political and social turmoil of the times, we often hear of the powerless speaking truth to power. But in Zen, we recognize a more personal dimension of power (J. *joriki*) that does not come from societal position, wealth, or other circumstances.

The specific effects of Zen practice on your daily life depend partly on your specific traits, such as physique, personality, and attitude, as well as the intensity of your zazen. But the latter will strongly affect all of the former. This is the nurturing of joriki. Our attitude in Zen is not one of passive acceptance, but an aggressive embrace of whatever confronts us in daily life. In Zen we surrender to the truth, rather than try to escape it.

An old adage has it that the yogi welcomes adverse circumstances, regarding them as opportunities for strengthening spiritual union, one meaning of the term "yoga." Similar figures of speech from the current vernacular include "That which does not kill us makes us stronger" and "I don't have the stomach for it." In Zen, we develop "stomach power" (J. *hara*) though meditation, both on and off the cushion. But mainly on the cushion.

The stomach is the center of our physical being, and the seat of our personal power. The gut is the emotional center where we feel confidence and, alternately, doubt or fear. In daily practice, we feed the thoughts, trials, and tribulations that assail us to our stomach, as if consuming them, like feeding fuel to a fire. This was my teacher's suggestion.

This is also the natural result of Zen's fostering personal power. Joriki enhances our ability to empathize with, and to persuade, others. They can feel your increased confidence, indirectly. This marks the development of what is called "other-power" (J. *tariki*). Not so much power over others, but in collaboration with them. This is one secret commonly associated with jujitsu or judo: turning your opponent's power to your advantage, meeting hardness with softness, or surrender. In confronting the monkey mind, this idea becomes our catchword. When it goes low, we go soft. Once we take this approach to heart, bending like the willow under assault by the storm, our relationships with others tend to become more harmonious.

You may even find that others suddenly find you more charismatic. You begin to exude a kind of gravitas. If so, do not let it go to your head. It is only a side effect of Zen. Charisma may be harnessed to nefarious purposes, of course, as so often seen in the actions of powerful political and religious leaders, as well as wayward celebrities.

However, it is unlikely that any individual who has the humility, and persistence, to stick with Zen long enough to develop its gut-level confidence to any significant degree will still harbor the kind of intent that leads to the misuse, or abuse, of others. But there are no guarantees. What you do with your newfound confidence is entirely up to you.

Personal and Interpersonal

The social aspects of meditation practice compose a less personal dimension of Zen, not separate from time on the cushion but more obviously interpersonal in nature. This is yet another comfort zone, the fourth, following on physical, emotional, and mental dimensions of zazen. Which, remember, is supposed to be the comfortable way. As we overcome discomfort in the posture, so also we become more relaxed with anxiety and other emotional reactions that come up, in zazen and daily life. Just as we come to embrace confusion in holding contrary, contradictory ideas in mind simultaneously—classic cognitive dissonance—we must be at ease with the investment of time required for Zen. We must also be prepared to deal with friends' and families' curiosity and concerns, and any negative predispositions they may harbor about Zen. This is especially true in the Bible Belt of the USA. Your comfort zone on the social level counts as much as the personal one, maybe more so.

Zen community, or Sangha, is the traditional arena for observing, and refining, the effects of our practice on our relationships with others. On a three-month practice period (S. *ango*), one of my teachers said that by living together in a Zen center, we rub the rough edges off each other, like pebbles polished in the bed of a tumbling mountain stream. Zen retreats often function as a microcosm of daily life, warts and all. It is a truism in Zen that any one of the Three Treasures falling away—Buddha or Dharma, as well as Sangha— marks the decline of Buddhism.

This communal aspect of Zen practice is emphasized in Western groups, perhaps more so in the individualistic West than in the ethnic enclaves of Zen's countries of origin, where community was historically a given. America, the world's melting pot, is undergoing an agonizing process of creating true community, under assault by the pressures of immigration. Which can be as difficult to find as real solitude, in our digitally connected, but ironically alienated, society. Zen centers may be in the vanguard in this endeavor.

But care must be taken to avoid substituting social engagement for personal practice. Overemphasizing relationships with others in the community can get in the way of progress in Zen. This is one example, of many, of misshapen practices I see as "substitution effects," countless sidetracks that come to supplant our original purpose in Zen. This particular one arises from too much emphasis on the social side of practice, misinterpreting another translation I have heard of the last line of Dogen's quatrain on studying the Way quoted above, paraphrasing, "To be enlightened by all things is to remove the barrier between self and other, and go on in traceless enlightenment forever."

If we take Dogen to mean "self and other(s)" in the social sense, instead of "self and other" in the most concrete, immediate sense—of a fundamental, personal bifurcation in reality—it reduces enlightenment to a kind of New Age, touchy-feely Aha Moment, in which we finally "get it." That other people are, after all, just like us, and we are just like them. So can't we all just get along and be more compassionate with each other?

While few would argue with this sentiment, it misses a more fundamental, existential point: the supposed barrier between self and other—in the objective sense of a being isolated from its environment—is, itself, a myth. While reified by the cult of the individual and reinforced by religious belief in the separation of spiritual and worldly life, this meme is only as real as any other dualistic take on reality.

In Zen, grasping the primordial relationship of my "self" to my "other" takes precedence over improving the relationships of ourselves to others. Even if, like Bodhidharma, we find ourselves sitting alone in a cave in a mountain fastness, far removed from anyone else, the imagined absolute separation of self and other is still present.

This is the primary relationship that we have to resolve in order to be in harmony with our surroundings, our mortality, and our fate. All other relationships—with other persons—fall into place, taking their position and priority from the resolution of this existential schism. The bifurcation of self, as opposed to other, is the seminal basis of all forms of alienation, personal or social. It is learned and can be unlearned.

Harmony in the Zen community is ultimately dependent on each member coming to terms with this fundamental dilemma. It is the central, existential koan, and the reason for being of the Sangha. Socializing, even at a Zen center among like-minded people, can become a comforting diversion from confronting this central, and most difficult, problem. We are called upon to thoroughly, and unsentimentally, examine the apparent distinction between self and other. Where is the dividing line, exactly?

However, none of this is to denigrate the place and importance of community in Zen. Sangha forms the third leg of the stool of Buddhism, along with study of the compassionate teachings (S. *dharma*) and direct experience of our innate Original Nature, our potential for awakening, on the cushion (S. *buddha*). We honor Matsuoka Roshi's point that if and when any one of these three components ends, Buddhism ends.

Protocol and Practice

Many modern people question why Zen temples and centers follow so many protocols of the ancient Masters. Actually, we do not. That is, we do our best. But nobody living and propagating Zen today would claim to be preserving, as in a bell jar, some sort of historical artifact. As a designer, I have an aesthetic appreciation for the rituals and trappings of Zen, hailing from India, China, Korea, Japan and other Eastern cultures. But we do not follow them slavishly or believe that, somehow, just going through the motions has some sort of magical effect on our understanding.

Standard protocols are cohesive to any community and, in a psychological sense, have a reinforcing effect on our own, personal practice. But Dogen clarifies their position in the hierarchy of Zen praxis, instructing: [125]

> Without engaging in incense offering, bowing, chanting Buddha's name, repentance, or reading scriptures, you should just wholeheartedly sit and thus drop away body and mind.

Dogen profiles protocols as yet another potential substitution effect, diverting us from the real work of Zen. He, himself, apparently did engage in incense offering and the rest. But we may surmise that it was not something he needed to do for his practice to be genuine. The basic idea is that through sheer repetition, the standards that we follow in entering and exiting the zendo, conducting service, and so on lose their weirdness and eventually fade into the background. They become empty in the sense of mystical import, though not meaningless.

Matsuoka Roshi talked about the familiar Zen bow (J. *gassho*) in terms of mindfulness, but mindfulness of Buddha's teaching. Placing the hands palm to palm in front of our face, we bow when entering the zendo, and we bow to the altar, to our place of sitting, and to each other before and after sitting, as well as in greeting or parting. Bowing with the hands together at the stomach (J. *shasshu*) is an informal, person-to-person greeting. In most cases in Zen company, when in doubt—bow. But it does not have religious overtones, such as prayer.

Bowing and Praying

Sensei explained that in the formal Buddhist bow, one hand represents our everyday self, the self that we yearn to improve. The other hand symbolizes our idealized self, or buddha-nature, the self to which we aspire. We speak of discovering, or recovering, this original nature, or true self, since it is always there. But it is hidden by ego-centeredness. One profound benefit of Zen is the realization that we do not really have to improve ourselves. We only have to uncover our original self.

Clasping our hands together, palm to palm, signifies that these two selves are not really separate but only appear to be, just as our hands appear to be distinct and separate but are actually parts of the same body. When we bow to each other, it signifies my recognizing your buddha-nature as the same as mine; your bow acknowledges the inverse. Sensei also said that "When the bowing ends, Buddhism will end."

But Zen's bowing can be misinterpreted in the current cultural context. It is not a form of prayer, the most common misunderstanding. Bowing to the altar is not a gesture of idolatry or of worshipping Shakyamuni Buddha, or whatever bodhisattva is represented in statuary. Bowing to these artistic representations of buddha-nature is, instead, an act of veneration for Zen's founder, ancestors, and lineage, simultaneously with your own buddha-nature. It expresses respect for Buddha's great discovery in lieu of a teacher, as well as our profound gratitude for his deciding to teach others for our sake. Bowing when entering the zendo and when approaching the cushion, is, similarly, an expression of simple appreciation for having a place to practice Zen meditation.

Over time, the practice of bowing loses any inappropriate, or unsavory, connotations we may associate with it. For example, that it conveys obsequiousness, or that it is a form of public religiosity. With repetition, bowing becomes empty of such imputed meanings. Then, like an empty tea cup, it can be refilled. Gradually, bowing takes on new, and deeper, meaning.

I think of the Buddhist bow as an expression of the Three Minds of Zen (J. *sanshin*): Magnanimous mind (J. *daishin*), embracing everything as dharma; Nurturing mind (J. *roshin*), encouraging each other in the sangha; and Joyful mind (J. *kishin*), enjoying our buddha-nature. We bow to everything in magnanimity. Others seeing us bow are encouraged, which is nurturing. And bowing returns to us the simple joy of bowing, within emptiness.

The bow eventually becomes a constant state of mind internally, whether we bow externally or not. When someone treats us unkindly, or even unfairly, we can bow in their direction in our heart and mind (J. *shin*), thanking them for teaching us the dharma in a way that we may not like and that they do not realize, wishing them well in their suffering. They are "negative bodhisattvas." Our happiness—and for that matter, our safety and sanity—entails realizing the magnanimous and nurturing aspects of our complete, joyous wisdom mind (S. *bodhicitta*) in traveling the dangerous pathways and negotiating with the unfriendly, indigenous tribes on the original frontier.

BENEFITING FROM ZEN IN EVERY WAY IMAGINABLE

What follows may appear somewhat redundant, since related points have been made heretofore, basically as prescriptions for practice. Here, we are revisiting certain aspects of Zen practice as descriptions of reality instead, reviewing benefits that flow from practicing Zen's prescribed activities in the context of today's realities. These bear repeating.

Most texts on Zen do not go into great detail describing the effects of zazen. There seems to be a near taboo against lauding the benefits of Zen practice, for similar reasons. We do not want to raise undue expectations by making overly optimistic claims for Zen, such as that it will foster prosperity, or fantastical ones—that it will develop your paranormal powers.

Both claims may have some basis in truth but do not rise to worthy goals in Zen. There is nothing more miraculous than the original mind, in all its ordinariness. This calls to mind a story from D. T. Suzuki, recording a Chinese government officer's insight:[126]

One day after his official duties were over, he found himself leisurely sitting in his office, when all of a sudden a clash of thunder burst on his ear, and he realized a state of Satori. The poem he then composed depicts one aspect of the Zen experience:

Devoid of all thought, I sat quietly by the desk in my official room,
With my fountain-mind undisturbed, as serene as water;
A sudden clash of thunder, the mind-doors burst open,
And lo, there sitteth the old man in all his homeliness.

And lo, there is that reference to "thunder" again, coming out of the silence. He hears an instance of mokurai. What is revealed in Zen is already completely present where you are. The Old Man is always with us, whether we know it or not. This is not a reference to a spirit, or God. It is just the ordinary, even homely, ever-present, living reality of Zen, from which we find ourselves largely estranged until we are not.

If you are new to meditation, or to Zen, it may be hard to believe that significant changes for the better may come about as a result of simply sitting still enough for long enough. But if Zen were not beneficially transformative, it would not have attracted the numbers of geniuses that it has throughout its history. Nor would it have spread so extensively around the world from its humble origins in India. You can fool some of the people all of the time, and all of the people some of the time, as Honest Abe reminds us. Of course, you could say the same for Christianity, or any other great world religion. But Zen is not a religion in the conventional sense of a belief system. It is a spiritual practice instead.

If you are already experienced in meditation, or Zen, you may unwittingly be settling for less than your practice can deliver. You may feel that you have gotten all that Zen has to offer, when in reality you are still wandering about outside the dharma-gate, looking in.

Turning Expectation into Aspiration

Because of these and other issues, judging the effectiveness of their own meditation, many feel like giving up from time to time. By far the largest cohort of Westerners who try Zen are the ones who give up too soon. For teachers of Zen, the public complexities can be equally daunting, in my case as the guiding teacher of a Zen community. Zen is simple, but establishing community practice in today's climate is not.

You will most likely become discouraged in your practice, sooner or later. It comes with the territory and actually may be a sign that your practice is maturing. Simple in concept, Zen is difficult in execution, particularly in the long run.

This is not the fault of Zen, but the natural resistance of the monkey mind, persisting in the face of expectations that consistently go unmet. Expectations are the problem. But it is nearly impossible to live without them. As is sometimes said of the opposite sex, you can't live with them either. Better to hold an aspiration, rather than an expectation, for Zen's promise: [127]

> Accord with the enlightenment of all the buddhas; succeed to the samadhi of the ancestors.

Which is why it would be foolish to develop any preconceived expectation. It is bound to fall short of these outsized aspirations.

One of the reasons the great Masters downplayed tangible benefits from Zen probably has to do with our all-too-human penchant for setting up expectations, goals, and objectives and then striving to achieve them. And then, when we fall short, giving up and looking for something else to occupy our time and attention. When Zen ancestors speak of "achieving enlightenment," it indicates an appreciation of the level of difficulty, the near impossibility, of such a thing. They are not setting up enlightenment as a goal, nor are they using the phrase tongue-in-cheek.

Good for Nothing

Zazen is not regarded as a means to achieve enlightenment, but as the full expression of Buddha's wisdom, just as it is. We do not seek to gain anything from zazen. We do not sit patiently, secretly waiting for enlightenment. We recognize that as soon as we take the upright posture, the whole of Zen is already actualized. It takes time for this attitude to take hold, mainly because we are so preoccupied with thoughts about enlightenment or other benefits that we imagine we will realize from Zen:[128]

> [Kodo] Sawaki Roshi ended a long talk on zazen by saying that it is good for nothing. People thought that he was joking. That, however, was not the case. As I have already said: wherever, whatever happens, I live out my life. As long as I maintain this attitude, I cannot go anywhere. There is nowhere to go. Since I have nowhere to go, it is natural to say that zazen is good for nothing. There is nothing to gain from it because it is universe-full.

Odd, that last expression, "universe-full." There may be a Japanese term that does not translate well. This does not mean that zazen does not deliver results. It is important to know, however, that the most-obvious benefits—those touted by all schools of meditation—are essentially side effects. Zazen is not good for that. But most of us need to be reassured of positive results—as enlightened-self-interest inducements to practice—until we begin to experience real benefits for ourselves. This is one reason Right View is emphasized as the first dimension of the Noble Eightfold Path. Who wouldn't want to have the right view of things?

Taking the Long View

And yet, we do not start with right view in actual practice. If we already had the right view, there would be little need for practice other than to reinforce our existing view. First and foremost, the operational mode of Zen practice is Right Meditation. One cannot simply dream up Zen's right view by thinking about it. Though listed last, zazen is where our process actually begins. And to which we return again and again, through thick and thin.

That one would automatically benefit from the practice of Zen might seem to be a given. But it is not necessarily so. Some teachers caution that if you are only going to dabble in Zen, looking for short-term benefits, it may be better to wait until you are ready for a more serious commitment. If you are not willing to take the long view and commit to serious practice, you may end up giving up too soon. This admonishment is not meant to discourage you from taking up Zen, but to forewarn you that it is not just another fad, an interesting hobby to check out for a while. Nor is it just another regimen of self-improvement.

Improving Yourself

You may have read popular literature in the self-improvement genre, whose authors often argue the case for physical and mental, as well as psychological, benefits of meditation. Many books on Zen do so as well. Practice based on this kind of motivation is sometimes called *bompu* Zen. So there is certainly no need for us to stress self-improvement here.

But if self-improvement is not the main goal of Zen, then what is? A comprehensive answer is difficult to put into words. Practicing Zen does not magically produce happy circumstances or eliminate unhappy ones. But it does help us accept the situations that emerge in our daily lives more graciously, many of which are beyond our control. But Zen goes deeper still.

We are encouraged not to settle only for the obvious beneficial results of Zen. However welcome such developments may be, they are bound to be impermanent. More to the point, in Zen the very self—that we wish so earnestly to improve—is called into serious question. We do not deny the existence of the self, outright. But we do differentiate between the imagined, or constructed, self—or ego—and the true self, the self-nature that is natural and unconstructed. But we have to see through this imaginary self in order to fully become our original self. This is where zazen comes in.

Of course, there are no guarantees. The true self, by definition, is not constrained by preconceptions, prejudices, and opinions of the constructed self. A Zen teacher who has been there and done that can help point out these deeply ingrained biases, both directly as they manifest and indirectly by example. But having a teacher is no substitute for meditation.

Those of us engaged in studying the self in order to forget the self, and committed to the propagation of Zen, recommend that you seek out and practice with a Zen group as well as an experienced teacher. If you do so, you will be able to engage Zen's social dimension with that community, along with the personal dimension on the cushion. Thus, you will actualize the double-edged benefit of the sword of Zen: the opportunity to change your life for the better, and to pay back to your local community. The two go hand in hand.

But people come and go in the Sangha, all the time. The Zen community is like a cloud, constantly evaporating and recondensing. But when people leave, we do not assume that their practice has ended. We follow the motto posted on his center in New York by the first Rinzai master to settle permanently in America, Sokei-an Sasaki (1882–1945): "Those who come here are welcome; those who leave are not pursued."

Many missing-in-action members come back to the Zen center after long periods of time, even decades. It usually turns out that they have been dealing with exigencies of life that precluded participation. "Life is what happens to you while you're busy making other plans" (Master Lennon). It is best to take the long view. Persistence pays back big time in Zen. That you have persisted in reading this text thus far is an auspicious portent.

The best-case outcome of your reading this book, the greatest potential benefit, is that you will be encouraged to begin, or rededicate yourself to, your Zen practice. If possible, seek out a Zen community and teacher to support your practice. A true lay Sangha is a collaborative community, in which all members strive to work in harmony with each other in the common goal of Zen practice. In particular the practice of zazen. And to integrate their practice with daily life, including at work, at home, and at play. If you do not find these traits, it may be best to move on to another group. The support of a guiding teacher and community can help you stick with Zen until its benefits begin to manifest in your life.

Sticking with It

I hope to bolster your resolve by sharing some of the benefits I think you may reasonably expect to enjoy as a result of your stick-to-it-ivity. The benefits of Zen practice have the power to infiltrate and permeate every dimension of your life. This is because Zen goes straight to the heart of the matter.

Starting at home, where all the trouble begins, Zen meditation offers a ready sanctuary, an efficient and effective method to offset the pressures, the hassles, and the hustle and bustle of the modern world. But at the same time, it provides a neutral, neural feedback process—the mirror of Zen—in which we see our world reflected, often with brutal but brilliant clarity.

The benefits that accrue to us from practicing Zen are primarily personal in their impact. But like ripples on a pond, they potentially touch everyone and everything else in our lives. This ripple effect may even encourage others to follow your example when they see that you can keep your head when all those about you are losing theirs (kudos, Kipling).

The effects of Zen often manifest in your outer behavior before becoming apparent to yourself. We may be blind to our own weaknesses, but we are also blind to our own strengths. Like a flower unaware of its own beauty, we may not be conscious of our true colors, our nurturing role, in the grand scheme of things or during the daily grind.

But with the practice of Zen, we can truly blossom. Like the flower, our unfolding may not be visible to us. So it is better not to look for change, especially for any imagined self-improvement. The benefits of Zen practice do not distinguish between self and others but permeate physical, mental, emotional, and social planes in one holistic cornucopia.

Dogen expresses the indeterminate nature of realization as inconceivable, which may be the ultimate in stating the obvious:[129]

The boundary of realization is not distinct, for the realization comes forth simultaneously with the mastery of buddha-dharma. Do not suppose that

what you realize becomes your knowledge and is grasped by your consciousness. Although actualized immediately, the inconceivable may not be
apparent. Its appearance is beyond your knowledge.

That the inconceivable may not be apparent would seem to go without
saying. But the monkey mind has a deep streak of arrogance. It may presume
that we can know that we are enlightened. If we think we are, this is but another, perhaps more refined, delusion. In the same tract, Dogen claims:[130]

Those who have great realization of delusion are buddhas; those who are
greatly deluded about realization are sentient beings. Further, there are those
who continue realizing beyond realization, who are in delusion throughout
delusion. When buddhas are truly buddhas they do not necessarily notice
that they are buddhas.

Sticking with Zen, and taking the long view, means that any and all preoccupations—such as being a buddha, versus being deluded—drop away. We
continue practicing in delusion throughout delusion and do not necessarily
notice if and when we cross the boundary of realization into the original
frontier.

Going Beyond

During my freshman year at the Institute of Design, one of the teachers would
often praise students' solutions to an assignment by saying that they had really
"gone beyond." This curious expression means going beyond the assigned
parameters, reinterpreting and finding deeper meaning in the exercise, rede-
fining its goals and scope. This kind of attitude is nurtured in the creative
professions, at least for students, while still in school. Later on in real-world
careers, this idealism is all too often squelched by constraints on design, particularly the corporate culture and economic objectives, the "dead hand of
management." Which is probably true of all professions, one reason why
professional in all fields become disenchanted, even cynical.

I believe that Zen practice can help you go beyond the limitations you
may currently find in your life at work, at home, even at play. I am confident
that Zen practice helps me do so. In Zen interviews (J. *dokusan*), issues with
right livelihood seem to occupy a great deal of attention for all age groups and
professions.

In Zen, going beyond has a similar meaning to that expressed by my design mentor. It signifies a transcendence of ordinary understanding. In the Heart Sutra, chanted frequently in most Zen centers, the ending invocation (S. *dharani*) declares:

Gate gate paragate parasam gate bodhi svaha!

Though dharanis are not usually translated, this means something like this: Gone, gone, to the other shore; gone completely beyond; enlightenment accomplished! Dharanis are usually chanted in the original language. The sounds of the original syllables are thought to be imbued with transformative power, the ability to transport us to the Other Shore of enlightenment.

In the first English translation of the Heart Sutra that we used at the Chicago Zen temple, the phrase "having never left" was added at the end of this dharani, contributed by my senior dharma brother, Kongo Richard Langlois Roshi, working with an early translation committee of American Zen priests.

We have never left the other shore. And as Dogen reminds us, the other shore actually comes to us. We do not go to it. We are already standing on the shore of Nirvana, in the midst of this world of Samsara. In Zen, "going beyond" redefines what is typically meant by how something usually works. We go beyond in our Zen practice when we give up preconceptions about how zazen works, or how we think it should.

Training Intuition

Studying Zen in the same way that we generally approach other areas of learning is not adequate to the task. We tend to regard learning as the assimilation of information, as knowledge to be applied, regurgitated, or critiqued. Zen training is more a matter of apprenticing yourself to a teacher, in a program of action. We recognize certain parallels to the Zen method in the arts, crafts, and sciences, as well as in higher learning and specialties, such as PhD and MD degree training programs. These disciplines are often taught in apprentice mode, where observation and intuition play as great or even greater a role than intellectual analysis, or accumulation of rote knowledge.

Pursuing any subject in the information-gathering mode, our discriminating mind runs its subroutines of comparison, categorization, and analysis. Such analytical processing usually serves us well in most areas of knowledge-based learning. But not so much for Zen. As a Ch'an poem reminds us:[131]

All is empty, clear, self-illuminating, with no exertion of the mind's power. Here thought, feeling, knowledge, and imagination are of no value. In this world of Suchness there is neither self nor other than self.

At extreme reaches of Zen experience, not only is the acquisition of knowledge of little or no value, but even thought, feeling, and imagination lose their power. These four elements of awareness, each connected to the other three, form a tetrahedron, an interactive model of conventional learning. That is, feeling affects knowledge, knowledge informs imagination, imagination conditions thought, thought defines knowledge, and so on. But intellectualization is of little or no avail when it comes to Zen wisdom. Nonetheless, such modeling enables us to systematize interconnections between the components, as well as their limitations, and to better intuit the comprehensive truth to which they are pointing. More importantly, at this far pass the conundrum of self is naturally resolved. There is neither self nor other in this singular awareness, characteristic of the original frontier.

Socializing Zen

Neither self nor other than self returns us full circle to Dogen's dropping of body and mind. This nondual nature applies to the societal level of the self, particularly the many roles that we play in life as a child, a parent, or a spouse, as well as in our professional lives. How we come to self-identify with the various roles is determinative of our persona. They become part of our makeup, our self-identity. But this makeup is largely made up. The degree of reality depends on the interactive functioning of it. That is, we are not a parent unless we behave as one. We are not a son, or a daughter, if we do not act like it. This is the basis of being filial, considered a value in Zen, probably derived from Confucianism in China.

To cite a familiar and common example of social self-identification: most people, if you ask them, will tell you that they are a Christian, a Jew, a Muslim, Buddhist, atheist, et al. Religious identity has historically been a matter of inheriting the belief system of the tribe and is still largely so in much of the world. In the West, there seems to be a modern migration from traditional religions to experimental forms. Zen qualifies as this kind of choice in a primarily Judaic and Christian culture.

Others may claim to be artists, actors, or musicians, even though they are waiting tables at the moment. We self-identify by professional and biological traits, as well as beliefs. In most cases this "living as if" bespeaks a harmless bit of aspiration, rather than self-delusion. Which should be encouraged; it underlines the reality of stiff competition in the arts. But one is not an artist simply because one declares oneself to be. We rise to the level of art when others recognize our work as such. Great actors, musicians, or artists are granted such status only when enough followers say that they are. And not all opinions are equal, for better or worse. Who it is that recognizes your ability often matters most, sometimes unfairly.

This is not to imply that if Shakespeare had never showed his plays to anyone or had never had them performed—or if they were all burned before anyone could read them—that he would not be an outstanding playwright, an artist, and a genius. It is only to say that the individual cannot be dissociated from the milieu in which she or he operates, whether recognized by contemporaries or not. Interdependency—including the interconnectedness of self-identity with the identity of others—is a traditional tenet of Zen.

So-called Zen masters are another example of this connectedness. Masters are recognized as such by their peers. They are teachers only when and if they have students. Self-declared adepts are merely that: self-anointed. Their claim may be true, but it doesn't matter to anyone else. And, like art—where the work may be valued more after an artist's death than during their lifetime—the test of an ancestor's legacy is found in the lives of their successors.

This argues indirectly for the importance of the Sangha, the harmonious community, in Zen training. But it also includes that of family, social community, and even the larger civic state, as extensions of Sangha. While Zen may regarded as an individual preoccupation, this introversion is balanced by the emergence of the true self in interaction with the larger world. The roles we play are constantly shifting to fit the context.

I am certainly not the Zen master, or guiding teacher, at home. That particular self is interdependent with my Zen students. No students: no teacher. No family: no parent, son, or daughter. We become an extended "dharma family" through Sangha, in which blood lines are no longer determinative. We become dharma brothers, sisters, fathers, and mothers, as well as dharma daughters, sons, uncles, and aunts. First and second cousins. Maybe even in-laws, to stretch the metaphor. Just one big, if not always happy, family.

Embracing the Extraordinary

When the "I" that ordinarily thinks—I think; therefore I am (Descartes)—begins to disintegrate, it can be an extraordinarily unnerving experience. Who, or what, is it that is disintegrating? Such a denouement is beyond the power of the intellect to rationalize. We must truly go out of our (thinking) mind to embrace it fully. Our familiar self cannot survive morphing into the true self.

Like a snake molting its skin, a cicada emerging out of its shell, or a butterfly from its cocoon, the old self dies and is reborn as the true self, the original self. But in this, nothing has materially changed. Transmogrification is transpiring continuously, moment by moment. But it is happening so quickly that we cannot perceive it. We have adapted, over time, to the rapid pulse of change, including our changing selves, becoming numb to it.

Seemingly extraordinary changes in perception, triggered by meditation (J. *makyo*) or, for that matter, from psychotropic drugs, may then actually be quite ordinary. But they are also ordinarily subliminal. Zen meditation does not, indeed cannot, reveal anything that is not already present, if unaccounted for. But the advent of genuine insight must seem shockingly unfamiliar.

Eventually, the emotional reactivity of our mind levels out, becoming familiar with the strange new landscape through sheer repetition. In this, Zen is a bit like aversion therapy. Or, more precisely, graded-exposure therapy. Acrophobic patients, for example, undergo incrementally greater exposure to heights. Agoraphobics spend measured time in crowded spaces. Others on airplanes, for those with fear of flying. They undertake a regimen of gradual confrontation, of familiarization, with their phobias. What the therapist wants to avoid, above all, is retraumatizing the patient by going too far too soon.

Likewise, repeated exposure to bare fluctuations of sensory data, in the gradual process of adaptation encountered in zazen, paradoxically renders our heart and mind more certain. We become more confident in going further, in confronting the unfamiliar. In the face of increasingly strange phenomena in meditation, our confidence grows to embrace the final ambiguity of life itself. Entering fully into Zen is, finally, not an exertion of will, nor is it conceived by intellect. It is a life-changing, holistic event on the original frontier.

Approaching the Singularity

When your body, mind, and heart come together—and you know it—clap your hands! This is the real zazen. The grand unification theory of Zen is not a matter of all being one but, more clearly, all together being not-two. From Dogen again:[132]

> The Buddha way is, basically, leaping clear of the many and the one.

Entering the final, original frontier of Zen is like being in thrall to a kind of singularity, of consciousness itself. Much like the concept from astrophysics, where all nearby physical material and energy are pulled into a massive black hole. Discrete constituents of being: physical, mental, and emotional, along with those of the environment: matter and energy, collapse inward, when practice-enlightenment reaches critical mass, into the singularity of emptiness. We pass an event horizon beyond which nothing can escape, a spiritual point of no return. In which there is no inner and outer; all dualities collapse into nonduality.

In the social realm, interactions with others are subsumed under this same change. Only if we are at peace with ourselves can we be at peace with others. This is true freedom.

Finding True Freedom

It bears repeating that any and all benefits we accrue from Zen, including Samadhi as an effect, begin with those associated with Zen meditation. And they end—well, they may never actually end, to all practical purposes, unless, and until, we stop meditating. And even then, we cannot prove any causal connection. But we go on collecting the residuals. Even Shakyamuni continued sitting for the rest of his life, after his profound awakening in his midthirties. It benefited him, as well as his followers, further clarifying his initial insight and standing as an example to all to "do thou likewise."

Initial self-centeredness in beginning zazen is of necessity, not by choice. Zen practice may contribute to the well-being of others by virtue of engendering within its followers a more balanced and compassionate way of life. But again, this is not Zen's primary function, nor its reason for being. Actions on behalf of Buddhism are both self-interested and other-directed. Not exclusively selfless, nor entirely selfish. This comprises another example of the harmony of sameness and difference.

You may have encountered texts extolling the virtues of Buddhism, expressed either as prescriptions for practice or as descriptions of enlightened reality. Sometimes it is difficult to tell the difference as to the intent of the teacher. Some describe experience and prescribe a path to its realization, simultaneously, in the same breath.

All Zen teachings, benefits of practice, and ripple effects on the larger community may be regarded as side effects of zazen Samadhi. Samadhi itself is the primary benefit, the profound and transformative stillness emerging from sitting still enough for long enough. A passage from the "Song of Zazen," by Rinzai Master Hakuin, expands upon this point:[133]

> The gateway to freedom is zazen Samadhi—beyond exaltation, beyond all our praises, the pure Mahayana. Upholding the precepts, repentance and giving, the thousand good deeds, and the way of right living all come from zazen.

True freedom is extolled as the gateway benefit of zazen Samadhi. But freedom of a different order is intrinsic to the founding of the United States, and fundamental to the mantra of American exceptionalism. How often do we hear that our enemies envy our freedom? Master Hakuin reminds us, however, that the only true freedom is that found through the Samadhi of zazen. This suggests a comparison that begs some clarification. Please bear with me while indulging a somewhat political aside.

Even in what is claimed to be the freest nation on Earth, liberties enjoyed by citizens of the USA are necessarily of a relative nature. They do not represent the thousand good deeds, and the way of right living, which would presumably embrace social justice. This would also suggest an equitable distribution of wealth to achieve a compassionate society. This is presumably an ideal of the rules (S. *vinaya*; J. *shingi*) of the original Order of Buddhist monastics in ancient India, as well as those adapted in China, Japan, and the Far East.

But all of the altruistic laws and policies in the world cannot ensure the ultimate liberation that may be realized in this lifetime, according to Zen soteriology. Absolute freedom cannot be granted by others, no matter the protestations of ideologues. This does not amount to an anti-American or antidemocratic sentiment. These teachings are centuries old, prior to the existence of democracy as we know it, and derived from different cultures and countries of origin. But the problems currently plaguing our world are universal to humanity. The gateway to freedom is one gate, found only on the original frontier.

Master Hakuin's devotion to zazen belies the notion that Zen can be practiced without zazen, though some of his Rinzai colleagues might disagree. Soto Zen holds that awakening cannot arise solely from study of sutras, or koans, no matter how extensive or intensive. Other auxiliary practices—such as observing precepts and repentance and practicing generosity—cannot take the place of zazen. Dogen makes the same point: "[Y]ou should just whole-heartedly sit and thus drop away body and mind."[134]

The operative word here is "wholeheartedly." If our sitting is half hearted, it can deliver only half a loaf, and half baked at that. It is not going to work, in other words, in any ultimate sense. In fact, again, unless you are going to devote yourself, wholeheartedly, to your practice, it may be better not to take up Zen at all. It may only make things worse in your life.

This is not meant to discourage, or intimidate, only to forewarn us, that the practice of Zen is not a quick fix. But it is not necessary to compromise your household, family, or work obligations in order to have a wholehearted lay practice. In lay Zen practice, we maintain a normal life, introducing zazen in an unobtrusive way into our lifestyle.

On the other hand, the ancillary trappings of Zen practice are not to be discarded out of hand. Dogen himself apparently codified, and practiced, extensive rituals and protocols. But we understand all protocols to be secondary to, and supportive of, Zen meditation.

However, following the formal protocols surrounding Zen should likewise not be half hearted. This is illustrated by a Zen anecdote in which a group of young students (J. *unsui*), beginning a period of training at a monastery, are told by the abbot not to imitate the senior monks. Later on, they observe the abbot following the same protocols as the others, and confront him with his apparent hypocrisy. He tells them that he only has his devotion this way. In other words, he was not imitating anyone. His practice of ritual had assimilated completely into Zen's all-inclusive embrace.

Depending on Independence

Dogen's first manual on the method and meaning of zazen (J. *Fukanzazengi*) was first published in English on the two hundredth anniversary of the Declaration of Independence. A fitting synchronicity, since in the tract Dogen points the way to true independence, while admonishing his followers to avoid word-study only (J. *kanna*): [135]

> You should stop pursuing words and letters and learn to withdraw and reflect
> on yourself. When you do so, your body and mind will naturally fall away,
> and your original Buddha-nature will appear.

Dogen is not suggesting that we reject studying buddha-dharma in any form whatever, such as the written record of sutras and commentaries. Nor is he implying that we should not listen to the spoken teachings of a living teacher, such as himself. But as a first principle, we should read our own book—direct experience—instead of the written leavings of others. He is clearly recommending against using zazen for anything else other than just sitting in upright meditation. Instead of contemplating an assigned koan, we sit without recourse to any specific object of attention. This amounts to a not-so-subtle critique of Rinzai Zen, the predominant Zen sect in the Japan of Dogen's time.

But for us today, Dogen offers a declaration of genuine, thoroughgoing independence. Freedom from the tyranny of conceptual learning, and the imagined prison of body and mind, is the gateway to true freedom. Conceptual learning, in our times, is so common a phrase that it seems redundant. Learning is by definition conceptual and is most commonly expressed in words and letters. Language is not just something we learn, but also our primary vehicle for learning.

Unlearning the Truth

But language is, demonstrably, not necessary to conceptualization itself. There was a time in each of our lives when, as a child, we did not yet have command of the native tongue. Which is the basis of most conceptual learning, especially the received wisdom taught to us by others. In many areas of intellectual endeavor, however, concepts are generated more often from nonlinguistic sources.

In music, for example, compositions are conceived as combinations of acoustical passages voiced by instruments, but not necessarily including language, except in the form of a lyric or libretto. Other examples of nonverbal learning and expression in the arts and crafts, as well as in the sciences, are too numerous to catalog here.

It can be argued that basic learning is not limited even to conceptualization. For example, early learning involves negotiating the physical constraints of our world, beginning with gravity at a very early age. A toddler has no concept of gravity, but it is a consistent and ever-present teacher that cannot be avoided or safely ignored. The same may be said for the natural suffering of aging, sickness, and death. What Buddhism teaches goes beyond conceptual frameworks or intellectual understanding.

Withdrawing from the world for a time, and reflecting on the self, our apparent body and mind will fall away, naturally. We don't have to force it. Zen prescribes a natural process of sensory unlearning, from which clearly seeing into our original nature may finally emerge. Dogen goes on to describe the refreshing quality of genuine practice-enlightenment:[136]

> The truth appears, there being no delusion. If you understand this, you are completely free, like a dragon that has obtained water or a tiger that reclines on a mountain. The supreme law will then appear of itself, and you will be free of weariness and confusion.

The Buddhist truth appears as primary, unmediated experience, not as secondary information from others. Thus, there can be no actual delusion. But what we consider delusion, in our deluded state, is what impedes insight. The central delusion is that there is such a thing as delusion. Truth is not simply what remains after getting rid of delusion. Zen's truth includes so-called delusion.

Ordinarily, we consider truth and delusion to be polar opposites, antipodes. But they are complementary monads, comprising a dyad that we may term reality. Reality has to be realized. It cannot be grasped, or understood, in the ordinary sense. That which we take to be delusional is, by definition, illuminating truth. Truth is reflected in delusion, as in a mirror.

Separating reality into truth versus delusion probably begins at an early age, with individuation, the process of distinguishing the individual self from all other, the environs. The self emerges somewhere in infantile mind, engendering a conviction that there is, indeed, an individual me: a substantial self. And by logical extension, an eternal soul. This suggests that our koan in zazen is to immediately, and intimately, see through delusion to the truth.

You and It; It and You

Things, beings, are real—including you and me—in that they are tangible and present. But they are not real in the sense that they are not permanent, or unchanging. In the case of external objects, we can accept this truth rather readily, and unsentimentally. But when it comes to our sense of self, we take the notion of Impermanence—along with its fellow travelers, Imperfection and Insubstantiality—very personally. These three I's are traditional marks of dukkha, existence, that lend it the quality of being unsatisfactory. We do not want to accept that we, ourselves, are not real—that is, impermanent and ever changing—in spite of overwhelming evidence to the contrary. Another Ch'an poem states this succinctly: [137]

You are not it, but in truth it is you.

The resolution of this dilemma is a matter of realization, not of conceptual understanding. This is not something we can "get" without undergoing fundamental change. That IT is you—but you are not IT—relieves us of the necessity of believing, or accepting, any concept of the nature of the true self. If and when we experience this resolution—merging of self and other, of mind and body—we can see that the problem itself does not exist. It was a category error, from the very beginning in the crib.

You Can't Do This

Dogen reminds us, time and again, that gaining insight into buddha-dharma is not something that is intentionally doable, but something that will "appear of itself." We have but to set the stage. The resultant transformation promises to be refreshing, like quenching the fiery thirst of the dragon. Dogen assures us that it is comforting, like coming home after a long absence. Like a tiger returning to its mountain lair.

Finally returning to our true home, relieved of the terrible thirst of craving, comprises the only real freedom according to Zen. It has nothing to do with exteriors, such as our financial circumstance, or the form of government, or laws, under which we live. Direct, unfettered realization is coming into harmony with the supreme Law, or universal Dharma.

Dogen assures us that not only does this realization relieve confusion plaguing our mind heretofore, but it also reveals the futility of other pursuits. He continues, extolling Zen's longer-term benefits:[138]

By virtue of zazen it is possible to transcend the difference between "common" and "sacred" and attain the ability to die while doing zazen or while standing up.

Finally transcending all perceptual, conceptual dualities, we bridge the supposed gap between the mundane and the sacred. That they are opposed is conventional common sense. That never the twain shall meet is reinforced by theistic doctrine, as well as Western philosophy. Dividing spirit from flesh, God from Caesar, angels from devils.

Emphasis on the afterlife—at the expense of the present life—is the predictable result. Escaping the many traps of dualistic thinking requires going beyond faith but is not subject to scientific evidence. It can come about only through a fundamental transformation—of both the observer and the observed—in nondual integration. Intrinsic to this insight is the nonduality of birth and death. The life of buddhahood comprehends both on this frontier.

Zen of the People, by the People, and for the People

Studying the Way entails mainly studying the self. But we do not practice Zen in a vacuum. In spite of its suspicion of the false self—or because of it—Zen is for everyone. It is a practice that truly can be of the people, by the people, and for the people. As such, we may regard Zen as being as American as apple pie, if not as tasty.

Any and all who give it a try will benefit, because it works. Zen is the well to which we return to quench our thirst for the living dharma, to revitalize commitment to our practice, and to reaffirm any insights we may have gleaned into the true meaning of daily life. Zazen reveals the meaning of Zen, enabling direct insight untainted by thought.

But our practice of meditation continues even after insight, as did Buddha's. There is no final, ultimate awakening that marks the end of Zen. Nor do we outgrow the utility of zazen. Because life itself is in a state of flux, delusion is inexhaustible. Which means that insight is inexhaustible also.

Because Zen's insight is not self-clarifying, continuing follow-up is called for. This is why Buddha continued meditating for the remainder of his life, and why Master Huineng hastened to practice with Master Hongren, the Fifth Patriarch in China, following his initial insight. Hongren helped him clarify the "Great Matter" within a span of nine months, the story goes. But that did not mark the end of his training in zazen.

Sitting, in upright meditation, comprises most of the personal work associated with Zen. Propagating Zen properly also demands a great deal of time and effort. Mainly because sharing a personal practice, such as zazen, demands person-to-person engagement in addition to spoken teaching or written collateral material. As does any apprentice-mode training.

Written documents of Buddhist teachings preceded assimilation of its practice in China, Japan, and the Far East, as well as later in the West. It is much easier to distribute documents, even when laboriously copied by hand, than to set up the one-on-one personal mentoring relationships necessary to genuine Zen training. Zen praxis consists primarily of direct experience in zazen, and only secondarily from the written record.

Of course, there is much more to Zen than just sitting. We revere the Three Treasures of Buddhism: Buddha, Dharma, and Sangha, which represent our highest values. Zen prescribes a balanced approach to life, maintaining a positive relationship to the Zen Sangha as well as secular society. We promote studying the teachings and their meaning, Dharma. But above all, practicing meditation itself, preferably under the supervision of an experienced teacher. We want to wake up completely and to help others do the same.

Meditation may be thought of as buddha-practice; study, as dharma-practice; and community service, as sangha-practice. Benefits of a well-rounded practice include positive, holistic effects on our personal worldview and behavior and, potentially, public health and happiness. These stem from a balanced program of meditation, study, and participation in Zen community. After exploring the original frontier, we naturally want to invite others to settle it. And we want to emulate the hearty pioneers who blazed trails in the wilderness.

FOLLOWING THE SAGES AS GUIDES TO THE FRONTIER OF ZEN

Dialectical models of the teachings of the sages of Zen include such formulations as the Four Noble Truths (attributed to Shakyamuni Buddha), Bodhidharma's four observations during meditation (the breath, physical sensations, emotional moods, and mental conceptions), the Five Ranks of Tozan Ryokai (founder of Soto Zen in China), and the four alternatives attributed to Lin-Chi (founder of Rinzai Zen in China):[139]

Sometimes I take away man and do not take away the surroundings; sometimes I take away the surroundings and do not take away man; sometimes I take away both man and the surroundings; sometimes I take away neither man nor the surroundings.

Sensei profiled the Five Ranks in one of his longer published talks, explaining the many choices, and differences, in Zen sects:[140]

Again the main practice was zazen, but the "finger pointing to the moon of enlightenment" took the form of the teaching of the five ranks. The five ranks were a system of symbols used to differentiate among levels of enlightenment. The ranks were the prince, the minister, the prince looking at the minister, the minister returning to the prince, and the prince and minister in harmony. As those of you who have practiced Soto Zen know, we do not discuss the five ranks. Instead, we practice zazen-only Zen.

It's worth noting that Dogen also questioned how the "Great Matter" could be reduced to the five ranks.

You get the idea, though you may not get the meaning. Some models reflect the well-known tetralemma of Indian logic, that for any proposition there are four possibilities: affirmation, negation, or both. It is, it is not, it both is and is not, or it neither is nor is not. Some suggest relatively discrete, programmatic stages that one may expect to undergo in meditation. The downside is that they tend to encourage forming expectations. We will not go into detail on these, since extensive coverage is widely available. My main point is that mental models can be useful, but they do not supplant experiential grasp of the teachings.

Such constructions were developed as aids to the application of skillful means between master and student—images pointing to the unimaginable. They are meant to encourage Zen students to penetrate to ever-greater depths of practice-experience. But intellectual modeling falls short of a full comprehension of Zen. We should not look to them for insight. They are like the well-known spaghetti thrown at the wall, hoping something sticks. A Taoist aphorism touches on this truth:[141]

Lao-tzu tells us that "Tao" (Way) is just a convenient term for what had best be called the Nameless. Nothing can be said of it that does not distract from its fullness. To say that it exists is to exclude what does not exist, although void is the very nature of the Tao. To say that it does not exist is to exclude the Tao-permeated plenum. Away with dualistic categories.

Here, "plenum" is used in the sense of universal space, not as part of your heating-and-cooling system. This nameless reality is, finally, inaccessible to intellectual analysis, inexpressible in language. It can be pointed at only in words or gestures, not captured. We all manifest this truth at all times, however, if unintentionally and on a nonverbal level.

Trusting Your Teacher

An ancient Ch'an teaching advises us to follow the wit and wisdom of the ancients: [142]

If you want to follow in the ancient tracks, please observe the sages of the past. One on the verge of realizing the buddha way contemplated a tree for ten kalpas, like a battle-scarred tiger, like a horse with shanks gone gray.

Old tigers and horses have earned their wisdom. They have the scars to prove it.

Variations on the ancient instructions for zazen found in Matsuoka Roshi's contemporaneous pamphlet represent relatively minor examples of adaptation to present realities. Old folks in the West need to sit on chairs instead of on the floor. But they also illustrate a major principle in the legacy of Zen: the absolute authority of the Master. Transmitted priests are given free rein to adapt Zen teachings and protocols to the requirements of the times. Zen doctrine is not holy writ. Indeed, it is their responsibility to contradict written teachings when necessary. To the degree that your teacher does so, he or she follows the sages of the past.

This distinguishing trait of Zen's lineage stands in stark contrast to dogged adherence to hierarchy, uncritical acceptance of inerrant scripture, or blindly following sacrosanct ritual. Zen priests are scouts, adjusting to circumstance, blazing the trails of the original frontier.

This absolute level of trust in the ancestors provides powerful testament to Zen's reliance on personal experience over and above doctrine. It bespeaks a profound confidence in the wisdom of Zen masters to reinterpret tradition as needed, for the sake of their students. And it is evidence of Zen's deep trust in human nature, a rarity in either religion or science.

An extreme example is the famous incident in which Ch'an Master Huineng made a public show of burning sutras. Contemporaneous practice had gone off the deep end, placing erudition ahead of genuine insight. This great genius of Zen responded with a shock tactic to make his point: the truth of Zen is not exclusively contained in written form. The real Zen is living Zen. It is manifest in enlightened people of today, who are "exactly as those of old" (Lung-Ya). This incident is one example of having the flexibility of mind not to only slavishly imitate but to innovate, when necessary, to clarify the essence of the teaching.

Speaking with One Voice

Comparing the verbal expressions of Zen by Matsuoka Roshi and Eihei Dogen, two great masters separated by nearly a millennium, illustrates another tradition of Zen: its unbroken lineage. Our Zen ancestors all spoke with one voice, that of buddha-nature. This does not suggest that they were mysteriously channeling Buddha, opening a mystical connection with Shakyamuni himself. But it is evident that their words are informed by a certain spiritual confidence, stemming from the same direct experience of buddha-dharma. All Zen ancestors speak with a clear voice, resonant with genuine insight. As can we for ourselves, if only we learn the backward step of doing the same nondoing that they did.

Tracing the Source of the Way

To trace the provenance of the original frontier, we need do no more than listen to its first explorer. If you go back to the original teachings of Shakyamuni, "sage of the Shakya clan," you will find the first descriptions of this very frontier, as reported by its historical discoverer. Just as Columbus reported his discoveries found in the land he had supposed would be India—the strange inhabitants, lifestyles and customs, and material goods—back to the queen of Spain, Buddha shared potent descriptions of his experience, such as the "First Sermon" and the "Heart Sutra." The latter is worth quoting at some length in this context:[143]

> Avalokiteshvara Bodhisattva, when deeply practicing Prajna Paramita, clearly saw that all five aggregates are empty and thus relieved all suffering. Shariputra, form does not differ from emptiness; emptiness does not differ from form: form itself is emptiness; emptiness itself form. Sensations, perceptions, formations, and consciousness are also like this. Shariputra, all dharmas are marked by emptiness: they neither arise nor cease, are neither defiled nor pure, neither increase nor decrease. Therefore, given emptiness, there is no form, no sensation, no perception, no formation, no consciousness. No eyes, no ears, no nose, no tongue, no body, no mind, no sight, no sound, no smell, no taste, no touch, no object of mind, no realm of sight, no realm of mind consciousness. There is neither ignorance nor extinction of ignorance; neither old age and death nor extinction of old age and death; no suffering, no cause, no cessation, no path, no knowledge, and no attainment.

That's a lot of "noes." It is as if everything we hold to be true is negated on the original frontier. Some terms may need explanation. Avalokiteshvara is the famous "Bodhisattva of Compassion" (C. *Quanyin*; J. *Kannon*), who is capable of relieving all suffering. This does not indicate a living person.

Shariputra is, however, and one of Buddha's ten most outstanding disciples. Buddha is explaining to Shariputra what the legend of the bodhisattva actually means in terms of direct experience in meditation. He is merely reporting back to this world, on the basis of his first personal survey of the new territory, of which Avalokiteshvara is a native.

This is from a much-longer sutra, condensed as a daily recitation capturing the heart of Buddha's teaching. It emphasizes relying on perfecting wisdom itself, "prajna paramita," in light of the fact that we can rely on nothing else, ultimately. Including this sutra.

In service, this is one long chant, without pause or punctuation. Its meaning, according to my teacher, is to be found in the chanting itself, not in the meaning of the words. We also occasionally chant in Sino-Japanese, which is a bit like reciting the Mass in Latin.

Down the Rabbit Hole

If we read between the lines of the Heart Sutra, however, we can see that, venturing into this original frontier, we enter into strange territory, indeed. Much like *Alice's Adventures in Wonderland* or *Through the Looking Glass*, we go down the rabbit hole and come out on the other side, forever changed.

The Five Aggregates (S. *skandhas*), after all, are nothing more than the familiar forms, sensations, perceptions, mental formations (volitions, motives, desires, etc.), and consciousness itself that we all experience on a daily basis. Within the boundaries of the frontier, however, they are all seen to be "empty." Whatever can this mean? Curiouser and curiouser.

In this strange land, form itself does not differ from emptiness. The very form of this writing—as well as the person reading it—is rendered empty of any permanent, substantial existence. The five aggregates—the most-familiar dimensions of our reality—disappear in a puff of smoke from the caterpillar's hookah pipe. They are the most immediate, in time and space, of all existent dharmas; five petals blooming in the consciousness of all sentient beings. All beings finds their true home, which is homelessness, in the original frontier.

That physical form is innately empty suggests that this formulation is not all that different from Einstein's stunning equation of matter and energy. Matter breaks down into constituent parts in a cascade of progressively smaller particles: molecules, atoms, subatomic nuclei, quarks, etc., on into the microcosmos of radiant energy. The cosmic rabbit hole.

I can't help but wonder whether Charles Dodgson, a.k.a. Lewis Carroll, may have come across this sutra before conjuring the cookies that make you large or small. Or talking flowers and doorknobs, images made visible by Walt Disney's animated movies, so influential in the formative years of my visual sensibilities. Did these two geniuses meditate, do you suppose?

The teacup, ubiquitous in Eastern as well as English culture, is frequently used to illustrate principles of Zen and appeared prominently at the Mad Hatter's tea party. Real teacups occupy "dharma-locations" in spacetime, one that no other object can occupy.

An anecdote related by Matsuoka Roshi concerns a teacup. A Zen master addressed an Indian guru, popular in America at the time, holding aloft a teacup: Where, precisely, does this teacup reside? Is it in your mind? Or is it in my mind? The guru demurred to answer.

A teacup is real, in that it functions as a teacup. It occupies a unique dharma-location. But this same teacup is empty of self-existence. It is composed of yet more dharma beings: microcosmic particles that make up the clay, the glaze, and the other components of the teacup. They likewise occupy their own unique dharma-locations. The teacup is not what it once was in the past. And one day, it will not be what it is now, in the future.

Owing to particle decay, if nothing else, nothing can be truly permanent. On the so-called classic scale of human perception, things seem to abide, unchanging, for some time. But perception, even consciousness itself, is subject to this same impermanence, according to Buddha's discourse. One of his dharma descendants, Bodhidharma, brought this insight, and the direct practice of zazen, to China. He expressed his understanding along similar lines.

Bodhidharma's Four Observations

The legendary Indian saint, and first ancestor of Zen in China, is credited with introducing Zen's direct approach to meditation (J. *shikantaza*) to China, where Indian Buddhism became Ch'an, or Chinese Zen. His observations for zazen compose a four-pointed model for directing our attention in zazen. He points to four areas of awareness, accessible to direct observation. The model itself is an example of a mental construct, the fourth area he mentions:

1. Breath Cycles   2. Physical Sensations   3. Emotional Feelings
4. Mental Constructs

These four objects of observation are not separate, but interconnected.

We scrutinize each in turn, with scientific detachment: our breathing cycles, in and out; physical sensory data; mood swings, ups and downs on the roll-ercoaster; and both natural and intentional thoughts. And not necessarily in that order. We revisit them again and again in meditation, going deeper with each cycle, like drilling for water. Recycling through what are, after all, only conceptual divisions in a holistic whole.

Bodhidharma's four-pointed model proves useful in focusing attention in zazen. Setting aside the overwhelming complexity of omnidirectional aware-ness, he homes in on four immediately present facets of being that shape and are shaped by zazen. Attention to the four major sense realms   seeing, hearing, feeling, and thinking, detailed above—is similarly targeted.

Visualized as a tetrahedron, the six connections between the four points become clear, illustrating their interactive transactions as mutual causes and conditions of our being. Zazen breathing gives us the grace to soften the impact of emotions upon our body. Stillness of the body, in turn, calms our mind. Calming our mind soothes the emotions. Taken altogether, the four facets with their six connections tune our internal dialogue and temper outer relationships.

All four areas are ever changing, impermanent, and insubstantial. Yet, each is intimately associated with our self-image, our identity. It is "I" that am Breathing, after all. I have Sensations of hot, cold, or tired. These are My Feelings, of elation or despair. My Ideas, about Zen, among others. My Philosophy of life. Eventually, however—through dispassionate observation—it becomes clear that all observable and conceivable components of our self-iden-tity are essentially empty of static existence, or of self-essence. They exist only in relation to each other, and only temporarily.

The upshot of all this direct observation is that our apparent, treasured self—the observer at the center of the observations—must also be imperma-nent, and empty, in essence.

Life Must Be You

Since everything intimately associated with you is evanescent, changing every moment, then so must be you yourself. The self itself must morph, over time. It is a shape-shifter, though appearing to remain the same. Case in point: you are both the same as—and different from—you when you were five years old.

But Zen argues that the true self is not limited to this constructed self. Dogen concurs, via analogy to fishes and birds:[144]

If a bird leaves the air it will die at once. If a fish leaves the water it will die at once. Know that the water is life and the fish is life. The bird is life and the fish is life. Life must be the bird and life must be the fish. It is possible to illustrate this with more analogies. Practice-enlightenment and people are like this.

The first four lines are relatively logical. But when he says that "life must be the bird and life must be the fish," we are thrust into the original frontier. He might have expressed the same idea differently: life is "birding"; life is manifesting as a fish. Dogen was known to use verbs as nouns, and vice versa, in order to undermine conventional interpretation.

Beings, expressed as nouns, including living things, are usually seen as discrete things, in the absolute sense. But life is expressing itself as a fish in one instance, and as a bird in another. So, life must be you as well. And life must be me. We are only operationally responsible for our own existence. Life is expressing itself, through us.

Insight into "nonself" may be considered a benefit of Zen, but it is certainly not tantamount to Buddha's awakening. It is the beginning of wisdom, however, and can be very humbling. Accepting this truth has the salutary effect of breaking down cherished myths of personal permanency, autonomy, and perfection. And the consequent mindless clinging to our misbegotten, self-serving self. It is also a great relief to realize that we are not totally in charge.

Observing Simplicity; Simplifying Observation

Like negative feedback, but in reverse, we begin to embrace Zen's overview. Much less inclined to bogging down, overreacting to any one area of difficulty. This leveling effect is zazen's hallmark. Zen is the great equalizer, cultivating harmony between internal and external, personal and social, dimensions of our existence.

On the social level, we compartmentalize interpersonal problems encountered in daily life in a similar way. We define the physical—aging and sickness—as originating in the body, in the environment, or both. Diseases can be communicated, some through breathing, and the world can wear us out through stress. Others are defined as emotional, psychosomatic "dis-ease." Still others are categorized as mental disorders, or disturbances of the mind. All can result in distortions of our worldview.

The determinative quality that all such observable aspects have in common is their impermanence. As a corollary to the Taoist teaching of the Nameless, anything that can be named—isolated as a perception or conception—must be impermanent.

Breathing, sensations, moods, and concepts—about all of the above—are all essentially impermanent, constantly coming and going, changing moment by moment. The self-observing self must, likewise, evolve over time. This calls into question the observer's own self-reality and mitigates against self-centeredness. In a Ch'an poem, we hear:[145]

> For the unified mind in accord with the Way, all self-centered striving ceases.
> Doubts and irresolutions vanish and life in true faith is possible.

If all that we can actually observe of the ego-self is impermanent, insubstantial, and imperfect, then so, ergo, must be the ego. However, that which observes impermanence must, by definition, be permanent. Conceiving of impermanence requires conceiving of permanence as its equal and opposite complement.

According to Zen, there can be neither permanence nor impermanence, in reality. The universe is both permanent and impermanent and is neither permanent nor impermanent. It is not-two.

Revering Buddhas and Ancestors

Zen transmits the essential method and experience of Buddhism's entire lineage, beginning with the historical Buddha's profound insight and its transmission to his successor, Kasyapa. Zen's lineage is venerated as a virtually unbroken, face-to-face transmission of realization, from teacher to student, down to the present day. Our eye of practice matures with time and experience, as did theirs. Quoting Dogen again:[146]

> Buddhas and ancestors of old were as we; we in the future shall be buddhas
> and ancestors. Revering buddhas and ancestors, we are one buddha and
> one ancestor; awakening bodhi-mind, we are one bodhi-mind.

We should take these assurances of the ancestors to heart and have confidence that though the landscape of the original frontier may appear foreboding, others have trod there before and have blazed the trails for us. All we have to do is find the markers.

One of the traditional chants regularly performed in all Zen centers, temples, and monasteries is a listing of the ancestors (J. *bussorai*), from Shakyamuni on down to your immediate teacher's dharma name. After repeated recitation of a hundred-plus names to date, and counting, the visceral reality of warm-blooded living human beings populating generations of Zen progenitors throughout centuries in India, China, and Japan begins to sink in.

But the true vehicle for Zen's transmission is sitting zazen. It does not solely rely on your teacher. Likewise, awakening Bodhi-mind does not depend on doctrine, ritual, or any other ancillary practices. The Chinese poem quoted at the beginning of this section indicates the requisite level of commitment, "contemplating a tree for ten kalpas," which may seem like a waste of time. But following this do-it-yourself path, through the original frontier, entails taking the long view.

While ten kalpas, or eons, may sound like a mighty long time, don't let that discourage you. You may have already been practicing that long, granting credit for time served in past lives. You may already be ripe and ready without knowing it.

Doing Thou Likewise

Observing the sages of the past seems possible only through the written record, by studying their lives and sayings. But following in the ancient tracks means Do thou likewise. Studying buddha-dharma and sitting in zazen are complementary, not competitive, activities. There is no dichotomy in Zen, no actual gap between experience and expression or between the living dharma and its documentation. The former is the moon; the latter, fingers pointing to it.

Master Dogen and my teacher were both insistent on this point, the centrality of zazen. And it is still the central mission of Zen to transmit this undiluted method. The provenance of the instructional pamphlet from the ZBTC becomes clear when compared with Dogen's seminal tract on the principles of zazen:[147]

At your sitting place, spread out a thick mat and put a cushion on it. Sit either in the full-lotus or half-lotus position. In the full-lotus position, first place your right foot on your left thigh, then your left foot on your right thigh. In the half lotus, simply place your left foot on your right thigh. Tie your robes loosely and arrange them neatly. Then place your right hand on your left leg and your left hand on your right palm, thumb tips lightly touching. Straighten your body and sit upright, leaning neither left nor right, neither forward nor backward. Align your ears with your shoulders and your nose with your navel. Rest the tip of your tongue against the front of the roof of your mouth, with teeth together and lips shut. Always keep your eyes open and breathe softly through your nose.

Once you have adjusted your posture, take a breath and exhale fully, rock your body right and left, and settle into steady, immovable sitting. Think of not thinking. Not thinking—what kind of thinking is that? Nonthinking. This is the essential art of zazen.

The similarity to Sensei's condensed version, designed as a take-home reminder for home practice, is obvious. Dogen's was also a reference for students to use in his absence and so goes into much-greater detail.

But the same inseparability of physical and mental dimensions of Zen, the integration of the practical with the profound, and the stunning simplicity of zazen itself come through with crystal clarity in both. Very few instructional teachings have this kind of millennial shelf life.

Relying on Nonthinking

Instead of giving specific techniques for controlling the mind, Dogen recommends that we set aside the operations of intellectual thinking altogether. He gives us a relatively prosaic, pragmatic and detailed description of doing zazen with the body. But throughout the text, he also expounds poetically upon the deeper meaning of Zen practice. It is noteworthy that these same instructions are still given in Zen centers today, virtually verbatim.

The translator's choice of nonthinking is a challenging term, and worth investigating in some detail. It is vintage Dogen coinage, a compelling example of his creative use of language, which stands out even in translation. Although Dogen's nonthinking is a prescription for practice, it is equally a description of reality: Zen's natural frame of mind.

We cannot do nonthinking intentionally, but we can certainly recognize it when it occurs. As soon as we recognize that, just now, we were not thinking there for a moment, of course it is no longer nonthinking. Suddenly, we are thinking again. However, we know for sure when we are not doing nonthinking, by virtue of the simple fact that, at the moment, we are obviously engaged in thinking. This awareness is what makes it possible for us to nurture nonthinking.

Nonthinking reflects a mindset of receptivity, rather than something that can be thought, done, or willed into being. It is reinforced by an approach characteristic of professional research—to let the information flow freely to us, rather than seeking to filter or control it. Dogen captures this subtle dimension of right effort in a memorable expression:[148]

To carry yourself forward and experience the myriad things is delusion. That the myriad things come forth and experience themselves is awakening.

This carrying yourself forward is our usual, goal-seeking way of using the thinking mind to accrue information and knowledge, and is ordinarily quite useful. So useful, in fact—in getting the good grades and the good jobs, and coping and competing in general—that it amounts to a Western mindset. It has unfortunately become a global default position, interculturally. Because of this, appealing to intellectualization amounts to playing to a certain weakness.

In zazen, however, this kind of effort is nearly useless and tends to interfere with the opening of the intuitive mind to a deeper level of knowing.

Nonthinking is not, however, not thinking. Zen does not recommend suppressing thought. The monkey mind simply pushes back if we try to silence it with brute force. Nonthinking may be taken as a synonym for bare awareness. It is sitting without relying on thinking. It represents the middle way between thinking—in both natural and intentional modes—and not thinking at all. Natural thinking is our innate reaction to any stimulus. Intentional thinking is often a form of self-centered, usually goal-oriented, striving. Natural thought is not a problem, nor is intentional thinking, but obsessive reliance on thinking can be, especially in areas of higher creativity and in meditation.

Doing Nondoing

When nonthinking emerges, it may be equally regarded as an instance of nondoing. What most people call meditation consists mainly of thinking differently, which is doing something. Through repetition, zazen becomes much more than habit, and far beyond second nature. Like driving a car, it does not require any thought. Zazen leads to the end of doing as well. We have to admit that we are sitting—but it has become nothing-doing.

The countercultural uniqueness of these ideas is obvious. Who sits without thinking? Fortunately, our nonthinking mind, intuition, can recognize whether intentional thinking is occurring or not. Owing to this innate capability, we can intentionally develop an aptitude for nonthinking.

In the early stages of Zen practice, many complain that they just cannot stop thinking. Monkey mind is winning. We remind them that emptying the mind of thoughts is not the goal of Zen. Eventually, it becomes crystal clear that the point is moot: we have little or no choice in the matter. The brain will continue thinking whether we want it to or not. Just as the body will continue breathing, whether or not we are conscious.

Thoughts that come up often have nothing to do with present. They consist of ruminating over the past, planning for the future, or daydreaming. They tend to be repetitious and are not especially relevant to zazen. Happily, whether thinking is happening or not is not crucial to where and how we direct our attention in zazen.

The more present and open awareness cultivated in Zen—doing and thinking nothing in particular—is closer to our original, childlike mind, which was operative long before we learned our native tongue. Following the acquisition of language, what we recognize as conscious thinking consists largely of verbal thoughts. This is not to suggest that the mind of a child is superior to that of an adult, or even capable of recognizing thinking or nonthinking, as such. But only that our original awareness is not obsessed with, or controlled by, thinking. Especially within the confines of language. "Childlike" is not the pejorative that "childish" is.

The fecklessness of language in dealing with reality is touched on in the last lines of the same, early Ch'an poem:[149]

Words! The way is beyond language, for in it there is no yesterday, no tomorrow, no today.

It would be difficult to choose three words that more perfectly characterize our concept of reality than yesterday, tomorrow, and today. They capture, after all, our first and most tangible grasp of our world, as clear as night and day. But on the original frontier, words fail to capture the true nature of time or of space.

CONCLUDING ZEN
AS IF THAT WERE POSSIBLE

If you have read all of the above, congratulations. You should now be able to appreciate how difficult it is to draw any pat conclusions regarding Zen, especially as to its benefits to our lives. It should also be obvious that it is impossible to bring Zen practice to a conclusion. Zen is not just a separate activity or hobby. It is integral to our lives. Everyone is practicing Zen, whether they know it or not. They just may not be doing it very well. Everybody is doing something to cope with their existence, if only running away from it.

Even if it becomes impossible to sit upright, owing to aging or injury, the effects of Zen persist no matter what posture we find ourselves in at the moment: standing or walking, sitting or lying down. Of course, anyone who has experienced the real zazen will continue to practice as long as they can, and to whatever degree their physical and mental health allows.

If you do quit practicing meditation, you may soon find yourself again looking for that "something" that is missing in your life. In that sense, you may feel you are right back where you were when you first started Zen. But Zen is not like that. Like art, when you return to it after a long hiatus, you are better; your Zen is better. Zen comes from, and returns to, life itself. You get credit for time served, on or off the cushion.

In reality, we do not ever actually begin Zen. We rediscover it in the midst of life. And so, we cannot ever really quit Zen either. In other words, we are all, already, forever on the path of Zen. We are living in the original frontier, whether we recognize it or not.

Zen Is Not about Life; Life Is about Zen.

We first hear about and then decide to approach Zen, thinking that it is about life. We will, it is hoped, learn something new that we can apply to our daily lives. But we come to see that life is about Zen, actually. It turns out that our real life is all about what Zen is pointing to—the central riddle, koan, or Mystery of life. And, in one way or another, we are all doing our best to resolve this koan. Only we may not be doing a very good job of it. The same applies to all of our efforts, including mine, in writing this text.

This is the meaning of "wholeheartedness" in Zen. If you live in a neighborhood where a lot of people go jogging, you can see that some are totally into the running, with little or no hesitancy, just flying along. Others, however, look like they are trying to stop with every step. Their body language conveys a half-hearted, even resistant, mindset. They are trying not to jog, in the midst of jogging.

Our Zen practice is like this. This is why we say that if you cannot throw yourself into it unreservedly, it may be better to drop it for now. Later in life, we may find the maturity, the desperation, or the certainty to engage Zen fully. Of course, a lack of conviction should not discourage you. If you are having difficulty, either in actual zazen practice on the cushion or with integrating Zen into your daily life, no worries. As my teacher would often say, "Don't give up!" Your meditation practice will not always be perfect.

We may also fail in our intention of observing and keeping the Precepts. In fact, we observe them precisely when we violate them. We learn each Precept by breaking it. At least, that is when their meaning, and relevance, becomes clear. Then we take the Precept again, internally and repeatedly. But these monkey-mind shenanigans should not dissuade us from the equally important Buddhist practices of taking refuge and repentance, and persevering.

Repentance for our mistakes is best addressed by wholehearted perseverance on the cushion. We take, and find, refuge, not only in the Three Treasures but in the sanctuary of zazen. Zazen is to our practice as the temple, or center, is to the larger community.

Matsuoka Roshi would often say that you should put your "whole self" into zazen. If you can put your whole self into this simple act of sitting, he would say, "You will gain the power to put your whole self into everything that you do, and you will become the strongest person in the world." Of course, he did not mean strong only in the physical sense, but in light of what he called spiritual confidence. Spiritual confidence, unlike the confidence that we know how to drive a car, for example, is independent of any specific situation or competency. It has universal application.

Zen Is Always Contemporary

This frequent saying of my teacher bears repetition with each new generation. Zen is universal in its scope and adaptability. It is especially accessible to the modern mindset and lifestyle, offering a simple and efficient style of meditation that you—or anyone, anywhere, anytime—can adopt without undue disruption to your daily life. Practicing zazen promises to pay dividends on your investment in it.

This may seem to be slipping down the slope of making wild, unsubstantiated claims for Zen, something untested in your life thus far. But again, this case cannot be made a priori, prior to your actually practicing zazen. This is not a cop-out, just the simple truth.

In this regard, Zen is no different than any other apprenticeship program or training discipline—in the professions in the arts and sciences, for example. Its practice is similar to the demands of an exercise regimen, of which minimum requisites must be met before any hoped-for results may be realized. Like most serious endeavors, Zen may require the usual 10,000 hours, or five years, to develop a basic degree of mastery. In this sense, Zen is very ordinary. But ultimately, it closes the gap between the ordinary and the miraculous.

Zen Is for Everyone

Not everyone may be ready for Zen, but Zen is for everyone. Including—most pertinently—you, dear reader. Zen offers a highly effective method to meet, head on, the seemingly endless and intractable challenges that we are confronted with every day in our personal as well as public life. Zen meditation is, in my experience, the indispensable method for overcoming, or at least living with, the vagaries of both nature and nurture.

The former include your natural mental and physical endowment, such as it may be, as well as your ingrained predispositions. The latter include learned attitudes and traits, inculcated through nurturing by parents and peers, along with the many compromises and constraints imposed by society.

We are all creatures of habit, conditioned by cultural custom and constrained by comfort level. Zen pushes this claustrophobic envelope to the breaking point. Eventually, you can experience a breakthrough. But you will not be able to know this for yourself unless and until you have practiced enough Zen. How much is enough? You will know for sure when it is enough. If there is any doubt in your mind, it is not yet enough.

Zen's Mission: Meditation

Zen is the meditation branch of Buddhism. We honor and emulate Buddha's accomplishment as our prototype. He mounted a mission in India in the form of an intentional community, the original Order of mendicant monks and nuns. Its unifying premise was, essentially, exploring the territory of the mind as the gateway to understanding reality, and our place in it. Its business model was the begging bowl.

In a very real sense, propagating Zen is still a mission, the burden of which was felt by Dogen upon his return to thirteenth-century Japan from his sojourn in China:[150]

I came back to Japan with the hope of spreading the teaching and saving sentient beings—a heavy burden on my shoulders.

He believed that the real Zen—particularly the emphasis on zazen, the centrality of which he discovered while training under his teacher in China—was what the Japan of his time needed.

I believe that the same mission is finding its rebirth here and now, in America, as my teacher, Matsuoka Roshi, predicted it would. He felt deeply that the Western mind, with its emphasis on individual self-sufficiency; its embrace of a creative, can-do mindset; and do-it-yourself mentality, would provide fertile ground for the planting of the Zen way of life. I hope that my life is a living example of his prescience. Dogen was in his midtwenties when he went to China, as was Sensei when he came to America. And as was I when first I met my teacher. They say that the brain finishes its hardwiring in the midtwenties, when we first become aware of our mortality. Coincidence? I think not.

If Not Now, When?

I also hope that this book arrives at a critical moment in your life, especially for those readers who find themselves assailed by escalating man-made and natural disasters in this era of uncertainty. I believe that Zen still offers an ancient refuge, an island of sanity, in the ocean of chaos that is our world. Yet, Zen is completely modern in its method, as evidenced by its increasing inclusion in psychology, medicine, social sciences, and brain studies. Zen is not proffered as an escape, or some sort of panacea, but as a direct and simple method for finding inner, personal peace.

Philosophically, and even politically, the inclusionary worldview of Zen offers us a viable alternative in critical areas of public and private life. It enables us to embrace increasing social diversity, with its disruption to societal norms. And to resist, and refute, the exclusionary trend of the politics of ideology, with its gridlock of opposing worldviews, divisiveness, and intransigent polarization.

Zen's embrace of nonduality suggests a way around the hardening positions that arise in conflicts, such as those between rational secularism and theistic dogmatism. Its equanimity can help us sort through issues with high social stakes, such as the ersatz debate between intelligent-design proponents and defenders of evolution, to take but one example. It can also help us see through, and beyond, the façade of special-interest and partisan politics.

Awakening to Reality

In the intervening two and a half millennia since Buddha's advent, many attempts have been made to clarify the meaning of his spiritual awakening. These begin with the spoken teachings of Buddha himself. Over the centuries, competing religious belief systems—notably the Abrahamic lineages of Judaism, Christianity, and Islam—arose to vie with one another. Today, religion is largely regarded as yet another arena of competition for our hearts and minds, one of many forces clamoring to capture our attention in the daily din.

Modern crusades between tribes and nation-states, as well as those between contending international corporations, continue to threaten the eradication of neighboring groups, along with their political and religious belief systems. Secular social structures, such as democracy and socialism, are not immune to these struggles. We are currently witness to the greatest number of displaced persons in history, owing to intertribal and ideological conflicts in troubled areas.

We would like to assume that what may have started as internecine, primarily doctrinal competition among ancient belief systems—Zen Buddhism—may have overtly far-reaching consequences for modernity. Not only to preserve the integrity of its opposing tribes, but even for the long-term survival of humanity itself. Zen offers the familiar ancient raft for us to safely cross to the other, unfamiliar shore of the original frontier.

If you are at all familiar with Buddhism, you know that its adherents do not proselytize. But we cannot simply withdraw from the fray either. Ignoring the suffering in the world, even if driven largely by ignorance of the truths propounded in Buddhism, is not the Zen way.

If you have read widely about Buddhism, or Zen in particular, you may have noticed that all commentators, from Buddha on down to my present poor effort, are, to a great degree, attempting to say the same thing, if in different ways. The teachings of Zen, as well as the many commentaries on them, are necessarily redundant. The ancestors all speak with one voice, but from disparate cultural contexts.

I hope to have corrected any misimpressions you may have had about Zen, which may or may not have been inadvertently inflicted upon you by other writers and commentators. For I am beating a horse here, one that I hope is not yet dead. Buddha is attributed with saying that seekers are either like slow horses or fast horses. The fast horse takes off running at full speed upon merely seeing the tip of the whip out of the corner of its eye. The slow horse, in contrast, you have to beat nearly to the bone. But far better to be the latter. Once slow horses get it, they really have it for good.

I hope you are a slow horse, and that you agree that Zen's message bears repetition. The message of Buddha's wisdom to those living today is summed up in the first mother of all Precepts: Do no harm. Combined with the Christian expression Do thou likewise, we have our marching orders. In other words, do what Buddha did himself. And do it yourself, which is quintessentially American. His last admonition to his followers is said to have been for them to work out their own salvation, to be a lamp unto their own feet, not to take his word at face value for the truth, but to check it out for themselves in meditation. Zen Buddhism is, and always has been, the ultimate in DIY. Zen is always modern, beckoning to us as the ancient but absolutely modern, and the original, frontier.

Exploring the Original Frontier

As Americans, we are captivated by the idea of the frontier in all its iterations. The geographical frontier represented by the North and South American continents in colonial times, the "final" frontier of outer space, and the frontiers of imagination and science, to name a few.

Now we are embarking upon the exploration of another order of frontier—that of the mind. Not only in science—which is making great strides in brain studies, understanding the intelligence of humans as well as other sentient beings—but also in terms of personal insight, as represented by the revival of contemplative and meditative traditions.

If you do find yourself drawn to Zen and its zazen, you will encounter something of the wonder, awe—and terror—characteristic of the frontiersman's experience. Not only that of those pioneers setting sail from Europe, who navigated the historical settlement of the northern and southern continents called America, or the earlier Vikings, or the prehistoric diaspora from Asia, but also those intrepid explorers of today—including insentient beings, a.k.a. robots—entering upon the frontiers of space and plumbing the depths of the planet's vast oceans. Not to forget those adventurers boldly exploring the scientific and technological boundaries of the future, such as genetics. Frontiers equally thrilling and terrifying in their potential for dystopian, or utopian, consequences.

But the original frontier—first discovered, explored, and reported back to the rest of us by Shakyamuni Buddha, and later settled and documented by his followers—is a frontier of a different order. It is not limited by geographical boundaries or the limits of science and technology, but only by those of consciousness itself. Its territory is universal, and absolute. Entering this frontier is entering the world of Zen. It is my world, and you are welcome to it.

THE
ORIGINAL FRONTIER

The frontier may be a tried-and-true analogy, and perhaps a bit tired from overuse. But I believe it is highly appropriate and apt in the context of Buddha's legacy. The "original frontier" has meaning only in the context of the old frontier of legend, and in contrast with the new frontiers of science, the chaos and uncertainty of relentless human population growth, and its consequences to the world. Zen's intrinsic sense of urgency embraces both the personal and the social spheres, as not-two in essence.

Remembering the Old Frontier

The idea, and ideal, of the frontier is burned into the American psyche like a cattle brand. But the place it holds on our imaginations may be mostly based on myth. Frontiersmen were reportedly bold and brave, self-reliant, and adventurous. Traits partially, if not completely, driven by necessity. The seemingly endless western frontier of the vast North American continent provided ample opportunity for adventure, freedom, independence, and initiative. The frontier represented an irresistible lure to something greater, calling many to their destiny. But it also provided resistance, exemplified by the necessity of man-handling Conestoga wagons over the Rocky Mountains, a feat of unimaginable grit and determination.

Even after the western edge of the continent, the great Pacific Ocean, was finally reached, the attraction of the frontier continued to speak to our spirit of adventure. Prompting the great migration westward, it was driven by economic prospects and necessity. "Go West, young man" promised an escape from a sometimes regrettable past, as well as from limited opportunities for fame and fortune in more-settled territories of the East. Its promise also attracted droves of immigrants from Europe, China, and the Far East. The economic frontier represented by the Western Hemisphere, now including the European Union as well as the USA, is still attracting a flood of immigrants.

We know, now, that the European conquest of the Americas was not the first incursion to take place on these shores. Vikings explored the northeastern coast long before Columbus landed in 1492. In the early mists of prehistory, the continent was settled by Asian pioneers, indigenous by the time of the European discovery of the New World. But new information is continually coming in on this front, challenging our conventional grasp of protohistory. It is somewhat ironic that the current propagation of Zen to America represents a kind of second invasion from the East, all these many millennia later.

Americans still aspire to emulate the admirable, if largely imagined, attributes of their forebears' character. Without, of course, facing the incredible hardships they endured. The urge to explore is as compelling as ever, however, as attested by the popularity of "the final frontier" of space, both in the form of science fiction and the real space program, now being privatized as another forward-thinking business frontier.

But the traditional idea of a frontier, in its limited geographical sense, is meaningful only in the context of its opposite: the presence of civilization, or settled, familiar territory. At some point in the early history of humankind, it could be said that the whole world was the frontier, beginning just beyond the circle of warmth around the campfire, or just outside the opening of the cave.

The original, spiritual frontier that Buddha discovered has nothing to do with the geography of the world. It is not confined to northern India, where he lived. It is still present with us, here and now. Wherever we find ourselves, whether on the planet or in outer space. Its boundary is only as far away as your cushion.

Recognizing the New Frontier

The allure of the frontier still attracts, though many may feel we have conquered them all. The promise of the promised land still beckons, just over the next horizon. Today, however, the geographical horizons are clearly more limited than they seemed just a few centuries ago. Humankind's great success story—in exploring and occupying nearly every nook and cranny of the globe—has come back to bite. The frontiers of the physical planet, as well as its resources, are clearly finite, and shrinking, relative to population. Today's unexplored physical frontiers are those of Earth's wide and deep oceans, and the celestial bodies—the moon and Mars, as well as other solar systems' "goldilocks" planets—floating in the ocean of outer space.

But we know that there are also new, and nearly infinite, nongeographic possibilities. The frontiers of technology, both mechanical and biological, are vast, opening the gates to both the micro- and macrocosmos. The revolution that brought us the digital age is undeniably, and irreversibly, altering our world, in ways yet to be fully realized. But even this sea change is said, by some, to have merely set the stage for a much-bigger revolution, for which the advent of the computer is only the prologue.

Mass information processing—with the storage capacity; the capability of visualizing, analyzing, mining, and manipulating vast quantities of data now available; fueled by enhanced number-crunching power; and regular increases in the blinding speed of calculation—provides the necessary basis for genetic engineering, presaging the potential for the most extreme of sci-fi fantasies to move forward. This portends a radical alteration in our ability to change biological reproduction, to tamper with the process of natural selection of evolution itself. This development opens up whole new—and, for many, terrifying—vistas of the future.

This may be the bottle to which the genie cannot be returned: a Pandora's box of tragic consequences. Or it may be the key to our wildest dreams of unprecedented health and well-being, as well as heretofore unimaginable longevity. Like all other historical transformations in innovation, controlling genetics may lead to either utopia or dystopia.

Exploring any frontier, physical or otherwise, can go either way. It may bring the rewards we seek, but is also fraught with danger. In any case, the new frontier will share a boundary with the familiar territory that we currently occupy. This is the jumping-off place, across the boundary between the familiar and the strange.

After embarking upon the alien landscape, turning back is still an option for some time, and at a certain distance. But at a far-enough remove, we reach the point of no return, where turning back is as treacherous as continuing on our journey. Like a swimmer reaching the halfway mark to the other shore, or an aerial acrobat releasing her grip on one trapeze in order to catch another. We reach a distinct turning point, one of irreversible intent and consequence, and there is no going back.

These characteristics are also true of the spiritual frontier, the one discovered by Buddha. But it has no existential limitations. I refer to this exotic realm as the original frontier. You are invited to enter the actual domain yourself, on your cushion.

Reentering the Original Frontier

One evening, the story goes, young prince Siddhartha sat down under a tree after pursuing various paths and disciplines for six years or so. Resolved to solve the conundrum of the intense suffering (S. *dukkha*) he had witnessed—or die trying—he sat for forty-nine straight days, according to legend. He did not die, fortunately for us and for all of humanity. However, what had been known as Siddhartha Gautama did cease to exist. The self, with its long list of unique human traits, was no longer determinative.

What arose from that long, dark night of meditation was Awake: buddha. The young prince was liberated from all prior causes and conditions, released from all self-limiting attributes and entanglements. But the actual circumstances of his life had not magically changed. Buddha himself had changed.

For cynics trained by our comic-book culture, this begins to sound a bit melodramatic. Siddhartha ducks into the telephone booth of zazen; realizes supreme, perfect awakening (S. *anuttara samyak sambodhi*); and, emerging, stands revealed as Shakyamuni, sage of the Shakya clan. But all sarcasm aside, in putting his life on the line, Buddha opened the original frontier for the rest of us. He is a genuine frontiersman, and a real superhero.

Buddha saw into the true conditions of life: the built-in, unsatisfactory limitations of existence—the true nature of suffering—as relentless change in this physical universe. While most of us seek various ways to avoid, ignore, or transcend the discomfiting attributes of impermanence, imperfection, and insubstantiality, Buddha's awakening brought them front and center. They stand as a sober and compassionate reassessment of his, and our, reality.

His last resort was to sit down in meditation—in desperation and in all humility—admitting to himself that even with all his learning and intelligence, he simply did not know that which he most needed to know. He sat upright, balanced and alert, directly confronting the same inconvenient truths and life-threatening unpleasantries that we confront in our own practice. Meeting the dictates of life head on in zazen was, and still is, the natural and most effective response to the problem of suffering. The fundamental koan is still with us, alive and well, today.

Buddha and his followers actively embrace change—universal suffering—as the absolute Way. We leave behind the received wisdom of our culture and discover a new world. One that is ancient yet ever present, and waiting to be explored, in the midst of everyday life.

Buddha reentered the real world. The same world that all human beings, indeed all sentient beings, inhabit, though most are unaware of it. He woke up completely. But only to what already was, and still is. In this awakening, there is no tangible change in anything, other than our own awareness. In other words, everything changes. Permanently, and for the better.

Siddhartha Gautama sat up in meditation all through that night, until the break of dawn, some 2,500 years ago, the story continues. Upon seeing the morning star, he awoke. He, alone and on his own, discovered the original frontier, thus coming to the end of his spiritual evolution. He had become Buddha, the Fully Awakened One. In other words, he had become none other than his own, true self.

He recovered the same buddha-nature as yours, and mine. He was the first to do so that we know of at that time, but he did not break the mold. For him, it was the end of becoming, marking his last birth, as he declared in his first sermon to his fellow monks. And the beginning of true being.

In the process of his awakening, Buddha directly realized the nature and meaning of existence itself, and of his own place in it. And, by extension, the place of all humanity: yours and mine. He was, as we are, finally and fully at home. In our True Home, in the heart of the original frontier.

The takeaway? Do thou likewise. Come home to Zen.

NOTES

Introducing the Original Frontier

1   John Daido Loori, *The Zen of Creativity: Cultivating Your Artistic Life* (New York: Random House, 2004), 1.

2   Yuho Yokoi and Daizen Victoria, *Zen Master Dogen: An Introduction with Selected Writings: Fukanzazengi* (New York and Tokyo: Weatherhill, 1990), 45.

3   T. Griffith Foulk, ed., *Soto School Scripture for Daily Services and Practice: Hokyo Zammai* (Tokyo: Sotoshu Shuucho / Soto Zen Text Project, 2001), 33.

4   Ibid.

5   Ibid.

6   Ibid.

Designing a Creative Zen Life

7   Kazuaki Tanahashi, ed., *Moon in a Dewdrop: Writings of Zen Master Dogen; Bendowa* (New York: North Point / Farrar, Straus and Giroux, 1995), 145.

8   Zuiho Menzan and Kosho Uchyama, *Dōgen Zen*, trans. Shohaku Okumura (Kyoto: Kyoto Soto-Zen Center, 1988), 173–174.

9   Zengaku Soyu Matsuoka, *The Method of Zen* (Chicago: Zen Buddhist Temple of Chicago, 1966).

10   Ibid.

11   Carl Bielefeldt, *Dogen's Manuals of Zen Meditation* (Berkeley and Los Angeles: of California Press, 1988), 112.

12   Matsuoka, *The Method of Zen.*

13   Bielefeldt, *Dogen's Manuals of Zen Meditation*, 169.

14   Matsuoka, *The Method of Zen.*

15   Ibid.

16   Zengaku Soyu Matsuoka, The Kyosaku: Soto Zen Teachings Archive, Volume I, ed. Michael J. Elliston (Atlanta: Atlanta Soto Zen Center, 2010), 165.

17   Matsuoka, *The Method of Zen.*

Differentiating Zen Meditation from All the Others

18   Daniel Goleman, *The Meditative Mind: The Varieties of Meditative Experience* (New York: G. P. Putnam's Sons 1988), *xxv.*

19   Ibid., xxii.

20   Erin McKean, *The New Oxford American Dictionary* (New York: Oxford University Press, 2005), <hang>www.oxfordreference.com/ search?q=meditation&searchBtn=Search&isQuickSearch=true.

21   Shohaku Okumura, *Realizing Genjokoan* (Boston: Wisdom Publications, 2010), 2.

22 Goleman, *The Meditative Mind: The Varieties of Meditative Experience*, xxiv.

23 Ibid., 39.

24 Kazuaki Tanahashi, ed., *Treasury of the True Dharma Eye: Zen Master Dogen's Shobo Genzo* (Boston: Shambhala, 2010), 439.

25 Kazuaki Tanahashi, ed., *Moon in a Dewdrop: Writings of Zen Master Dogen; Genjokoan* (New York: North Point / Farrar, Straus and Giroux, 1995), 70.

26 Zengaku Soyu Matsuoka, *Mokurai: Soto Zen Teachings Archive, Volume II*, ed. Michael J. Elliston (Atlanta: Lulu.com, 2010), 12.

27 Goleman, *The Meditative Mind: The Varieties of Meditative Experience*, 88.

28 Charles Luk, *The Surangama Sutra* (New Delhi: Mushiram Manoharlal, 2001), 201–202.

29 Tanahashi, *Moon in a Dewdrop: Writings of Zen Master Dogen; Bendowa*, 146.

30 Richard B. Clarke, trans., *Hsin-hsin Ming: Verses on the Faith-Mind by Seng-ts'an Third Zen Patriarch* (Buffalo, NY: White Pine, 1984).

Finding Work-Arounds for Your Lousy Excuses

31 Clarke, trans., *Hsin-hsin Ming: Verses on the Faith-Mind by Seng-ts'an Third Zen Patriarch*.

32 John Locke, *An Essay concerning Human Understanding, Volume One*, ed. John W. Yolton (New York: E. P. Dutton, 1961), 78.

33 Foulk, *Soto School Scripture for Daily Services and Practice: Hokyo Zammai*, 34.

34 Tanahashi, ed., *Moon in a Dewdrop: Writings of Zen Master Dogen; Bendowa*, 146.

35 Ibid., 147.

36 Clarke, *Hsin-hsin Ming: Verses on the Faith-Mind by Seng-ts'an Third Zen Patriarch*.

37 Bielefeldt, *Dogen's Manuals of Zen Meditation*, 194.

38 Yuho Yokoi and Daizen Victoria, *Zen Master Dogen: An Introduction with Selected Writings: Fukanzazengi*, 45.

39 Shunryu Suzuki, *Zen Mind, Beginner's Mind: Informal Talks on Zen Meditation and Practice* (New York: Weatherhill, 1991), 21.

40 Willis Harman and Howard Rheingold, *Higher Creativity: Liberating the Unconscious for Breakthrough Insights* (New York: Jeremy P. Tarcher / Putnam, 1984), 34.

41 Tanahashi, *Moon in a Dewdrop: Writings of Zen Master Dogen; Bendowa*, 147.

42 Yuho Yokoi and Daizen Victoria, *Zen Master Dogen: An Introduction with Selected Writings: Fukanzazengi*, 46.

43 Tanahashi, *Moon in a Dewdrop: Writings of Zen Master Dogen; Bendowa*, 145.

44 Clarke, *Hsin-hsin Ming: Verses on the Faith-Mind by Seng-ts'an Third Zen Patriarch*.

45 Ibid.

46 Bodhidharma, *The Zen Teachings of Bodhidharma*, trans. Red Pine (New York: North Point / Farrar, Straus and Giroux, 1987), xv.

Deconstructing Your Senses in the Most Natural Way

47   Bodhidharma, *The Zen Teachings of Bodhidharma*, 91.

48   T. Griffith Foulk, ed., *Soto School Scripture for Daily Services and Practice: Sandokai* (Tokyo: Sotoshu Shuucho / Soto Zen Text Project, 2001), 30.

49   T. Griffith Foulk, ed., *Soto School Scripture for Daily Services and Practice: Hannya Shingyo* (Tokyo: Sotoshu Shuucho / Soto Zen Text Project, 2001), 28.

50   Yuho Yokoi and Daizen Victoria, *Zen Master Dogen: An Introduction with Selected Writings: Fukanzazengi*, 47.

51   Loori, *The Zen of Creativity: Cultivating Your Artistic Life*, .

52   Paul Reps and Nyogen Senzaki, *Zen Flesh, Zen Bones: A Collection of Zen and Pre-Zen Writings* (Garden City, NY: Doubleday, 1989).

53   Ingrid Fischer-Schreiber, Franz-Karl Ehrhard, and Michael S. Diener, *The Shambhala Dictionary of Buddhism and Zen* (Boston: Shambhala, 1991), 24.

54   Eihei Dogen, *Eihei Koso Hotsuganmon: Dogen's Vow*, https://sanfranciscozencenter.blob.core.windows.net/assets/29_Eihei_Koso_Hotsuganmon.pdf.

55   Clarke, *Hsin-hsin Ming: Verses on the Faith-Mind by Seng-ts'an Third Zen Patriarch*.

56   Ibid.

57   Luk, *The Surangama Sutra*, 118–121.

58   Reps and Senzaki, *Zen Flesh, Zen Bones: A Collection of Zen and Pre-Zen Writings*, 136–155.

59   Clarke, *Hsin-hsin Ming: Verses on the Faith-Mind by Seng-ts'an Third Zen Patriarch*.

60   Wikipedia, *Einstein's Thought Experiments*, https://en.wikipedia.org/wiki/Einstein%27s_thought_experiments.

61   Yuho Yokoi and Daizen Victoria, *Zen Master Dogen: An Introduction with Selected Writings: Fukanzazengi*, 82.

62   Clarke, *Hsin-hsin Ming: Verses on the Faith-Mind by Seng-ts'an Third Zen Patriarch*.

63   Wikipedia, *Sapir-Whorf Hypothesis*, https://en.wikipedia.org/wiki/Linguistic_relativity.

64   Clarke, *Hsin-hsin Ming: Verses on the Faith-Mind by Seng-ts'an Third Zen Patriarch*.

65   Dwight Goddard, ed., *A Buddhist Bible* (Boston: Beacon, 1994), 101–102.

66   Fischer-Schreiber, Ehrhard, and S. Diener, *The Shambhala Dictionary of Buddhism and Zen*, 24.

67   Clarke, *Hsin-hsin Ming: Verses on the Faith-Mind by Seng-ts'an Third Zen Patriarch*.

68   Katsuki Sekida, *Zen Training: Methods and Philosophy* (Boston: Shambhala, 2005), 108–110.

69   Yuho Yokoi and Daizen Victoria, *Zen Master Dogen: An Introduction with Selected Writings: Fukanzazengi*, 47.

70   Calvin Tompkins, "In the Outlaw Area," *New Yorker; Profiles* (1966), www.newyorker.com/magazine/1966/01/08/in-the-outlaw-area.

71   Foulk, *Soto School Scripture for Daily Services and Practice: Hokyo Zammai*, 34.

72   Bodhidharma, *The Zen Teachings of Bodhidharma*, 13–15.

73   Ibid., 43.

74   Ibid.

75   Luk, *The Surangama Sutra*, 36.

76   Foulk, *Soto School Scripture for Daily Services and Practice: Sandokai*, 31.

77   Foulk, *Soto School Scripture for Daily Services and Practice: Hokyo Zammai*, 33.

78   Philip Kapleau, *Zen: Dawn in the West* (Garden City NY: Doubleday, 1979), 182.

79   Ibid., 28.

80   Wikipedia: The Free Encyclopedia. Article: *George M. Stratton* (https://en.wikipedia.org/wiki/George_M._Stratton).

81   Eihei Dogen, *Master Dogen's Shobogenzo: Hotsu-Bodaishin*, trans. Gudo Nishijima and Chodo Cross (London: Windbell, 1997), 3:265.

82   Anecdotal; David Finklestein, GA Tech.

83   T. Griffith Foulk, ed., *Soto School Scripture for Daily Services and Practice: Fukanzazengi* (Tokyo: Sotoshu Shuucho / Soto Zen Text Project, 2001), 81.

84   Irmgard Schloegl, trans., *The Wisdom of the Zen Masters* (New York: New Directions Books / James Laughlin, 1975), 62.

85   Yuho Yokoi and Daizen Victoria, *Zen Master Dogen: An Introduction with Selected Writings: Fukanzazengi*, 47.

86   Luk, *The Surangama Sutra*, 20–21.

87   Andrija Puharich, *The Sacred Mushroom: Key to the Door of Eternity* (New York: Doubleday, 1974).

88   Luk, *The Surangama Sutra*, 202.

89   Wikipedia, https://en.wikipedia.org/wiki/Makyo.

90   Timothy Leary, Ralph Metzner, and Richard Alpert, *The Psychedelic Experience: A Manual Based on the Tibetan Book of the Dead* (New York: Citadel / Kensington, 1964), 67, 135.

91   Foulk, *Soto School Scripture for Daily Services and Practice: Sandokai*, 30.

92   Tanahashi, *Moon in a Dewdrop: Writings of Zen Master Dogen; Bendowa*, 146.

93   Eihei Dogen, *Master Dogen's Shobogenzo: Ippyakuhachi-Homyomon*, trans. Gudo Nishijima and Chodo Cross (London: Windbell, 1997), 4:255.

94   Dogen, *Eihei Koso Hotsuganmon: Dogen's Vow*, https:/sanfranciscozencenter.blob.core.windows.net/assets/29_Eihei_Koso_Hotsuganmon.pdf.

95   Eihei Dogen, *Master Dogen's Shobogenzo: Keisei Sanshoku*, trans. Gudo Nishijima and Chodo Cross (London: Windbell, 1997), 1:86.

96   Tanahashi, *Moon in a Dewdrop: Writings of Zen Master Dogen; Bendowa*, 147.

97   Eihei Dogen, *Master Dogen's Shobogenzo: Gabyo*, trans. Gudo Nishijima and Chodo Cross (London: Windbell, 1997), 2:278.

98   Luk, *The Surangama Sutra*, 118.

99   Ibid., 121.

100 Tanahashi, *Moon in a Dewdrop: Writings of Zen Master Dogen; Bendowa*, 147.

101 *New Oxford American Dictionary*, www.oxfordreference.com/search?q=limbic+system&searchBtn=Search&isQuickSearch=true

Embracing Nonduality without Losing Your Grip on Reality

102 Clarke, *Hsin-hsin Ming: Verses on the Faith-Mind by Seng-ts'an Third Zen Patriarch.*

103 Buckminster Fuller, *Anthology for a New Millennium*, ed. T. K. Zung (New York: St. Martin's Griffin, 2002), 245.

104 Ibid., 247.

105 Clarke, *Hsin-hsin Ming: Verses on the Faith-Mind by Seng-ts'an Third Zen Patriarch.*

106 Tanahashi, *Moon in a Dewdrop: Writings of Zen Master Dogen; Genjokoan*, 70.

107 Shohaku Okumura, ed., Gengo Akiba , *Sitting under the Bodhi Tree: Lectures on Dogen Zenji's Bendowa; "Dropping off Body and Mind,"* trans. Yoshie Akiba (Soto Zen Education Center, 2001), 94.

108 Yuho Yokoi and Daizen Victoria, *Zen Master Dogen: An Introduction with Selected Writing: Fukanzazengi*, 47.

109 Eihei Dogen, *Zazenshin: Acupuncture Needle for Zazen*, trans. Shohaku Okumura, www.thezensite.com/ZenTeachings/Dogen_Teachings/Genjokoan_Okumara.htm.

110 Ibid.

111 Ibid.

112 Ibid.

113 Ibid.

114 M., *The Gospel of Sri Ramakrishna*, trans. Swami Nikhilananda (New York: Ramakrishna-Vivekananda Center, 1942).

115 Tanahashi, *Moon in a Dewdrop: Writings of Zen Master Dogen; Genjokoan*, 70.

116 Ibid., 72.

117 Ibid.

118 Ibid.

Applying Zen to Your Life by Applying Your Life to Zen

119 Jack Kornfield, *After the Ecstasy, the Laundry: How the Heart Grows Wise on the Spiritual Path* (New York: Bantam Books / Random House, 2000)

120 Charlotte Joko Beck, *Nothing Special: Living Zen* (New York: HarperCollins, 1993), 168.

121 Eckhart Tolle, *The Power of Now: A Guide to Spiritual Enlightenment* (Novato, CA: New World Library, 1999).

122 Elizabeth Wurtzel, *Prozac Nation: Young and Depressed in America; A Memoir* (New York: Riverhead Books / Penguin Putnam, 1995).

123 Clarke, *Hsin-hsin Ming: Verses on the Faith-Mind by Seng-ts'an Third Zen Patriarch.*

124 Foulk, *Soto School Scripture for Daily Services and Practice: Sandokai*, 31.

125 Kazuaki Tanahashi, ed., *Moon in a Dewdrop: Writings of Zen Master Dogen; Jijuyu Zammai* (New York: North Point Press / Farrar, Straus and Giroux, 1995), 145.

Benefiting from Zen in Every Way Imaginable

126 William Barrett, *Zen Buddhism: Selected Writings of D. T. Suzuki* (New York: Three Leaves / Random House, 2006), 124.

127 Foulk, *Soto School Scripture for Daily Services and Practice: Fukanzazengi*, 84.

128 Kosho Uchiyama, *The Zen Teaching of "Homeless" Kodo*, trans. Koshi Ichida and Marshall Mittnick (Libri Books on Demand), 122.

129 Tanahashi, *Moon in a Dewdrop: Writings of Zen Master Dogen; Genjokoan*, 72.

130 Ibid., 69.

131 Clarke, *Hsin-hsin Ming: Verses on the Faith-Mind by Seng-ts'an Third Zen Patriarch*.

132 Tanahashi, *Moon in a Dewdrop: Writings of Zen Master Dogen; Genjokoan*, 69.

133 Kapleau, *Zen: Dawn in the West*, 182.

134 Tanahashi, *Moon in a Dewdrop: Writings of Zen Master Dogen; Jijuyu Zammai*, 145.

135 Yuho Yokoi and Daizen Victoria, *Zen Master Dogen: An Introduction with Selected Writings: Fukanzazengi*, 46.

136 Ibid.

137 T. Griffith Foulk, ed., *Soto School Scripture for Daily Services and Practice: Precious Mirror Samadhi* (Tokyo: Sotoshu Shumucho, 2001), 36.

138 Ibid.

Following the Sages as Guides to the Frontier of Zen

139 Heinrich Dumoulin, *Zen Buddhism: A History*, trans. James W. Heisig and Paul Knitter (New York: Macmillan, 1988), 1:219.

140 Matsuoka, Mokurai: Soto Zen Teachings Archive, Volume II, 17.

141 John Blofield, *Taoism: The Road to Immortality* (Boston: Shambhala, 2000), 3.

142 Foulk, *Soto School Scripture for Daily Services and Practice: Hokyo Zammai*, 36.

143 Foulk, *Soto School Scripture for Daily Services and Practice: Hannya Shingyo*, 28.

144 Tanahashi, *Moon in a Dewdrop: Writings of Zen Master Dogen; Genjokoan*, 72.

145 Clarke, *Hsin-hsin Ming: Verses on the Faith-Mind by Seng-ts'an Third Zen Patriarch*.

146 Eihei Dogen, *Eihei Koso Hotsuganmon: Dogen's Vow* https://sanfranciscozencenter.blob.core.windows.net/assets/29_Eihei_Koso_Hotsuganmon.pdf.

147 Yuho Yokoi and Daizen Victoria, *Zen Master Dogen: An Introduction with Selected Writings: Fukanzazengi*, 82.

148 Tanahashi, *Moon in a Dewdrop: Writings of Zen Master Dogen; Genjokoan*, 69.

149 Clarke, *Hsin-hsin Ming: Verses on the Faith-Mind by Seng-ts'an Third Zen Patriarch*.

Concluding Zen as If That Were Possible

150 Tanahashi, *Moon in a Dewdrop: Writings of Zen Master Dogen; Genjokoan*, 7.